FIGHTING POWER

Recent Titles in Contributions in Military History

The Art of Leadership in War: The Royal Navy From the Age of Nelson to the End of World War II
John Horsfield

A Wilderness of Miseries: War and Warriors in Early America
John E. Ferling

Iron Arm: The Mechanization of Mussolini's Army, 1920-1940
John Joseph Timothy Sweet

American Sea Power in the Old World: The United States Navy in European and Near Eastern Waters, 1865-1917
William N. Still, Jr.

A Hollow Threat: Strategic Air Power and Containment Before Korea
Harry R. Borowski

The Quest for Victory: The History of the Principles of War
John I. Alger

Men Wanted for the U.S. Army: America's Experience with an All-Volunteer Army Between the World Wars
Robert K. Griffith, Jr.

Bullets and Bureaucrats: The Machine Gun and the United States Army, 1861-1916
David A. Armstrong

General John M. Palmer, Citizen Soldiers, and the Army of a Democracy
I. B. Holley, Jr.

History of the Art of War: Within the Framework of Political History, The Middle Ages
Hans Delbrück, translated by *Walter J. Renfore, Jr.*

"Dear Bart": Washington Views of World War II
Glen C. H. Perry

FIGHTING POWER

GERMAN AND U.S. ARMY PERFORMANCE, 1939–1945

Martin van Creveld

Contributions in Military History, Number 32

Greenwood Press
Westport, Connecticut

Copyright Acknowledgment

The figures on pages 15 and 16 are reprinted by permission of the publisher from David M. Mantell, *True Americanism: Green Berets and War Resisters*, (New York: Teachers College Press, copyright © 1974 by Teachers College, Columbia University. All rights reserved.)

Library of Congress Cataloging in Publication Data

Van Creveld, Martin L.
Fighting power.

(Contributions in military history, ISSN 0084-9251 ; no. 32)
Bibliography: p.
Includes index.
1. Germany. Heer—Evaluation. 2. United States. Army—Evaluation. 3. Germany. Heer—History—World War, 1939-1945. 4. United States. Army—History—World War, 1939-1945. 5. Germany. Heer—Statistics. 6. United States. Army—Statistics. I. Title. II. Series.
UA712.V256 355'.02 81-23732
ISBN 0-313-23333-0 (lib. bdg.) AACR2

Library of Congress Catalog Card Number: 81-23732
ISBN: 0-313-23333-0
ISSN: 0084-9251

First published in 1982

Greenwood Press, 88 Post Road West, Westport, Connecticut 06881
An imprint of Greenwood Publishing Group, Inc.

Printed in the United States of America

10 9 8 7 6

In war, the moral is to the
physical as three to one.

Napoleon Bonaparte

CONTENTS

TABLES AND FIGURES

TABLES

FIGURES

ACKNOWLEDGMENTS

In its final form, the present study owes a great deal to many different people who, at various stages in its development, read the manuscript, made corrections, criticized or just listened to me talk. Though no list could embrace them all, even a short one must include Prof. Manfred Messerschmidt, scientific director of the Militärgeschichtliches Forschungsamt, Freiburg i.B.; Dr. Wilhelm Deist, of the same institute; Prof. Yehuda Elkana and Drs. Benjamin Kedar, Amnon Sella, and Moshe Zimmerman of the Hebrew University, Jerusalem; Mr. Tovia Ben Moshe, also of the Hebrew University; Prof. Frederick Roberts of Atlanta, Georgia; Dr. Barry Rubin of the Institute for International and Strategic Studies, Georgetown University, Washington, D.C.; Dr. Steve Canby, Prof. Edward Luttwak, and Col. (ret.) Trevor N. Dupuy, all of Washington, D.C.

The number of librarians and archivists who, in Freiburg, Jerusalem and Washington, D.C., have always proved more than willing to help me find what was often obscure material is too large to allow a list to be drawn up. My gratitude is extended to them all.

I wish to take this opportunity to thank Mr. and Dr. R. Deissmann of Freiburg i.B. to whose incomparable kindness and hospitality my family and I owe more than it is possible to put into words. To list the ways in which they have assisted in the writing of this book would amount to a definition of friendship.

Finally, generous financial support for writing this book has come from the Alexander von Humboldt Foundation in Bonn. It was largely thanks to its assistance that what could have been merely an interesting year in Germany has also proved to be a very pleasant one.

Freiburg i.B., May 1981

FIGHTING POWER

THE PROBLEM ______ 1

Throughout history, some armies have been better than others. The Romans in the age of Caesar, the Mongols at the time of Genghis Khan, the French during the Napoleonic period—all these were superior fighting organizations.

Though military excellence is inconceivable without victory, victory is by no means the sole criterion of military excellence. A small army may be overwhelmed by a larger one. Confronted with impossible political and economic odds, a qualitatively superior force may go down to defeat through no fault of its own. Not the outcome alone, but intrinsic qualities as well must therefore figure in an attempt to measure military (or any other) excellence; omit to do this, and the very notion of quality becomes impossible to sustain.

Within the limits set by its size, an army's worth as a military instrument equals the quality and quantity of its equipment multiplied by what, in the present study, will be termed its "Fighting Power." The latter rests on mental, intellectual, and organizational foundations; its manifestations, in one combination or another, are discipline and cohesion, morale and initiative, courage and toughness, the willingness to fight and the readiness, if necessary, to die. "Fighting Power," in brief, is defined as the sum total of mental qualities that make armies fight.

While weapons and methods of warfare change, the nature of fighting power does not; though the relative proportion of the individual qualities listed may vary from time to time, the qualities themselves, for the most part, are the same today as they were for Caesar's veterans 2,000 years ago.[1] Though good equipment can, up to a point, make up for deficient fighting power (the reverse is also true), an army lacking in the latter is, at best, a brittle instrument. History, including recent history, bristles with examples of armies that, though ostensibly strong and well equipped, disintegrated at the first shock of combat through sheer lack of fighting power.

In what lies the secret of fighting power? Writers from Xenophon on have sought to answer this question by pointing to national character, the relationship between armed forces and society, the powerful influence of religious and ideological beliefs, and primary group cohesion, among other factors. It is, in fact, easy to conjure up a mental picture of an ideal fighting army; such an army should consist of men who are born fighters, are held in high esteem by their society, are well trained, well disciplined, and well led. To describe an organization that will foster and maintain these qualities, however, is far more difficult. The present study will attempt to do this by way of a historical organization that developed fighting power to an almost awesome degree: the World War II German Army.

History is said to consist of reputations; if the reputation of an army is a measure of its quality, the German Army certainly stands second to none.[2] Most historians simply note its superiority in passing, but some have sought to explain its origins.[3] A few have used it to explain all kinds of otherwise incomprehensible facts; for example, that *Ultra* did not have as much effect on World War II as might have been expected.[4] The high fighting quality of the German Army has led to its being used as a rod against which other less successful forces can be measured.[5] Finally, at least one historian has written an entire book with the express intention of showing that the German Army in World War II was NOT better than any other—only to conclude that "in the early years of victory [the Wehrmacht] was to prove so spectacularly successful, and in the years of defeat so tenacious in defence, that its high place in the history of warfare is assured."[6]

If victory is taken as a measure of military quality, the German Army has certainly had its fair share of victories. Its campaigns in France (1940), Russia (1941), and North Africa (1941 and 1942) are still regarded as masterpieces of the military art and have indeed become almost legendary. Its operations in Norway (1940) and Crete (1941) are examples of smaller-scale triumphs achieved through hair-raising boldness. Confronted with opponents smaller than itself, as in Poland and the Balkans, the Wehrmacht displayed unequalled self-assurance and determination.

A point to be noted about the most important of these victories is that, far from resting on material superiority, they were waged by the Germans in the teeth of considerable numerical odds and, as often as not, inadequate logistic preparations.[7] As numerous writers have pointed out, the Wehrmacht in 1939 was not prepared for a conflict that, by Hitler's timetable, should have broken out four years later. Owing partly to time pressure and partly to a deliberate choice on the part of the National Socialist leadership, rearmament in depth had not taken place, leaving much of the army's equipment out of date and 80 percent of its units dependent on horse-drawn transport. Even within the vaunted Panzer divisions, to cite but a single example, two-thirds of the tanks had been designed with nothing but training purposes in mind. Condemned to fight a poor man's war, the German Army compensated by developing a high degree of fighting power that enabled it, even though actually inferior in numbers of both men and machines, to defeat France in six weeks, though four months were required for a crushingly superior Allied Force to drive it out again. In Russia a strongly outnumbered Wehrmacht needed only five months to reach the gates of Moscow; to drive it back to its starting line took an (by then immeasurably superior) opponent fully two-and-a-half years.

It is, however, not on its victories—regardless how splendid—that the German Wehrmacht's reputation for fighting power is mainly based. For here the historian is confronted with an army that, depending on the particular front and category of arms one cares to select, was outnumbered three, five, even seven to one. Yet it did not run. It did not disintegrate. It did not frag its officers. Instead, it doggedly fought on. It fought on even though Hitler's war was never at any time really popular in Germany.[8] It fought on even though its homeland was being bombed to smithereens behind its back. It fought on even though many of its generals—and numerous subsequent historians as well—regarded its commander in chief as little better than a raving lunatic.[9] It fought at Narvik and it fought at Alamein. It fought on for years after the last hope for victory had gone. Even as late as April 1945, to quote the Allied Intelligence Summary, its troops went on fighting wherever the local tactical situation was at all tolerable.[10] By that time it had already suffered 1.8 million casualties in dead alone and almost half as many again in captives who were to disappear forever in Soviet prison camps.[11] Yet for all this, its units, even when down to 20 percent of their original size, continued to exist and to resist—an unrivalled achievement for any army.[12]

As a final criterion of excellence, Colonel (ret.) Trevor N. Dupuy of the U.S. Army has made two separate attempts to measure the German Army's performance by quantitative means. The first of these involves the construction of a mathematical model of battle; that is, a series of fairly complicated equations that take into account such factors as the numbers involved on both sides, their arms, terrain, posture, and the effect of airpower where present. Fitting the formulas with data from seventy-eight World War II engagements, it was discovered that the actual outcome (that is, victory or defeat, each assigned a mathematical value) could only be predicted when it was assumed that, man for man and unit for unit, the Germans were 20 to 30 percent more effective than the British and American forces facing them. To put it in a different way: even after all material factors affecting the outcome of an engagement have been taken care of by the model, there still remains between German and Allied units a gap that must be explained.[13]

The second and much simpler way to measure the German performance against that of other forces is to count the number of casualties inflicted by the troops of both sides on a man to man basis. For this purpose, it is necessary first of all to determine the number of men who fought on each side. Second, the number of casualties—defined as killed, wounded, and missing, but excluding prisoners taken after the engagement—must be established from the war diaries and casualty reports of both sides. Third, the "score," that is, average number of casualties inflicted on the enemy by "blocks" of one hundred men on each side, is calculated. Finally, "score effectiveness" is arrived at by dividing the "score" by a constant (derived from the model discussed in the previous paragraph) whose value differs in accordance to posture; that is, 1 for Attack (A); 1.3 for Hasty Defense (HD); 1.5 for Prepared Defense (PD); 1.6 for Fortified Defense (FD); and 1.2 for Delaying Resistance (Del).

Table 1.1 shows Dupuy's data in a slightly modified form. In the column on the right the German score effectiveness was divided by the Allied one in order to obtain the differential.

average differential in 65 Allied attacks	1:1.56
average differential in 13 German attacks	1:1.49
average differential in 50 engagements between US and German units	1:1.55
average in all 78 engagements	1:1.52

The figures in table 1.1 may be broken down in different ways. Similar ones can be drawn up for the Eastern Front or for World War I, and this has in fact been done. That the German superiority was not due to Allied inexperience can be shown by using the data from the forty-one, 1944 engagements alone, which yields a differential of 1.45 (1.43 against the Americans only). For our purpose, all this does not matter. Suffice it to quote Dupuy's summing up:

> [The] record shows that the Germans consistently outfought the far more numerous Allied armies that eventually defeated them. . . . On a man for man basis the German ground soldiers consistently inflicted casualties at about a 50 percent higher rate than they incurred from the opposing British and American troops under all circumstances. This was true when they were attacking and when they were defending, when they had a local numerical superiority and when, as was usually the case, they were outnumbered, when they had air superiority and when they did not, when they won and when they lost.[14]

The fact that Hitler and his High Command made numerous strategic blunders, beginning at Dunkirk and running through Stalingrad all the way on to the Battle of the Bulge, does not affect this conclusion. Indeed, the reverse may well be true: for not the least astonishing aspect of the matter is that the Wehrmacht fought equally well in victory and in defeat,

TABLE 1.1
German and Allied Combat Effectiveness in 78 Engagements

ENGAGE-MENT[a]	ALLIED UNIT[b]	POS-TURE[c]	SCORE EFFECT	GERMAN UNIT[d]	POS-TURE[c]	SCORE EFFECT	DIFFEREN-TIAL
1	B46ID	A	1.02	16Pz	PD	3.85	1:3.77
2	B56ID	A	0.99	16Pz	PD	2.75	1:2.77
3	US45ID	A	1.12	16Pz	HD	2.45	1:2.18
4	US45ID	HD	1.96	16&29Pz	A	2.51	1:1.28
5	B46ID	HD	1.78	HG Pz	A	2.30	1:1.29
6	B56ID	HD	1.61	16Pz	A	3.86	1:2.39
7	B46ID	HD	1.59	HG Pz	A	1.74	1:1.09
8	B56ID	A	0.98	16Pz	Del	2.02	1:2.06
9	US45ID	A	0.96	16&26Pz	Del	2.44	1:2.54
10	B7AD	A	0.68	15Pz Gr	PD	2.05	1:3.67
11	B56ID	A	1.08	HG Pz	PD	3.94	1:3.23
12	US3IID	A	0.75	HG Pz	PD	2.50	1:3.33
13	US45ID	A	1.26	3&26Pz	Del	1.22	1:0.96
14	US34ID	A	0.58	3Pz Gr	Del	1.66	1:2.86
15	B46ID	A	0.51	15Pz Gr	PD	2.94	1:5.76
16	US34ID	A	0.89	3Pz Gr	Del	1.33	1:1.49
17	B46ID	A	0.93	15Pz Gr	PD	1.73	1:1.86
18	B7AD	A	0.75	15Pz Gr	PD	1.60	1:2.13
19	B&AD	A	0.96	15Pz Gr	PD	1.06	1:1.10
20	B56ID	A	0.76	HG Pz	PD	2.20	1:2.89
21	US34ID	A	1.28	3Pz Gr	PD	3.28	1:2.56
22	US3IID	A	1.34	3Pz Gr	FD	2.82	1:2.10
23	US45ID	A	0.54	3Pz Gr	FD	1.59	1:2.94
24	B56ID	A	0.81	15Pz Gr	FD	2.06	1:2.54
25	B56ID	HD	0.42	15Pz Gr	A	2.24	1:5.33
26	US3IID	A	0.66	3Pz Gr	FD	1.36	1:2.06
27	B56ID	A	1.25	15Pz Gr	FD	3.27	1:2.16
28	B46ID	A	0.84	15Pz Gr	FD	2.95	1:3.51
29	US36ID	A	0.59	15&29Pz	FD	1.82	1:3.08
30	BIID	A	0.81	3Pz Gr	HD	4.60	1:5.67
31	BIID	HD	0.73	3Pz Gr	A	1.10	1:1.50
32	BIID	A	0.87	3Pz Gr	PD	1.71	1:1.96
33	BIID	HD	3.14	HG Pz	A	3.11	1:0.99
34	BIID	HD	1.56	3Pz Gr	A	1.47	1:0.94
35	US45ID	HD	1.40	65ID	A	1.33	1:0.95
36	BIID	HD	1.35	HG Pz	A	2.08	1:1.54
37	US45ID	A	1.77	715Lt	HD	1.50	1:0.84
38	US45ID	HD	1.88	4 divs	A	1.26	1:0.67
39	B56ID	HD	1.88	65ID&4Pa	A	4.56	1:2.42
40	US45ID	PD	0.78	114Lt	HD	1.28	1:1.64
41	US88ID	A	3.09	94&71ID	FD	2.33	1:1.10
42	US85ID	A	2.62	94ID	FD	4.46	1:1.70
43	US88ID	A	2.89	94&71ID	Del	1.95	1:0.67
44	US85ID	A	1.98	94ID	FD	3.04	1:1.53
45	US88ID	A	2.10	94ID	HD	2.33	1:1.10
46	US85ID	A	2.06	94ID	HD	2.77	1:1.34
47	US88ID	A	1.50	94ID	Del	3.14	1:2.03

TABLE 1.1 *Continued*

ENGAGE-MENT[a]	ALLIED UNIT[b]	POS-TURE[c]	SCORE EFFECT	GERMAN UNIT[d]	POS-TURE[c]	SCORE EFFECT	DIFFEREN-TIAL
48	US85ID	A	1.64	94ID	HD	4.34	1:2.64
49	B5ID	A	2.43	4Pa	FD	1.92	1:0.79
50	B1ID	A	2.48	65ID	FD	1.58	1:0.63
51	US1AD	A	2.04	3&362ID	FD	1.74	1:0.85
52	US31ID	A	2.48	362ID	FD	2.94	1:1.18
53	US85ID	A	1.43	29Pz	HD	1.47	1:1.02
54	US1AD	A	3.84	362ID	FD	3.54	1:0.92
55	US34ID	A	2.29	3Pz Gr	FD	1.45	1:0.63
56	US45ID	A	2.34	65ID	FD	1.76	1:0.75
57	B51ID	A	1.81	4Pa	FD	1.60	1:0.88
58	US34ID	A	1.97	3Pz Gr	FD	2.24	1:1.13
59	US1&45ID	A	2.02	3&65ID	FD	2.16	1:1.06
60	B1&51ID	A	2.36	4Pa	FD	2.44	1:1.03
61	USXX Cp	A	1.20	1 Army	PD	1.48	1:1.23
62	USXX Cp	A	1.09	1 Army	Del	1.60	1:1.46
63	USXX Cp	A	1.11	1 Army	HD	1.76	1:1.58
64	US7AD	A	1.97	1 Army	HD	2.24	1:1.13
65	US7AD	A	1.03	48ID	PD	2.13	1:2.13
66	US35&26& 4AD	A-HD	1.14	XIII SS Cp	FD-A	3.21	1:2.81
67	US4AD	A	0.87	361ID	Del	3.54	1:4.06
68	US4AD	A	1.27	Pz Lehr& 361ID	HD-A	1.98	1:1.55
69	US4AD	A	1.41	Pz Lehr& 361ID	HD	1.26	1:0.89
70	US4AD	A	1.54	Pz Lehr	HD	1.17	1:0.75
71	US4AD	A	1.01	Pz Lehr	Del	0.76	1:0.75
72	US4AD	A	0.73	11Pz& Pz Lehr	PD	1.93	1:2.64
73	US4AD	A	0.92	25Pz Gr &11Pz	FD	1.52	1:1.65
74	USXII Cp	A	1.69	XIII SS& LXXXIX Cp	Del	2.97	1:1.65
75	USXII Cp	A	1.75	XIII SS& LXXXIX Cp	Del	2.54	1:1.45
76	USXII Cp	A	1.45	XIII SS& LXXXIX Cp	Del	1.82	1:1.25
77	USXII Cp	A	1.13	XIII SS& LXXXIX Cp	Del	1.29	1:1.14
78	USXII Cp	A	1.39	XIII SS& XC Cp	Del	1.47	1:1.05

SOURCE: T. N. Dupuy, *A Genius for War* (London, 1977), appendix E.

[a]For a list of engagements, see appendix B of this book.

[b]B-British; ID-Infantry Division; US-United States; AD-Armored Division; Cp-Corps

[c]A-Attack; HD-Hasty Defense; PD-Prepared Defense; FD-Fortified Defense; Del-Delaying Resistance

[d]Pz-Panzer; Pz Gr-Panzer Grenadier; HG-Herman Goering; Lt-Light; Pa-Paratroopers

at the gates of Tobruk and in the deathtrap that was Tunisia. It is the secret of this consistently high performance, not the ups and downs of Hitler's military "genius," that forms the theme of the present study.

To bring out the secret of the German performance, it was essential to have a background against which it could be silhouetted. For this purpose, the World War II U.S. Army was selected, not because it was a priori believed to be very different—like other armies around the world, it had copied much of its organization, including in particular the General Staff system, from the German model—but simply because more information about it was available in print than about any comparable force. The choice later turned out to be an inspired one because the U.S. Army, backed by vast economic and technological resources, developed an entirely different style of war. Whether the study does indeed succeed in its aim of bringing out the secret of the German Army's fighting power, however, remains for the reader to judge.

NOTES

1. This is hardly the place to discuss the changing demands made on soldiers through the ages, which would require a separate book. In any case, fighting power could very well be defined as that part of a soldier's mental makeup which does NOT change through time.

2. Asked to rate the Red Army, the U.S. Army, the Bundeswehr, and the former Wehrmacht by military quality, 74.5 percent of West Germans interviewed put the last named force at the head of the list. See R. Weltz, *Wie steht es um die Bundeswehr?* (Hamburg, 1964), p. 31.

3. Most recently, W. V. Madej, "Effectiveness and Cohesion of the German Ground Forces in World War II," *Journal of Political and Military Sociology* 6 (1978):233-48.

4. R. Lewin, *Ultra Goes to War* (London, 1978), pp. 155, 344.

5. R. A. Gabriel and P. L. Savage, *Crisis in Command; Mismanagement in the Army* (New York, 1978), especially chs. 1 and 3.

6. M. Cooper, *The German Army 1933-1945* (London, 1978), ch. 12 and page 166.

7. See M. van Creveld, *Supplying War: Logistics from Wallenstein to Patton* (Cambridge, 1977), chs. 5 and 6.

8. M. Messerschmidt, *Die Wehrmacht im NS Staat* (Hamburg, 1969), pp. 480-92; M. G. Steinert, *Hitlers Krieg und die Deutschen* (Düsseldorf, 1970), pp. 588-98. That Hitler was aware of this fact is brought out by S. Haffner, *Anmerkungen zu Hitler* (Munich, 1978), p. 56.

9. I have put down my views on this question in "Warlord Hitler; Some Points Reconsidered," *European Studies Review* 4 (1974):57-79. Whether Hitler was really a military ignoramus is debatable; that the quarrels between him and his generals had a negative effect on Germany's war effort is certain.

10. SHAEF (Supreme Headquarters, Allied European Forces) Weekly Intelligence Summary for Psychological Warfare, No. 28, 9 April 1945, file 332/52/268 at the National Archives (NA), Washington, D.C.

11. Figures from B. Mueller-Hillebrand, *Das Heer,* 3 vols. (Frankfurt am Main, 1968-), 3:248-66.

12. C. Barnett, "The Education of Military Elites," *Journal of Contemporary History* 2 (1967):26.

13. T. N. Dupuy, *Numbers, Predictions and War* (New York, 1979).

14. T. N. Dupuy, *A Genius for War* (London, 1977), pp. 234-35. The question as to why the second method should yield a greater differential than the first has been the subject of some correspondence between Colonel Dupuy and myself. It may be accounted for by two factors; namely, (*a*) the second method disregards the qualitative superiority of many German Army weapons, such as the Panther tank, the 88 mm antitank gun, the submachine guns MP 38 and 40, and the machine gun MG 42 (the latter, such an excellent weapon that it is still in use) and (*b*) combat effectiveness as calculated by the first method, as opposed to score effect as calculated by the second, takes the outcome into consideration. This has led Colonel Dupuy to conclude that "the ratio of the casualty-inflicting capabilities of forces is the square ratio of the ratio of their relative combat effectiveness" (letter to M. van Creveld, 15 May 1981). On the whole, combat effectiveness is probably a better measure of a force's Fighting Power as defined in this chapter than is its score effectiveness.

THE ROLE OF NATIONAL CHARACTER 2

As even a cursory look at history will reveal, some societies have always been more warlike than others. However, attempts to correlate this quality with other factors (geography, climate, social life, and sexual repression, among others) have not to date met with noticeable success.[1] The problem is compounded by the fact that every national group necessarily contains men of many different types and that the waging of war also requires many different and sometimes conflicting qualities. Furthermore, to speak of modern troops as "warlike" in the same sense that the term is applied to more primitive societies may be misleading, since present day warfare requires brains as well as brawn. A goodly supply of not-too-sophisticated cutthroats may still be essential, but it is no longer quite sufficient.

If all this were not enough, a further complicating factor is introduced by the fact that a people's fighting qualities may change, sometimes with remarkable speed. The German people, the subject of this inquiry, were not regarded as particularly good soldiers before the middle of the last century, when they suddenly emerged as the world's most formidable military nation. The Vietnamese, regarded as more or less useless by their French overlords before 1939, decisively defeated those very overlords in 1954 and then promptly split into two halves, one of which was indeed useless, while the other went on fighting magnificently for another two decades. The Arab defeat of 1967 called into being a character known as the "amoral familist," whose social nature allegedly rendered him incapable of cooperating with others; though amoral familists had probably not become an extinct species by 1973, fighting the Arab armies undoubtedly did.[2]

Given these methodological difficulties, it is perhaps not surprising that scientific—that is, statistical—material on the "warlikeness" of this or that society is exceedingly hard to come by. Accordingly, the following pages do not claim to do more than touch upon the problem.

If the propensity to go to war is any indication of a people's fighting qualities, there would, by Quincy Wright's data, appear to be little to choose from between Prussia/Germany on the one hand and the United States on the other. In considering table 2.1, it should by no means be overlooked that Germany is located right in the center of Europe, whereas the United States is so isolated as to constitute virtually the sole power in an entire hemisphere.

TABLE 2.1
Wars in German and American History

NAME OF WAR	DATES	INVOLVEMENT PRUS./GER.	INVOLVEMENT U.S.	DURATION IN YEARS PRUS./GER.	DURATION IN YEARS U.S.
American Revolution	1776-1783		x		7
Bavarian Succession	1777-1779	x		2	
1st Coalition	1792-1797	x		5	
Tripoli-U.S.	1801-1805		x		4
3rd Coalition	1806-1807	x		1	
War of 1812	1812-1814		x		2
4th Coalition	1813-1814	x		2	
5th Coalition	1815	x		0.15	
Algiers-U.S.	1815		x		0.3
Mexico-U.S.	1846-1848		x		2
Denmark-Germany	1848	x		3	
U.S. Civil War	1861-1865		x		4
Prussia-Denmark	1864	x		1	
Prussia-Austria	1866	x		0.15	
Franco-German	1870-1871	x		0.8	
Spanish-American	1898		x		1
Boxer Expedition	1900	x	x	1.5	1.5
Mexican Expedition	1912		x		1
World War I	1914-1918	x	x	4	1.5
World War II	1939-1945	x	x	5.5	3.5
TOTAL		12	11	26.1	27.8

SOURCE: Q. Wright, *A Study of War* (Chicago, 1965 ed.), tables 36-42, pp. 645-46.

Had the post-World War II years been taken into account also, the United States figures would have risen to 14 wars and 37.3 years respectively. The comparison, therefore, fails to show that the German people as a whole are significantly more trigger happy than the American one.

What direct comparisons between Germans and Americans have been made, mostly belong to the "hunt the Nazi" type of study popular in the years following World War II and are not very helpful to our purpose. One series of questionnaires among youths of both countries found Germans to be distinctly in favor of obedience to authority, whereas Americans tended toward independent decisions and actions;[3] however, even this cliché—it is at least two hundred years old[4]—has been denied by another study which, surprisingly enough, found postwar German youths more inclined than American ones to ask for the reasons behind an order.[5] In any case, since modern war requires intelligent cooperation on all levels rather than unquestioning obedience (see on this point chapter five) it is doubtful whether a nation of automatons would make good soldiers.

Again on the basis of questionnaires, it has been claimed that Germans are more callous than Americans, since they regard disobedience to established authority and loss of face, rather than violent offenses against other persons, as the worst of all conceivable crimes. This conclusion is certainly not supported by the homicide rates for both countries; though it must be remembered that, during the period in question, many of Germany's worst murderers had donned uniforms and were exercising their profession under official auspices behind barbed wire.[6]

Finally, one comparative study has reached the conclusion that German youths, unlike American ones, regard hard work as an end in itself "because it demonstrates that the person has control over his selfish impulses to be lazy, etc."[7] The "etc.," of course, is especially enlightening.

What comparative studies exist, in other words, do not allow the conclusion that Germans make better soldiers than Americans and may indeed not allow any sort of conclusions at all. Attempting to shed light on the question, we shall next turn to the numerous attempts that have been made, again mostly during the immediate postwar period, to understand the German nation's "collective soul."[8] It has been claimed, for example, that German social patterns were distinguished from others in the Western world by the "strongly authoritarian character of the father-son relationship ... also by a much more rigidly formalistic and hierarchical occupational system."[9] German children feared authority, developed obsessive traits of orderliness, and, if they were boys, acquired a "manliness," by which is meant the suppression of impulses of tenderness, pity, or regret.[10] "Partial constants of the German national character" were discovered by one author to be thoroughness, love of order, lack of good form or manners, self will, ecstasy, and fanaticism.[11]

All this, no doubt, is the result of toilet-training at too early an age, to which German mothers are said to be prone.[12] Using the ideas of Wilhelm Reich, some pscyhologists have concluded that the German people possess a compulsive anal erotic character. This causes them to become rigid, disciplined, and unable to let go. Their attitude toward women is "often marked by conscious and unconscious fear, aggression, and contempt."[13] (It is interesting to find one study claiming American men, allegedly brought up by women to a greater extent than anywhere else, possess exactly the same traits.)[14]

The "Reich German," to continue our survey, is said to have a harsh and aloof German father, who dominates the household and resents the little boy's gratifying tender ties with his indulging mother, who in turn acts as a mediator between the child and his father and is ambivalently hated and loved by both. This results in acute romantic rebellion in adolescence, plus the emergence of a "lonely genius" syndrome. The final outcome is said to be a "peculiar combination of rebellion and obedient submission," a person who is "harsh with himself and with others."[15]

Summing up the results of his investigations of the German "national character," one psychiatrist wrote that German national culture is "psychotically inclined"; surely no way to explain why Germans make or made good soldiers![16]

Since the available literature makes it impossible to show that Germans are (or are not) particularly warlike by character, how about Americans? Here we are fortunate to possess one, albeit small-scale, quantitative study that points toward interesting conclusions.[17] This study, published in 1974, consists of an attempt to define the socio-psychological profiles of two clearly delimitated groups of Americans, namely volunteers for war (Green Berets) on the one hand, and conscientious objectors on the other. Methodologically the study is, in many ways, a model of its kind: representatives of both groups were identified, matched for age, given a long series of questionnaires, and also interviewed in considerable depth.

As compared to the control group of conscientious objectors, the Green Berets—excellent soldiers by most people's standards—typically were raised in families that were less harmonious. One of the parents tended to dominate the other. Much greater emphasis was put on respect for material possessions, social status, work and industry, order and cleanliness, discipline, conformity, obedience and physical prowess, as opposed to goodness, joy in life, and individual achievement, which values were held in high esteem by the families of conscientious objectors. Stealing, lying, vandalism, and disobedience were regarded as the cardinal sins among parents of Green Berets, whereas those of conscientious objectors put far greater emphasis on inconsiderateness. In the families of Green Berets, moreover, punishments and threats were far more prevalent.

Conscientious objectors tended to regard women as equal partners and sex as a shared experience. Though capable of superficial relationships, they neither laughed at women nor despised them. Green Berets, by contrast, tended to be "remarkably unscrupulous and unfeeling" in their relationships to women. They were also male chauvinists in the sense of wanting to restrict sexual freedom to men only. This in turn meant that any woman who slept with them was automatically an object of contempt.

To find out which of the two groups were more representative of American life, they were compared with a third group consisting of conscripts. Five tests were carried out, of which two are reproduced in figures 2.1 and 2.2.

FIGURE 2.1
Group Mean Values on the Edwards Personal Preference Schedule

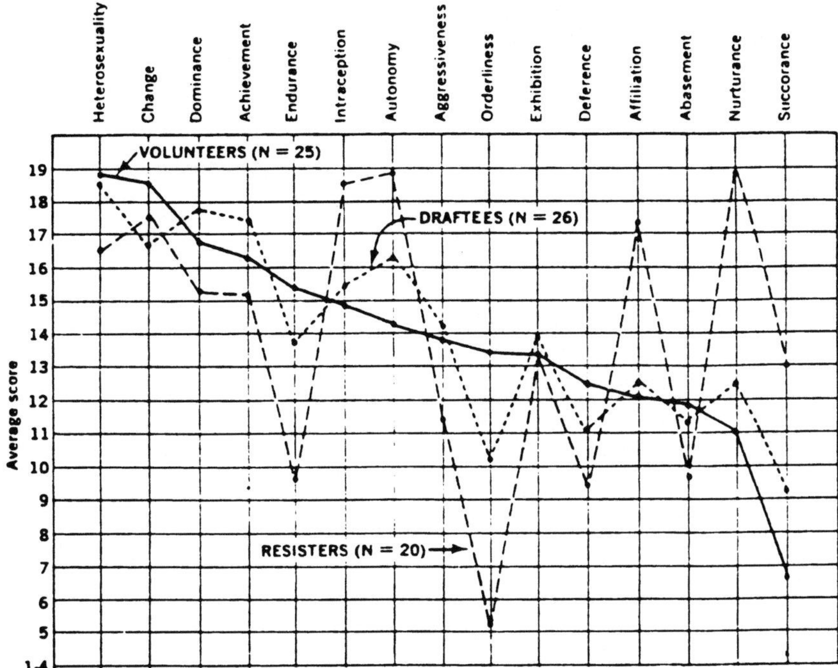

SOURCE: D.M. Mantell, *True Americanism: Green Berets and War Resisters, a Study of Commitment* (New York, 1974), p. 206.

While the numbers involved are admittedly small, these results clearly show that the American population at large has far more in common with the Green Berets than with the conscientious objectors. It may be worth adding that the results of the remaining three tests (measuring a person's evaluation of historical personalities, his moral attitudes, and his mental defects) lead to the same conclusion.

Our inference from all this is that Americans, by upbringing, education, and personality make first-class soldier material, a statement that can be supported by quotations ranging from Winston Churchill and Bernhard Montgomery to William Westmoreland and Moshe Dayan. Paradoxically, the same cannot be proven of Germans, though it may very well be true. This chapter must therefore end with the disappointing conclusion that, from the available evidence, there is no reason to believe the German national character to be more or less suitable to war than the American one.

FIGURE 2.2
Mean Scores on the Fascism, Traditional Family Ideology, Political-Economic Conservatism, Rigidity, and Dogmatism Scales

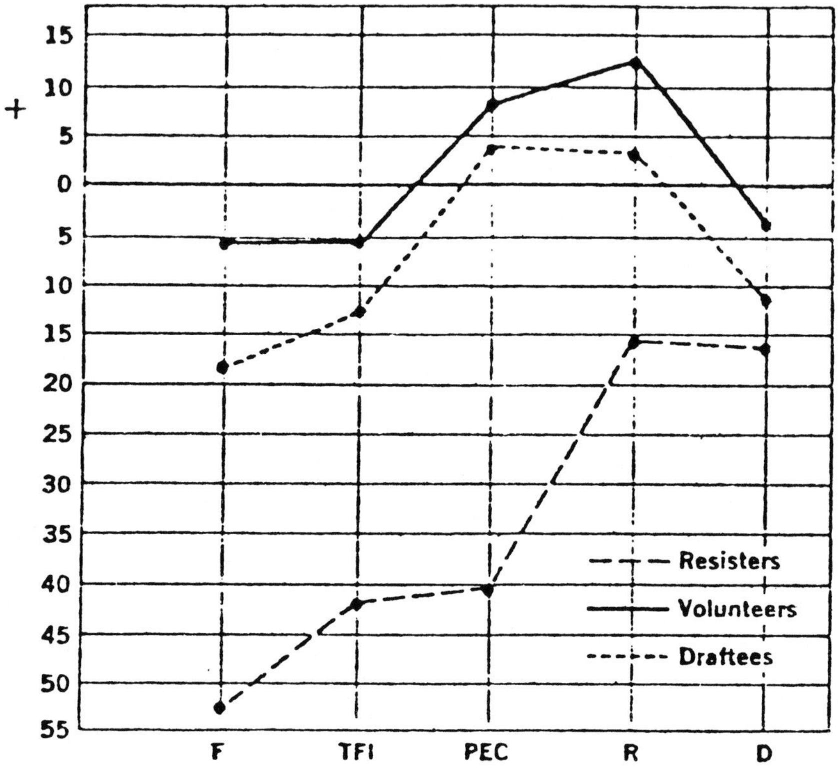

SOURCE: D. M. Mantell, *True Americanism: Green Berets and War Resisters, a Study of Commitment* (New York, 1974), p. 215.

F-Fascism
TFI-Traditional Family Ideology
PEC-Political-Economic Conservatism
R-Rigidity
D-Dogmatism

NOTES

1. S. Andreski, *Military Organization and Society* (Berkeley, 1968) p. 12; see also S. Bidwell, *Modern Warfare* (London, 1973) p. 145, and W. Nöbel, "Das Verhalten von Soldaten im Gefecht," *Wehrwissenschaftliche Rundschau* 28 (1979):115.
2. Y. Harkabi, "Basic Factors in the Arab Collapse during the Six Day War," *Orbis* 2 (1967):677-91.
3. D. V. Granahan, "A Comparison of Social Attitudes among American and German Youth," *Journal of Abnormal and Social Psychology* 41 (1946):244-47, 255.

4. Baron von Steuben, the Prussian drillmaster of the Continental Army, once put it as follows: "The genius of this nation is not in the least to be compared with that of the Austrians, Prussians, or French. You say to your soldier, 'do this,' and he doeth it; but I am obliged to say: 'this is the reason you ought to do that,' and he doeth it."

5. D. C. McClelland, J. F. Sturr, R. N. Knopp, and H. W. Wendt, "Obligations to Self and Society in the US and Germany," *Journal of Abnormal and Social Psychology* 56 (1958):253.

6. In 1937 Germany, with a population of 68 million, had 516 cases of murder and homicide. In 1938, 1,089 American cities, combined population 37.5 million, had 1,189 cases of murder and manslaughter. See *Statistisches Jahrbuch für das deutsche Reich*, vol. 57 (Berlin, 1938), p. 610, and FBI, ed., *Uniform Crime Reports for the US and Its Possessions* (Washington, D.C., 1939), p. 19.

7. D. C. McClelland, "The United States and Germany; a Comparative Study of National Character," in *The Roots of Consciousness* (New York, 1964), p. 81.

8. A useful summary is P. Loewenberg, "Psychohistorical Perspectives on Modern German History," *Journal of Modern History* 47 (1975):229-79.

9. T. Parsons, *Essays in Sociological Theory* (Glencoe, Ill., 1954), pp. 312-13.

10. B. Schaffner, *Father Land; a Study of Authoritarianism in the German Family* (New York, 1948), p. 55.

11. W. Hellpach, *Der deutsche Charakter* (Bonn, 1954), p. 185.

12. D. Rodnick, *Postwar Germany* (New Haven, 1948), p. 18.

13. P. Kesckemeti and N. Leites, "Some Psychological Hypotheses on Nazi Germany," *Journal of Social Psychology* 27 (1948):96.

14. H. Elkin, "Aggressive and Erotic Tendencies in Army Life," *American Journal of Sociology* 51 (1946):408-13.

15. E. Erikson, *Childhood and Society* (London, 1965 ed.), ch. 9. Erikson's contentions are unsupported by any kind of statistical evidence.

16. R. M. Brickner, "The German Cultural Paranoid Trend," *American Journal of Orthopsychiatry* 12 (1942):611-32.

17. D. M. Mantell, *True Americanism: Green Berets and War Resisters, a Study of Commitment* (New York, 1974), pp. 206 and 215.

ARMED FORCES AND SOCIETY 3

THE ARMY'S SOCIAL STATUS

A high social status for the armed forces within society is important for several reasons. It probably contributes to an army's morale. It may help in attracting and keeping high-quality manpower. It may be useful in helping the military to obtain a larger share of the national budget.

German Army

In Germany, beginning at the Wars of Unification, the army was highly regarded by most of the people and was considered the pride of the nation.[1] Esteem was extended more or less automatically to any member of the army and endowed him with a certain prestige that was graduated according to rank, position, arm of service, and regiment. In general, being a soldier or an exsoldier was regarded as an important social advantage and working girls gladly paid for the privilege of a uniformed date.[2]

Army service was officially defined as a duty-of-honor.[3] It presupposed the right to bear arms. A prison sentence involving the loss of civil rights also carried the loss of the right to bear arms, followed by an assignment to a labor battalion. To be dishonorably discharged from the army or navy was regarded as a heavy punishment and implied considerable social stigma. The consequences to a person's career in civilian life could also be unpleasant.

Before 1914, since universal conscription was not in fact put into practice, the opportunity existed for normally well-to-do, well educated youth to volunteer for one year's service. In 1912 alone 64,000 made use of this opportunity.

Things military—weapons and uniforms—were surrounded by a kind of awe that was spread by the press and literature. For parades, there were always crowds of enthusiastic spectators to be had. As the proverb had it, the soldier both was considered and regarded himself as "the first man in the state."

Organized in military-minded leagues, adoring civilians—mostly of middle-class origins—surrounded the army. The Kyffhäuser Bund, an organization of ex-servicemen founded in 1898, had 1,220,615 members in 1898, 2,097,527 in 1903, and 2,528,667 in 1909.[4] Founded in 1912 to pressure the Reichstag into making available larger funds for the military, the Wehrverein (Defense-Union) could count 300,000 members after a single year. Even more phenomenal was the success of General Colmar von der Goltz's Jungdeutschland, a paramilitary youth movement whose membership reached 750,000 within three years of its establishment in 1912. All together, therefore, the number of people associated with one proarmy organization or another exceeded 3.5 million in a population of 65 million.

The officer was the idol of society, a fact which in itself made him a target of Social-Democratic criticism. Bismarck had said that humanity starts with the rank of lieutenant. Society modelled itself on its darlings, a practice that could be carried to extremes as ridiculous as they were significant. Appearing in front of the Reichstag for the first time in 1909, Chancellor Bethmann-Hollweg wore a major's uniform. Five years later it was apparently thought he could not properly carry out his duties without being promoted to honorary lieutenant general.

To carry the rank of a reserve officer—normally that of a lieutenant or captain, rarely that of major—was an important status symbol. It was also not without value in professional life. Among higher officials the rank of reserve officer was regarded virtually as a patriotic duty. A widely circulated story had it that an old and famous professor, granted an audience with the kaiser and asked to make a request, he raised his glaucomous eyes and, with a shaking voice, begged to be made a second lieutenant of the reserve.

An officer's pay was low. Until 1909 he lived, as the title of a popular book put it, in "Splendid Poverty." Even afterwards, a junior officer earned only between 125 and 200 marks per month and was thus dependent on aid from parents and relatives.[5]

A good measure of the officer's exalted social status is provided by the sums that cadets had to dish out from their own resources in order to be taken into a regiment.[6] This varied from as little as 50 marks per month in some infantry regiments to 200 marks in the Fifth Cavalry Regiment. For commissioned lieutenants the sums varied between 20 and 200 marks, the average being 64. To this the cost of initial equipment, anything between 250 and 600 marks, had to be added. This was at a time when the average clerk could expect to earn about 70 marks per month.

To be an officer was to live in the best of all possible worlds. Friedrich Sachsse, himself an officer who was killed in July 1941 at the age of 29, remembered what it was like during the Weimar period:

> Often there were officers among the guests. They were big and loud men. Talking to them gave one a fright, when they bent down and shook [a boy's] shoulder with their hard hands. "Well my boy, what do you want to be when you're grown up! Officer, right! Ha ha ha!" They laughed loudly and carelessly. To them it was a matter of course that every boy wanted to become an officer, that he was burning to become one![7]

U.S. Army

The status of the armed forces in American society has always been problematic. Summing up the interwar experience, N. F. Parish wrote:

> Ground and air officers alike stubbornly carried out their duties among a people hoping and trying to believe that all officers were as useless as their sabre chains. It was a weird, almost furtive existence, like that of a fireman trying to guard a wooden city whose occupants pretend it was fireproof. In such an atmosphere of unreality officers sometimes felt a little ghostly or bewildered, or turned to the affectation of imported uniforms and mannerisms, the imitation of the well-to-do and the horse culture. These psychic manifestations of a sense of social uselessness appeared in surprisingly few officers. Most plodded grimly along, stubbornly reminding themselves and each other that they were real, after all, and that the things they were doing were necessary.[8]

Historically in the American democracy, military values were felt to be so alien that the army was considered and felt itself a neglected stepchild.[9] The idea that large military forces form a threat to liberty, that they endanger democracy, that they imperil economic prosperity, and that their very existence undermines peace—all these are said to have been "fairly constantly characteristic" of American attitudes toward the army.[10]

During the interwar period in particular, the dominant business culture rejected militarism as a vestige leftover from a barbarous past. Reform minded liberals, by contrast, were prepared to retain the army, but only insofar as it shed its military character and became an instrument of social reform. The military officer, a *New Republic* writer declared, "is a man cherishing an attitude towards life that belongs to the dark ages."[11] His standards of honor, obedience, and loyalty were looked upon as either hypocritical or positively dangerous.

Besides being the butt of criticism, the U.S. Army had to fight its historical isolation. A big step forward was taken in 1911 when Congress passed a law imposing a $500 fine on commercial establishments showing a "No Soldiers Admitted" notice. Fven in 1951, after half a century of public relations, the *Social Register* for New York, Boston, and Chicago listed fewer than 1 percent officers—and those lucky few owed their places not to military rank but to social pedigree, connections, and money.[12]

The Army's low prestige was reflected in spoken language. "To soldier" meant to loaf; the expression was replaced by "goldbricking" during World War II, but resumed its original meaning thereafter.[13]

Considering all this, it is remarkable how well the officer (but not the enlisted man) did in opinion polls regarding the comparative social prestige of various trades and professions. In a series of surveys dating from 1925 on, officers consistently appeared among the upper 25 percent of all professions; for example, 9th among 45 in 1925, 8th among 40 in 1935, 6th among 27 in 1947, 9th among 26 in 1949, and 6th among 25 in 1951.[14] In the same surveys, enlisted men figured 30th, 28th, 19th, 20th, and 25th respectively.

In 1955 a nationwide survey found officers ranking 7th on a scale of 17, below physicians, scientists, college professors, lawyers, ministers, and public schoolteachers, but above farm owners, carpenters, mail carriers, bookkeepers, plumbers, radio and TV announcers, owners of small stores, mechanics, enlisted men in the armed forces (number 16 on the list), and truck drivers.[15]

Possibly because the results could easily be predicted, no systematic attempt was made to study the social status of the German Army during the interwar period.[16] However, a survey was carried out in 1955. At that time the prestige of things military in the Federal Republic had touched rock bottom; 40 percent of all West Germans were for but 45 percent were against the reconstitution of a German armed force, and only 17 percent thought the army represented any positive values whatsoever.[17] Nevertheless, even at this time the esteem in which German officers were held by their public was greater—though only slightly so—than that accorded to their American counterparts in a comparable study.[18]

THE ARMY'S SOCIAL STRUCTURE

Another indication of an army's social status, fully as important as any external sign, is its social structure. It is to be assumed that, given the very real handicaps surrounding the life of a soldier, only a highly regarded force will be able to attract society's higher classes; conversely, its ability to do so may well determine its quality, since it is often among the higher classes that society's main reservoirs of educated, trained, and skilled manpower are to be found.

German Army

Owing to the fact that German militarism at one time was the major historical interest, the social origins of the Prussian/German officer corps have been investigated with comparative thoroughness. In Germany, as in other European states, a caste that had originally been the almost exclusive preserve of the nobility was gradually penetrated by scions of middle-class families during the nineteenth century. In Germany at any rate, this development was by no means the result of the nobility's reluctance to serve; rather, the rise of mass conscript armies after about 1870 brought in its wake such an increased demand for officers that it became necessary to turn, in the words of Kaiser William II, from the "nobility of the blood" to the "nobility of the mind." Consequently in 1913, only 30 percent of all officers were of the nobility.[19]

World War I brought a further huge increase in the demand for officers. Numerous sons of middle- and even lower-middle-class families who did not stand a chance of being accepted into a regiment in time of peace were thereby given an opportunity to obtain a commission. The army did not turn democratic, however. With certain rare exceptions, even deserving soldiers and non-commissioned officers (NCOs) were refused promotion into the officer corps—a bad error which was to come in for much criticism after the war. Keeping an eye on the future political reliability of the army,[20] the war ministry strove to maintain social standards as best it could.

Immediately after 1918, the nobility was reluctant to serve in the army of the Weimar Republic. This soon changed, however, and as early as 1921 an article appeared in the German nobility's journal calling on blue-bloods to resume the tradition of "the best for officers."[21] So successful was the campaign to recruit noblemen that their percentage among newly commissioned officers in 1931-32 actually exceeded the 1913 figure.[22] Nor was this fact due simply to favoritism: a scrutiny of the lists of officers dicharged as unsuitable each year shows that the share of noblemen never fell below 20 percent and stood at 23.2 percent for the period 1924-32. The high number of noblemen was due rather to the fact that many patents, especially among senior officers, were of recent origin.[23]

Put into tabular form, these facts can be summed up as shown in table 3.1.

TABLE 3.1
Social Origins of the German Officer Corps

YEAR	OFFICERS WHO WERE NOBLEMEN (%)	YEAR	GENERALS WHO WERE NOBLEMEN (%)
1913	30.00	1911	67
1920	21.70		
1926	20.50	1925	38
1932	23.80	1932	33

During the Nazi years, another huge increase in the demand for officers caused the nobility to be completely swamped. Once again, however, this was by no means due to any reluctance on its part to enter the service; even during these years, the names of many noble families appeared several times in the army lists.[24]

Although the Nazis did much to democratize the army, they could not—possibly owing to the short time at their disposal—prevent the continued dominance of nobles among the officer corps' top ranks. Even as late as May 1943, 17.6 percent of 681 field marshals, colonel generals, generals, and lieutenant generals were of the nobility. Among field marshals alone, there were actually more noblemen in 1944 than there had been in 1932.[25] These facts show that army personnel policy during the Nazi years was hardly revolutionary; they also serve as additional proof that the army had by no means lost its traditional ability to attract the highest classes of society.

Distributed according to their fathers' professions, officers entering the War Academy presented the picture shown in table 3.2.

TABLE 3.2
Origins of the German Officer Corps by Fathers' Professions

FATHER'S PROFESSION	1912	1926	1921-1934
officers	24.56(%)	44.34(%)	34.93(%)
professionals or senior civil servants	39.88	41.51	36.50
landowners	7.87	4.73	4.76
agrarian managers	1.69	0.94	1.59
merchants and industrialists	15.41	6.13	9.52
NCOs	4.74	1.41	7.94
others	5.85	0.94	4.76

Throughout this period, therefore, an officer's career was sufficiently highly regarded for the army to be able to attract those classes in the population who, by reason of property and education, did have a choice.

U.S. Army

Turning now from the German to the American Army, we are handicapped by the fact that the only available figures do not refer to the officer corps as a whole but to generals only. The social origins of this group present the picture shown in table 3.3. Table 3.4 further delineates the social status of this group.

TABLE 3.3
Origins of American Generals by Fathers' Professions

FATHER'S PROFESSION	1910-1920	1935	1950
business	24 (%)	16 (%)	29 (%)
professional and managerial	46	60	45
farmer	30	16	10
white collar	—	6	11
worker	—	2	5
other	—	—	—

SOURCE: M. Janowitz, *The Professional Soldier, a Social and Political Portrait* (New York, 1960) pp. 67-69.

TABLE 3.4
Origins of American Generals by Fathers' Social Status

CLASS	1910-1920	1935	1950
upper	26 (%)	8 (%)	3 (%)
upper-middle	66	68	47
lower-middle	8	23	45
upper-lower	0	1	4
lower-lower	0	0	1

SOURCE: M. Janowitz, *The Professional Soldier, a Social and Political Portrait* (New York, 1960) pp. 67-69.

One might therefore conclude that, for generals at any rate, the view of the U.S. Army as a haven for those who do not have a choice does not hold water.

Finally, table 3.5 is a comparison of self-recruitment (the percentage of officers who were officers' sons) in the two armies. It is especially interesting, since it represents one measure of the officers' satisfaction with their jobs and status. The figures speak for themselves.

TABLE 3.5
Self Recruitment in German and American Officer Corps

YEAR	SELF RECRUITMENT AMONG U.S. OFFICERS (%)	YEAR	SELF RECRUITMENT AMONG GERMAN OFFICERS (%)
1910	7	1911	27
1920	10	1925	29
1935	23	1933	29
		1939	15
		1941	16
		1944	14
1950	11		

A LADDER FOR SOCIAL MOBILITY?

German Army

Comparatively little information is available on the German Army's function as a social ladder; that is, a vehicle through which talented and ambitious men might reach society's highest ranks. It would seem, however, that during the Imperial period, the feeling among officers was that even the humblest cadet carried the field marshal's batton in his knapsack; the same must have been true during the Weimar period with its heavy emphasis on an equitable administration of the promotion system.[26, 27]

While the army's growth during the Nazi years undoubtedly created opportunities for social advancement of every kind, no detailed figures are available. It is merely known that, among sixteen field marshals in 1944, seven came from long established families, seven from families that had been steadily advancing in the world for several generations back and could look upon a marshal's batton as the culmination of progress, and two, from humble families.[28] At this time the German Army also carried on its lists eleven generals who had risen from the ranks.

In spite of its relatively small size (29,000 before 1914, a mere 4,000 during the Weimar period, still only 10,800 in 1936) the officer corps was an excellent avenue for social mobility, as table 3.6 data on the origins, profession, and education of cabinet ministers shows.

TABLE 3.6
Officers' Sons, Officers, and Kriegsakademie Graduates among German Cabinet Members, 1980-1933

CABINET MEMBERS DURING:	OFFICERS' SONS	OFFICERS	KRIEGSAKADEMIE GRADUATES
pre-1914 (monarchy)	9.1 (%)	16.9 (%)	15.8 (%)
1919-1932 (republic)	4.9	7.4	2.5
1933 (Hitler)	12.1	18.2	12.1
average	8.7	8.5	10.1

SOURCE: M. E. Knight. *The German Executive, 1890-1933* (Stanford, 1952), pp. 36, 41, 45.

The share of officers' sons and officers among cabinet members was far from negligible. The high figures on the right are especially interesting, since they meant that on the average the chances of an officer who had passed through the Kriegsakademie of attaining cabinet ranks were some forty times as good as those of university graduates.[29]

U.S. Army

In the U.S. between 1892 and 1949, only 0.5 percent of all cabinet ministers were exofficers. A breakdown of senior civil servants during the same period fails to show any officers, nor are military academies named among the schools from which they graduated.[30]

While no studies are available for the interwar years, table 3.7 shows the results of a 1952 study comparing the social background of generals with that of business leaders.

TABLE 3.7
Social Origins of American Generals and Businessmen, by Fathers' Professions

FATHER'S PROFESSION	GENERALS, (1950)	BUSINESS, (1952)
business	30	26
professional and managerial	44	29
farmer	10	8
white collar	11	19
worker	5	15
other	—	2

SOURCE: M. Janowitz, *The Professional Soldier, a Social and Political Portrait* (New York, 1960), p. 93.

From this study one might conclude that, even at a time when a vastly expanded U.S. Army reached the peak of its prestige, it still offered fewer opportunities for social advancement than did American business.

NOTES

1. The following remarks are based on Militärgeschichtliches Forschungsamt, ed., *Handbuch zur deutschen Militärgeschichte*, 7 vols. (Frankfurt am Main, 1968), 5:83-84.
2. M. Kitchen, *The German Officer Corps, 1890-1914* (Oxford, 1968), p. 140.
3. Wehrgesetz (Law of National Defense) of 21 May 1935.
4. Figures from Kitchen, *The German Officer Corps*, pp. 129, 132, 136.
5. H. Meier-Welcker, *Untersuchungen zur Geschichte des Offizier-Korps* (Stuttgart, 1962), p. 20.
6. H. Rumschöttel, "Bildung und Herkunft der bayerischen Offiziere 1866 bis 1914," *Militärgeschichtliche Mitteilungen* 2 (1970):125-26.
7. F. Sachsse, *Roter Mohn* (Frankfurt am Main, 1972), p. 142.
8. "New Responsibilities of Air Force Officers," *Air University Review* 3 (March-April 1972):15-16. This essay was originally published in 1947.
9. R. F. Weigley, "A Historian Looks at the Army," *Military Review* 52 (February 1972):26.
10. S. P. Huntington, *The Soldier and the State* (Cambridge, Mass., 1957), p. 155.
11. Quoted in ibid., pp. 155-56.

12. M. Janowitz, *The Professional Soldier, a Social and Political Portrait* (New York, 1960), p. 204.

13. The word is used in this sense by W. Menninger, *Psychiatry in a Troubled World* (New York, 1948), p. 177; Menninger was the army's chief psychiatrist during World War II. See also B. von Haller Gilmer, *Industrial and Organizational Psychology* (New York, 1972), p. 441.

14. See C. H. Coates and R. J. Pellegrin, *Military Sociology; a Study of American Military Institutions and Military Life* (Washington, D.C., 1965), pp. 45-46.

15. Janowitz, *The Professional Soldier*, p. 227.

16. The nearest thing available is a 1930 Munich Ph.D. dissertation that traces social mobility among exofficers during the Weimar years. It was found that those (normally senior) officers who could live on their pensions managed to stay in society's higher classes, as did those, for example, physicians and chemists, whose skills were readily transferrable to the civilian market. The rest, however, had to take up new trades and thereby went down the social ladder. See J. Nothaas, "Social Ascent and Descent among Former Officers in the German Army and Navy after the World War" (New York, 1937), pp. 10-11.

17. R. Weltz, *Wie Steht es um die Bundeswehr?* (Hamburg, 1964), pp. 5-8. Even in September 1956, 43 percent of all West Germans wanted to abolish the Bundeswehr and only 38 percent wanted to retain it.

18. J. J. Wiatr, "Social Prestige of the Military; a Comparative Approach," in *Military Profession and Military Regimes*, ed. J van Doorn (The Hague, 1969), p. 77.

19 K. Demeter, *Das deutsche Offizierkorps* (Berlin, 1965), p. 27.

20. Ein Stabsoffizier, *Das alte Heer* (Charlottenburg, 1920), pp. 34-35.

21. Captain von Kortzfleisch, "Der Offizierberuf im Reichsheer," *Deutschen Adelsblatt* 39, no. 22, p. 338.

22. Demeter, *Das deutsche Offizierkorps*, p. 55.

23. D. N. Spires, "The Career of the Reichswehr Officer" (Ph.D. diss., University of Washington, 1979), pp. 260, 261.

24. Demeter, *Das deutsche Offizierkorps*, p. 54.

25. N. von Preradovich, *Die militärische und Soziale Herkunft des deutschen Heeres 1 Mai 1944* (Onasbrück, 1978), p. 13.

26. K. Hesse, *Der Geist von Potsdam* (Mainz, 1967), p. 27.

27. Spires, "The Career of the Reichswehr Officer," pp. 232-33.

28. Preradovich, *Die Militärische und Soziale Herkunft*, p. 5.

29. In any average year, students would outnumber Kriegsakademie students 250 to 1, yet they were only 6 times as numerous in the various cabinets.

30. R. Bendix, *Higher Civil Servants in American Society* (Boulder, Colo., 1949), pp. 56, 92.

DOCTRINE AND THE IMAGE OF WAR ______ 4

GERMAN ARMY

The best way to understand the German Army's views as to what really matters in war is to quote directly from the official manual *Truppenführung* (roughly translated as "Command of Troops") of 1936.[1] Its two volumes are signed by two successive commanders in chief, Generals Kurt von Hammerstein Equord and Werner von Fritsch.

Introduction

1. War is an art, a free creative activity resting on scientific foundations. It makes the highest demands on a man's entire personality.
2. The art of war is in a state of constant development. New weapons cause it to assume ever-changing forms. The advent of these weapons must be foreseen in good time, and their effect correctly assessed. Thereupon they must be quickly taken into service.
3. The situations arising out of war are infinitely varied. They change often and unexpectedly and can rarely be foreseen in advance. Often it is precisely those factors that cannot be measured that are of the greatest importance. One's own will is confronted by the enemy's independent one. Friction and errors are everyday occurrences.
4. It is impossible to exhaustively lay down the art of war in regulations. The latter merely serve as guiding lines that must be applied in accordance with circumstances.

   Simplicity and consistency in action present the best way of obtaining results. . . .
10. The advance of technology notwithstanding, the role of the individual remains decisive. His significance has been further enhanced by the dispersion characteristic of modern warfare.

    The emptiness of the battlefield demands independently thinking and acting fighters who exploit each situation in a considered, determined, and bold way. They must be thoroughly conscious of the fact that only results matter.

Habituation to physical effort, hardness against oneself, willpower, self-confidence, and courage enable a man to master the most difficult situations.

11. The quality of commander and men determines the fighting power[2] of a unit which must be properly backed up by high quality supply and maintenance.

    High fighting power can cancel out numerical inferiority. The higher this quality, the stronger and the more mobile the conduct of war.

    Superior leadership and superior troops are secure bases for victory....

15. From the youngest soldier upward, the independent commitment of all spiritual, intellectual, and physical facilities is demanded. Only thus can the full power of the troops be brought to bear in action. Only thus is it possible to develop men who are brave and decisive in times of danger and who are capable of pulling others along in bold exploits.

    Thus decisive action remains the first prerequisite for success in war. Everybody, from the highest commander to the youngest soldiers, must be conscious of the fact that inactivity and lost opportunities weigh heavier than do errors in the choice of means. [Emphasis in the original]

Having said this, the regulations proceed to enumerate some of the ways in which victory must be sought:

28. One cannot be strong enough at the decisive point. Whoever disperses his forces or employs them on secondary missions sins against this rule.

    By making use of speed, mobility, longer marches, night and terrain, surprise, and deception, the weaker can defeat the stronger at the decisive point.

29. Space and time must be correctly used, favorable situations quickly recognized and exploited with determination. Each advantage over the enemy reinforces one's own freedom of action....

32. Surprise is a crucially important means to bring about success. Actions based on surprise, however, can only yield results when the enemy is given no time to take effective countermeasures.

    The enemy will also attempt surprise. This is to be taken into account.

To this, little can or should be added. It is worth bearing in mind, however, that geography has placed Germany in the center of Europe; frequently finding themselves compelled to fight a combination of numerically superior enemies, the Germans responded by developing a very heavy emphasis on operations (defined as "the interplay of attack, defense, retreat, counterattack, and so forth") to the detriment, not to say neglect, of other functions, which were regarded as merely supportive. In particular, military doctrine put a heavy emphasis on the attack as the sole means of ending wars rapidly and decisively. An analysis of the index to the two volumes of the *Truppenführung* brings out the order of priorities listed in table 4.1.

TABLE 4.1
Analysis of the Index to the *Truppenführung*, by Subject

		SUBJECT
Total no. entries	650	
Entries with subentries	172	
Total no. subentries	746	
Entries with the largest number of subentries		
attack	53	a
defense	34	a
delaying resistance	32	a
combat	23	a
retreat	19	a
reconnaissance	18	a
cavalry	18	e
order (Befehl)	17	b
march	16	c
leader	16	b
communications	15	b
supply	14	c
resistance	12	a
signals	12	b
shelter	12	c
pursuit	10	a
shelter-place	10	c
security	10	a
fighting vehicle	10	d
artificial fog	10	d
Total	361	

SOURCE: Heeres Dienstvorschrift 300, *Truppenführung* (Berlin, 1936).
NOTE: To a (various forms of combat) belong 211 subentries, or 28.3 percent of the total; to b (leadership, command, signals) 60, or 8 percent; to c (logistics and factors pertaining thereto) belong 52, or 6.9 percent; to d (technical means) 20 or 2.6 percent; and to e (units or arms of service) 18, or 2.5 percent. Entries in category a are 9 in number and average 23.4 subentries each. Entries in category b number 4 and average 15 subentries. Those in category c also number 4 but average 13 subentries. Category d sports 2 entries averaging 10 subentries each. Apart from category e, where cavalry with 18 entries forms an anomaly as conspicuous as it is intriguing, the emphasis on operations as well as the entire order of priorities are therefore quite clear.

U.S. ARMY

The 1941 edition of the U.S. Army's Field Service Regulations (FM 100-5), signed by General Marshall, does not have an introduction on the nature of war. Instead there is prefaced to the volume an untitled page from which we quote.

> While the fundamental doctrines of combat operations are neither numerous nor complex, their application is at times difficult. Knowledge of these doctrines and experience in their application provide all commanders a firm basis for action in a particular situation. This knowledge and experience enable the commander to utilize the flexible organization with which he is provided to group his forces into task units most suitable for the accomplishment of his mission.
>
> Set rules and methods must be avoided. They limit imagination and initiative which are so important in the successful prosecution of war. They provide the enemy a fixed pattern of operations which he can more easily counter.
>
> It is a function of command to coordinate the tactics and techniques of various arms and services so as to develop in the forces employed on a given task the teamwork essential to success.

Having said this, the manual devotes its first two chapters to the organization of the army and to the functions of each arm and service, then goes on:

> 98. Man is the fundamental instrument in war; other instruments may change but he remains relatively constant. Unless his behavior and elemental attributes are understood, gross mistakes will be made in planning operations and in troop leading.
>
> In the training of the individual soldier, the essential considerations are to integrate individuals into a group and to establish for that group a high standard of military conduct and performance without destroying the initiative of the individual.
>
> 99. War places a severe test on the physical endurance and moral stamina of the individual soldier. To perform his duties efficiently, he must not only be well equipped and technically trained but he must also be physically qualified to endure the hardships of field service and be constantly fortified by discipline based on high ideas of military conduct. . . .
>
> 100. In spite of the advances in technology, the worth of the individual man is still decisive. The open order of combat accentuates his importance. Every individual must be trained to exploit a situation with energy and boldness and must be imbued with the idea that success will depend upon his initiative and action. . . .
>
> 107. The combat value of a unit is determined in great measure by the soldierly qualities of its leaders and members and its will to fight. Outward marks of this combat value will be found in the set up and appearance of the men, in equipment and in the readiness of the unit for action. Superior combat value will offset numerical inferiority. Superior leadership combined with superior combat value of troops constitutes a reliable basis for success in battle. . . .

111. The first demand in war is decisive action. Commanders inspire confidence in their subordinates by their decisive conduct and their ability to gain material advantage over the enemy.

Proceeding now to "Doctrines of Combat" the manual goes on:

112. The ultimate objective of all military operations is the destruction of the enemy's armed forces in battle....

113. Simple and direct plans and methods with prompt and thorough execution are often decisive in the attainment of success....

115. Through offensive action a commander exercises his initiative, preserves his freedom of action, and imposes his will on the enemy. A defensive attitude may, however, be deliberately adopted as a temporary expedient while awaiting an opportunity for counteroffensive action, or for the purpose of economizing forces on a front where a decision is not sought. The selection by the commander of the right time and place for offensive action is a decisive factor in the success of the operation.

Numerical inferiority does not necessarily commit a command to a defensive attitude. Superior hostile numbers may be overcome through greater mobility, better armament and equipment, more effective fire, higher morale, and better leadership. Superior leadership often enables a numerically inferior force to be stronger at the point of decisive action....

116. Concentration of superior forces, both on the ground and in the air, at the decisive place and time and their employment in a decisive direction, creates the conditions essential to victory. Such concentration requires strict economy in the strength of forces assigned to secondary missions. Detachments during combat are justifiable only when the execution of tasks assigned them contributes directly to success in the main battle.

117. Surprise must be sought throughout the action by every means and by every echelon of command. It may be obtained by fire as well as by movement. Surprise is produced through measures which either deny information to the enemy, or positively deceive him, as to our dispositions, movements and plans. Terrain which appears to impose great difficulties on operations may often be utilized to gain surprise. Surprise is furthered by variation in the means and methods employed in combat and by rapidity of execution....

118. To guard against surprise requires a correct estimate of enemy capabilities, adequate security measures, effective reconnaissance, and readiness for action of all units. Every unit takes the necessary measures for its own local ground and air security. Provision for the security of flanks and rear is of especial importance.

Thus, though entire sentences were clearly lifted straight from the German regulations, the overall effect is subtly different and, indeed, indicative of a dissimilar conception of the nature of war. Thus, the German view is that war is a "free creative activity resting on scientific foundations"; the American one, that it is a question of properly understanding and applying "doctrines" in such a manner as to "utilize the flexible organization with which [a commander] is provided . . . for the accomplishment of his mission." The emphasis on scientific management is thus evident.

From Carl von Clausewitz, the German Army adopted the idea that war is the clash of independent wills, and consequently dominated by friction. In the U.S. Army's manual by contrast the enemy is not mentioned except as a factor that may disrupt one's own pattern of activity, the Clausewitzan influence being instead obvious in the overriding emphasis put on decisive battle.

"Simplicity and consistency" in action constitute, in the German view, the key to success in war; the U.S. Army Manual renders this, characteristically, as "simple and direct plans."

The German manual emphasizes that "it is impossible to exhaustively lay down the art of war in regulations"; the American one, though it does recognize the need to avoid "set rules and methods" as a means of misleading the enemy, expects to provide commanders with "a firm basis for action in a particular situation." Possibly for this reason, it is not nearly as strong in its call for independent action on all levels—which comprises the real essence of the German regulations—and goes into considerably more detail at every point.

While both manuals emphasize the role of the individual vis-à-vis modern technology, the German one makes "the highest demands" on him; the American one, on the other hand, seems to regard him merely as one "instrument" among many, one whose "elemental attributes" must be understood if "gross mistakes" are to be avoided.

An interesting aspect of the U.S. manual, which has no direct equivalent in the German one, is the heavy emphasis laid on teamwork (with the implied prerequisites of coordination and control) and unit cohesion; the latter point constituting a perfectly sound doctrine which, as we shall see, was not put into practice.

Overall the U.S. Army's view of war was therefore considerably more managerial than the German one, putting far heavier emphasis on doctrine, planning, and control. One reason for this was probably the comparative inexperience of the majority of troops and commanders who, civilians until yesterday, required a higher degree of supervision from above. In the main, however, it reflects the experience of an army that, traditionally assured of overwhelming material superiority, simply did not have to rely on fighting power to the same extent that the Germans did. Given this difference (compare the means by which both armies sought to overcome numerical inferiority), considerably less emphasis was put on operations in the German sense and more on the organization and logistics required to ensure the most effective deployment of available material resources. This again is borne out by an analysis of the index to the U.S. Army regulations in table 4.2. This analysis was carried out in a manner similar to the analysis of the index to the *Truppenführung* (see table 4.1 on page 30 and the note thereto).

TABLE 4.2
Analysis of the Index to FM 100-5, by Subject

		SUBJECT
Total no. entries	287	
Entries with subentries	104	
Total no. subentries	1,210	
Entries with the largest number of subentries		
defense	63	a
attack	57	a
marches	57	c
river lines	42	c
cavalry	38	e
combat aviation	34	e
reconnaissance	32	a
armored division	30	e
signal communications	30	b
field artillery	28	e
security	26	a
mountain operations	25	a
tanks	24	d
troops transported by air	24	c
orders	22	b
snow and extreme cold	22	c
infantry	22	e
total	576	

NOTE: To a (various forms of combat) belong 203, or 16.7 percent of all subentries; to e (units or arms of service) belong 152, or 12.5 percent; to c (logistics and factors pertaining thereto) 145 or 11.9 percent; to b (leadership, command, signals) 52, or 4.2 percent; and to d (technical means) only 24 or 1.9 percent.

It can thus be shown, quantitatively, that American doctrine was much less single-minded than the German one with its emphasis on operations, choosing instead to stress a balanced development of operations, organization and logistics.

NOTES

1. Heeres Dienstvorschrift 300, *Truppenführung* (Berlin, 1936). This remained in force to the end of the war.
2. Kampfkraft.

COMMAND PRINCIPLES 5

The importance of a proper command system, leading to a correct distribution of authority and responsibility among the various echelons of the military hierarchy, does not require elaboration. Without striking a correct balance between centralization and decentralization, discipline and initiative, authority and individual responsibility, it is impossible for any human organization—let alone a military one, operating as it does in an environment where disorder and confusion are endemic—to function or, indeed, exist.

While the above is undoubtedly true about war in any period, a few words on the character of modern war may be in place. From the point of view of a command system, modern war is distinguished above all by its speed and by the need for close cooperation between many kinds of specialized troops. This means that, other factors being equal, a command system that allows for initiative on the lowest level, and for intelligent cooperation between subordinate commanders, is likely to be superior to one that does not. It is with these considerations in mind that the following sections should be read.

GERMAN ARMY

Contrary to the widely held clichés about "blind obedience"[1] and "Prussian discipline" the German Army had, from the time of Moltke the Elder at the latest, always emphasized the crucial importance of individual initiative and responsibility, even at the lowest levels. It was, in this respect, well ahead of German industry, where the authoritarian view of command from above-obedience from below continued to prevail until deep into the second third of the twentieth century.[2]

Even as early as 1906, the army regulations read: "in particular, combat demands thinking, independent leaders and troops capable of independent action." The idea was taken a step further in the regulations of 1908: "from the youngest soldier upwards, the total *independent* [emphasis added] commitment of all physical and mental forces is to be demanded. Only thus can the full power of the troops be brought into action."

Parallel to and as a direct outcome of the emphasis placed on independent action by subordinate commanders the German Army, again from the time of Moltke on, developed its system of Auftragstaktik (best translated as "mission-oriented command system"), which to this day forms a key element in West German military doctrine. The best short explanation of the system is provided by Bundeswehr General von Lossow who, interestingly, notes that it originated with Hessian troops who brought it back from the War of the American Revolution:

1. The mission must express the will of the commander in an unmistakable way.
2. The objective, course of action, and mission constraints, such as time, must be clear and definite without restricting freedom of action more than necessary in order to make use of the initiative of individuals charged with the tasks to be accomplished.
3. Limits as to the method of execution within the framework of the higher commander's will are imposed only where essential for coordination with other commands.[3]

Under a mission-oriented command system, in other words, commanders are trained to tell their subordinates what to do, but not how. Provided only that they keep within the framework of the whole, wide latitude is granted the latter to devise and carry out their own measures. Such a system, of course, presupposes uniformity of thinking and reliability of action only to be attained by thorough training and long experience. More important still, complete confidence of superiors in their subordinates and vice versa is absolutely indispensable.

Provided the above conditions can be met the system's advantages, again in General von Lossow's words, are considerable:

1. Leaders of all echelons are forced to analyze their own situations as well as that of the next highest[4] command.
2. Transmission of orders from one command level to another is expedited.
3. Measures taken at the scene of action are in harmony with actual conditions.

Returning now to the Heeres Dienstvorschrift 300, *Truppenführung* of 1936 already quoted, we find a heavy emphasis both on the independence of subordinate commanders and on Auftragstaktik:

36. The basis of command is formed by mission and situation.

The mission consists of the objective to be attained. The person responsible for it should never leave it from his sight. A mission consisting of many parts easily diverts attention away from the main purpose.

Confusion concerning the situation is the normal state of affairs. Only rarely will exact details about the enemy be known. While the attempt to find out about him is a matter of course, waiting for news in a difficult situation is a bad error.

37. On the basis of mission and situation a decision is formed. When the mission is overtaken by events the decision must take changed circumstances into account. Whoever alters a mission or fails to carry it out must report on so doing and assume responsibility for the consequences. He is ever to act within the framework of the whole.

The decision must state a clear purpose, to be pursued with all available forces. It must be carried by the commander's strong will. Often the stronger will wins.

Once a decision had been made it is not to be altered unless for really important reasons. Given the fluctuating circumstances of war, however, inflexible adherence to a decision once made may lead to errors. The art of leadership consists of a timely recognition of the circumstances and moment demanding a new decision.

To the extent that his purpose is not endangered thereby a commander must leave freedom of action to his subordinate commanders. He is not, however, to delegate to them decisions for which he himself is responsible. . . .

73. An order should contain everything a subordinate must know to carry out his assignment independently, and only that. Accordingly, an order must be brief and clear, definite and complete, tailored to the understanding of the recipient and, under certain circumstances, to his nature. The person issuing it should never neglect to put himself in the shoes of the recipient.

74. The language of command must be simple and understandable. Clarity which excludes any doubt is more important than correct form. Clarity is not to suffer owing to brevity.

75. Orders should be binding only insofar as circumstances can be foreseen. Nevertheless, the situation will often make it necessary for a commander to issue orders in the dark.[5]

76. Above all, orders are to avoid going into detail when changes in the situation cannot be excluded by the time they are carried out. In case of larger operational situations involving orders for several days in advance this problem is to be taken into account. In such cases the overall objective gains overriding importance; an order should accordingly lay special emphasis on the purpose at hand. Guiding lines for the imminent warlike actions are to be laid down, the method of execution is to be left out. In this way an order turns into a directive.

U.S. ARMY

For reasons that are hard to fathom but which may have something to do with the fact that scientific management was first developed and widely applied in the United States, American commanders never developed anything resembling Auftragstaktik, the principles of which, according to General Patton,[6] many of them found difficult to understand. America, after all, was the home of Taylorism; a system of management that tried to foresee and dictate the operative's every movement with the aim of turning him into a human machine as reliable as the mechanical ones he attended.

Be the reason what it may, the FM 100-5, though lifting entire phrases straight out of HDv 300, strikes a very different tone. What is more, it does many of the things which the German regulations warn commanders not to do. It attempts to foresee many different situations. It goes into considerably more detail. On the other hand, it has nothing to say concerning the independent responsibility of subordinate commanders. We quote:

> 127. In any tactical operation the commander must quickly evaluate all the available information bearing on his task, estimate the situation and reach a decision.
>
> 128. The commander's estimate of the situation is based on the mission of his unit, the means available to him and to the enemy, the conditions in his area of operations including terrain and weather, and the probable effects of various lines of action on future operations.... On the basis of these factors he considers the lines of action open to him which, if successful, will accomplish his mission, and the lines of action of which the enemy is physically capable and which can interfere with such accomplishment. He analyzes the opposing lines of action, one against the other, to arrive at conclusions as to the probability of success for each of his own lines of action. On the basis of this analysis he then considers the relative advantages and disadvantages of his own lines of action, and selects that line of action which most promises success regardless of what the enemy may do. If two or more lines of action appear equally promising he chooses that one which will most favor future action.
>
> 129. The estimate often requires rapid thinking with consideration limited to essential factors. On campaign exact conclusions concerning the enemy can seldom be drawn. To delay action in an emergency because of insufficient information shows a lack of energetic leadership and may result in lost opportunities. The commander must take calculated risks....
>
> 132. The estimate of the situation culminates in the decision. A decision once made is not changed without some compelling reason. In combat the will and energy of the commander must persist until the mission is accomplished. Estimation of the situation is, however, a continuous process, and changed conditions may, at any time, call for a new decision. Too stubborn an adherence to a previous decision may result in costly delay, loss of opportunity for decisive action, or downright failure....
>
> 150. Orders may be either complete or fragmentary. The order is complete when it covers all essential aspects and phases of the operation. Complete orders include missions to all subordinate units charged with the execution of tactical operations in carrying out the commander's plan.
>
> Fragmentary orders are used when speed in delivery and execution is imperative. Fragmentary orders are issued successively as the situation develops and decisions are made, and consist of separate instructions to

one or more subordinate units prescribing the part each is to play in the operation or in the separate phases thereof....

151. Orders should be originated sufficiently early and transmitted in such form as to permit subordinate commanders the maximum periods to reconnoiter, to estimate their own situation, to issue their orders, and to prepare their troops for the contemplated operation....

152. In many situations it may be necessary or desirable to issue an order to warn of impending operations (warning orders). A warning order contains information which enables subordinate commanders to make preparations for a contemplated operation. Its principal purpose is to gain time for preparatory measures and to conserve the energy of the troops.

153. An order should not trespass on the province of a subordinate. It should contain everything that the subordinate must know to carry out his mission but nothing more.

154. Orders must be clear and explicit and as brief as is consistent with clarity; short sentences are clearly understood. *Clarity is more important than technique.* [Emphasis in original] The more urgent the situation, the greater the need for conciseness in the order. Any statement of reasons for measures adopted should be limited to what is necessary to obtain intelligent cooperation from subordinates. Detailed instructions for a variety of contingencies, or prescriptions that are a matter of training, do not inspire confidence and have no place in an order. Trivial and meaningless expressions divide responsibility and lead to the adoption of half measures by subordinates. Exaggerated and bombastic phrases invite ridicule and weaken the force of an order. Expressions such as "attack vigorously," if used in orders, are not only verbose and meaningless but tend to weaken the force of subsequent orders in which such expressions do not appear.

Insofar as further sections are concerned with pure technical detail, we shall cut short our quotation at this point. There does, however, exist another document which brings out the differences between the German and American concepts of command in a unique way. In 1953 a group of former Wehrmacht officers, led by exchief of the General Staff Franz Halder, who had planned the French and early phases of the Russian campaign, was asked by the U.S. Army to comment on a new edition of FM 100-5 then being drafted to incorporate the lessons of the war. We quote:

The task of Regulations—besides transmitting basic information and points of view concerning command and battle—is to educate.

We deliberately put the educational aspect of the matter first of all.

The German High Command has indicated the following as the main goals for any education:

1. A high degree of independence at all grades of command;
2. The need for a mission-oriented discipline, i.e the inner duty always to handle in accordance with the mission given;
3. Free creativity;

4. Making "whole," i.e, clear and unambiguous decisions and carrying them out by concentrating all forces;
5. Continuous care for the troops and maintenance of their battle-worthiness.[7]

Having said this, Halder's group proceeded to criticize the American regulations in detail. The following represents a summary of the main points raised:

a. As compared to the German conception of war, the American regulations display a repeated tendency to try and foresee situations and lay down modes of behavior in great detail. This procedure limits a commander's freedom of action and, by rendering him incapable of handling in accordance with the actual situation, robs him of a very important prerequisite for victory.
b. The regulations do not do justice to the importance in modern war of the individual warrior.
c. Given their historical material superiority, the American regulations display a marked tendency to underestimate the importance of surprise, maneuver and improvisation.[8]
d. Owing to the attempt to foresee each situation in advance, the regulations tend to be stereotyped.[9]
e. The regulations tend to underestimate the psychological and bodily-physical aspects of war.
f. Putting his finger on the crux of the different images that the German and U.S. Armies held of war, Halder suggested that the following words be added to the Manual: "In war, the qualities of the character are more important than those of the intellect."

The last two points, of course, represent a repetition of the German concept of war already discussed in chapter 4; whereas the first four constitute a masterful analysis of just why the U.S. Army's command system, as expressed in its regulations, was unsuited to modern war.

NOTES

1. German: "Kadavergehorsam," literally "corpse-like obedience."
2. W. Schall, "Führungsgrundsätze in Armee und Industrie," *Wehrkunde* 14 (1964): 15.
3. W. von Lossow, "Mission-Type Tactics versus Order-Type Tactics," *Military Review* 57 (June 1977): 87-91. As often happens, attempts to translate key German terms into English result in awkward combinations since real equivalents simply don't exist.
4. Here an anecdote may be in place. An American exofficer and social scientist who read an early version of this study underlined the word "highest" and wrote: "lowest?"

5. German: "ins Ungewisse zu befehlen," literally "to order into the unknown."

6. M. Blumenson, ed., *The Patton Papers 1940-1945*, 2 vols. (Boston, 1974), 2: 486.

7. F. Halder, "Gutachten zu Field Service Regulations," U.S. Army Historical Division Study No. P 133 (Bonn, 1953), pp. 1-2.

8. On the disinterest shown by the U.S. Army in these factors, see also R. F. Weigley, "To the Crossing of the Rhine, American Strategic Thought to World War II," *Armed Forces and Society* 5 (1979): 302-20; also M. van Creveld, *Supplying War; Logistics from Wallenstein to Patton* (Cambridge, 1977), ch. 7.

9. German: schablonenhaft.

ARMY ORGANIZATION ______ 6

The purpose of military organization is to so deploy available human and material resources in order to produce the greatest possible effectiveness in combat. In the following sections, we shall present an overview of the different ways in which the German and American Armies tried to cope with this problem.

GENERAL PRINCIPLES

Organization by its very nature involves a series of balances. Among other things, a balance must be struck between the need for control from above and for initiative from below; between headquarters' desire to employ available resources where most needed and the need to have them locally at hand; and between headquarters' wish to set policy on one hand while avoiding excessive detail on the other. Overlapping responsibilities must be avoided, and authority must be firmly and clearly divided.

Above all, an organization should ever keep in mind the purpose for which it was created; this involves striking a balance between productive (output-related) and administrative (function-related) tasks, the latter to be adequate but limited to the minimum possible. Under no circumstances should function-related tasks be allowed to equal, much less exceed, the output-related ones in importance. This should be reflected in the organization's doctrine and structure.

Insofar as they make for efficiency, the cardinal virtues of any organization are simplicity, consistency, and interchangability of parts. Human beings, however, resent being handled like so many uniform, interchangeable building blocks; if the organization of which they form part is to be at all cohesive, the differences between individuals as well as their social and psychological needs should be taken into account.[1]

German Army

That Germany's supreme war-conducting organization in World War II presented a chaotic picture cannot be denied and must, indeed, be regarded as a not unimportant factor in her ultimate defeat. The rivalry between the Armed Forces High Command (OKW-Oberkommando der Wehrmacht) and the Army High Command (OKH-Oberkommando des Heer), each of which were responsible for handling the war on one or more fronts, is too well known to require elaboration. So is the confusion created by Hitler's assumption of the role of army commander in chief and his distrust of the General Staff which he regarded as too intellectual, too prudent, and altogether antiquated and lacking in National Socialist fanaticism.

Yet the German Army's wartime structure also comprised a number of interesting features which, possibly because they existed on a level below the highest one and were not directly connected to the spectacular business of operations and conquest, have largely escaped the attention of historians. There was, to begin with, the fundamental distinction between the Field Army (Feldheer) and the Replacement Army (Ersatzheer). The Field Army came under the direct control of the commander in chief (first Walter von Brauchitsch, then from December 1941, under the Fuehrer himself) and his staff at field headquarters who were thus able to devote their attention primarily to military operations. All other army business—induction of new recruits, training, replacements, procurement, administration, and so on—were entrusted to the Home Command in Berlin. All units and men stationed in the Zone of the Interior (Heimat) came under the Replacement Army. It and the Home Command were united under General Friedrich Fromm, a superbly able officer whose fundamental importance in running Germany's war effort has to date gone largely unnoticed.[2]

German troops were divided into combat units (fechtende Truppen) and supply units (Versorgungstruppen). Since German commanders seldom hesitated to use special troops in roles for which they had not been intended, however, this distinction was less fundamental than that between the Field and Replacement Armies, a system which enabled the former to concentrate on military operations secure in the knowledge that everything else was being taken care of in the rear.

Very great emphasis was laid on maintaining close connections between the Field and Replacement Armies. Not only was each corps tied to one of seven (later, thirteen) Wehrkreise, or defense districts, but personnel—mainly instructors—were constantly being rotated between the two. Since each division received its replacements from a given unit of the Replacement Army, the commanders on both sides were expected to maintain close personal ties by means of correspondence, mutual visits, and so forth.

Units and headquarters of all types were regarded as part of a vast pool from which withdrawals could be made at will to form task forces tailored to specific missions. Since missions and circumstances vary almost infinitely, few such forces were ever alike, and units above the division level were properly nothing but frameworks for command. The organization was thus both rigid and flexible; rigid in that the basic building blocks or units were as similar to each other as possible, flexible in that all were available to construct any type of combat organization needed to accomplish a given mission. Task forces were tactically and administratively independent and were never made to depend on other units to carry out their missions.

Fundamentally and in principle, units of all sizes consisted of five component parts as follows:

1. The commander and his staff.
2. Headquarters troops, including (in the case of a division) the divisional maps department, a troop of dispatch riders, military police, and divisional signals troops.
3. The unit proper, always consisting of three subunits.
4. Special troops of various kinds, such as a heavy battalion (engineers and antitank troops) for the infantry regiment, an artillery regiment for the division, various corps troops (for example, heavy artillery and bridging companies) for the corps.
5. Support troops (Trosse) including, in the case of a division, troop trains, supply columns, administrative units, sanitary and veterinary services, and the like.

In principle at any rate, all these units were organic. However, the higher the level of command and the longer the war went on, the more pronounced the tendency to commandeer units and bits of units (not, however, individuals) and put them together into improvised battle groups. Thanks to the excellent common training, these usually functioned admirably.

Divisions were known by their arabic number, corps by their roman one. Most divisions also carried names. There existed a tendency, even in official documents, to call units after their commanders; for example, Armeegruppe Rundstedt, Panzergruppe Kleist, Panzergruppe Guderian, and so on. Troops belonging to the second of these formations had a song composed for them containing rhymes on their commander's name ("Carried by the Fuehrer's Geist/We are Panzergruppe Kleist"). Those forming part of the third habitually painted their vehicles with a white "G."[3]

Improvised units could be counted by the hundred during the final stage of the war. Invariably known after their commanders as "Battle Group X," these units often showed a resilience and flexibility that remain among the more outstanding aspects of the German Army's performance.

Partly for historical reasons, but partly also as a lesson consciously drawn from World War I, German units from divisions down were normally formed on a "national" basis; that is, made up of Prussians, Bavarians, Saxonians, Würtembergians, and so on.[4] It was recognized, for example, that a Prussian among Bavarians, or vice versa, might face social difficulties to the point of being driven to suicide.[5] Hence the army's determination to maintain its units' national character in spite of the administrative difficulties that this entailed.

Given the alternatives of either keeping existing divisions up to strength by means of replacements or using the replacements to set up new divisions, the German Army, prodded by Hitler, opted for the latter. This arrangement has been much ridiculed by subsequent critics who saw in it merely an unbusinesslike obsession with numbers; and it is undeniable that, since combat troops are used up faster than staffs and services, some waste was involved in not keeping divisions up to establishment strength. On the other hand, German commanders unhesitatingly used troops in functions for which they had not been intended, thus eliminating at least part of this waste. Furthermore, the large number of divisions made possible the rotation of units in and out of the line right down to the end of the war. Above all, this policy meant that German divisions, especially at the lowest levels, were and remained tight bunches of men who suffered, fought, and died together.

Thus the divisions' social homogeneity, as well as the fact that they were NOT continually brought up to strength, goes far to explain their remarkable cohesion as measured by the number of desertions and surrenders. Always a fairly rare phenomena, these appear to have been most common in units hastily thrown together toward the end of the war in which Austrians, Czechs, and Poles were often randomly intermixed or in divisions which had been formed out of stragglers originating in different outfits. Formations in which this was not the case, however, suffered little from either desertions or surrender.[6]

U.S. Army

Unlike Germany, whose rickety OKW-OKH command system has been described above, the U.S. in World War II possessed a uniform organization for commanding all land and air (but not sea) operations in the form of the War Department General Staff. As the name implies, however, this body was both a War Department and a General Staff; it was not divided into a Field and Home Headquarters (the fact that the U.S. waged war overseas would have made such a division meaningless in any case) so that administrative matters occupied a more important place by far. Likewise, the land forces' two basic components, the Army Ground Forces (AGF) and the Army Service Forces, (ASF) were not geographically separated, since both maintained installations and units in the Zone of the Interior and overseas. Training was in the hands of AGF; the replacement system, however, came under ASF—with very bad results.

Apart from the fact that a larger proportion of U.S. troops were contained in nondivisional units, American organization resembled the German system in that units were regarded as parts of a pool to be assigned by General Headquarters in accordance with circumstances; attempts to create type corps and type armies were made early in the war but abandoned later on. Unit structure also resembled the German model, except that it was less simple and less consistent. At various times during World War II, divisions had more or less than three regiments, and intermediary headquarters were formed only to be abolished again.[7] As the war went on, these anomalies tended to disappear.

American commanders, too, often improvised battle groups tailored to carry out particular missions, though an examination of the index to the U.S. Army's official history suggests that they did so less frequently than their German opposite numbers. Possibly because the American system put greater emphasis on the "industrial" production of firepower, U.S. commanders were more reluctant to use specialist and line-of-communication troops in missions for which they had not been intended, with the result that much manpower was allowed to stand idle.[8]

Like their German counterparts, American units were known by either roman or arabic numbers. Most also had nicknames, though the enormous variety of whimsical designs—belligerent dogs, ducks, centipedes, spiders, bees, bulls, birds, monkeys, wolves, bears, horses, pigs, and cats, among others—that accompanied American units into combat suggests that these meant little to the troops. Except for Meril's Marauders, an outfit operating against the Japanese, I know of no case in which an American formation was known after its commander.

During World War I, American divisions had frequently been built up on the basis of a single small region. As happened to the British "pal divisions" also, some of these units took heavy casualties and the resulting losses to entire communities led to the system being changed.[9] World War II American divisions were accordingly made up of men called up from any part of the nation's 3,615,000 square miles without regard to geographical origin.

The U.S. Army in World War II activated 91 divisions of which 89 saw combat. The comparatively small number meant that units could seldom be rotated; worse still, the policy of constantly replacing casualties in order to keep up Table of Organization (T/O) strengths undermined cohesion and prevented the consolidation of primary groups. German divisions sacrificed some strength but remained bunches of men who suffered, fought, and died together. American divisions, on the other hand, preserved the teeth to tail ratio by acting like some huge meat-grinding machines that processed men on their way from the replacement system in the rear to becoming casualties at the front.

THE STRUCTURE OF STAFFS AND HEADQUARTERS

From the basic principles governing the organization of the German and U.S. Armies, we now pass to the structure of their tactical headquarters. Not only is this structure capable of yielding important clues as to the underlying philosophy and modus operandi; it also provides a rough and ready method for gauging the efficiency of the two armies by comparing the size of the directing brains with that of the respective bodies. There can be no doubt that there exists a point beyond which the expansion of headquarters no longer contributes to efficiency and may indeed reduce it; the problem, of course, is to identify that point.

German Army

German staffs at all levels were operational and tactical organs above all; that is, their primary function was to provide leadership in combat while devoting only the minimum effort possible to all other tasks. At each level of the hierarchy, therefore, it was the Operations Officer (Ia) who was known as the First General Staff Officer (erster Generalstabsoffizier); a primus inter pares where he was not actually superior in rank and position, his activity was controlling (massgebend) for all other departments.

The structure of a division staff was as shown in figure 6.1.

FIGURE 6.1
German Divisional Staff Organization

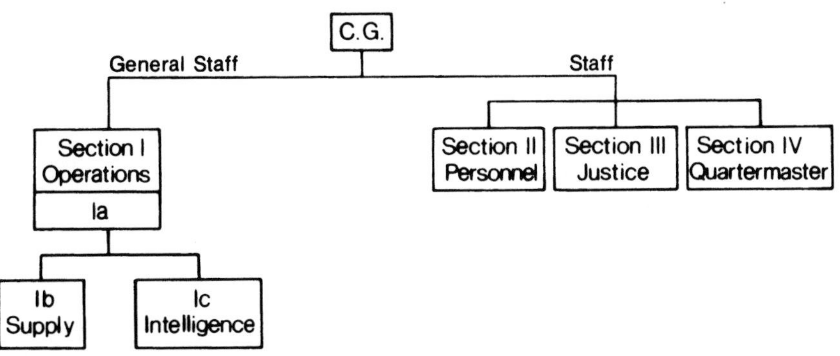

The operations officer doubled as chief of staff. The emphasis on operations is brought out more strongly still by the name of Section I; by the fact that all of the division's three general staff officers were concentrated in it, and by the subordination of the Ib and Ic to the Ia in his capacity as chief of staff. Under Section IV, nevertheless, the division had all those experts (on administration, motor vehicles, and fuel, among others) essential to function as an independent unit. Also included in this section were medical and veterinary officers and the chaplain.

A corps staff was constructed as shown in figure 6.2.

FIGURE 6.2
German Corps Staff Organization

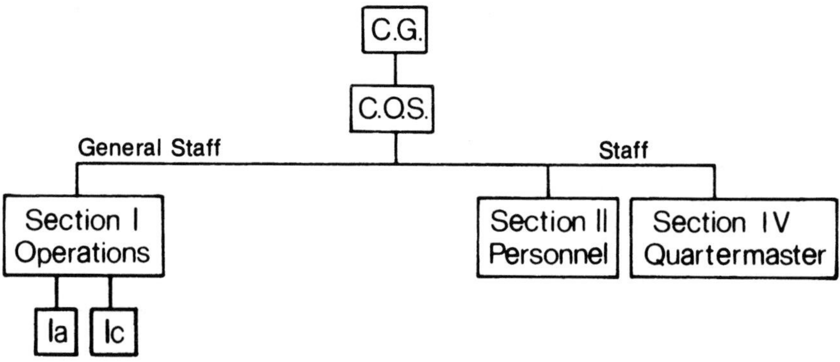

Since the corps commander did not possess juridical powers, Section III was not needed. Corps headquarters, moreover, was even more strongly specialized for operations than was the division, and its Section IV only had two officers instead of five.

The next highest headquarters, that of an army, are shown in figure 6.3.

FIGURE 6.3
German Army Staff Organization

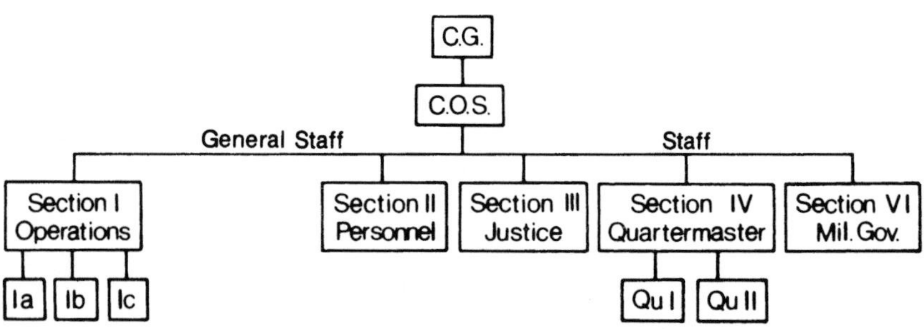

The division of the quartermaster department into two was made necessary by the fact that the army was the main logistic and administrative unit dealing directly with the OKH and thus bypassing the next highest headquarters, that of an army group, which resembled the corps in that it was a tactical and operational headquarters exclusively. In any event, the very heavy emphasis put on operations turned out to be excessive. As the war went on the impossibility of commanding a corps or an army group without control over logistics also was recognized, and the respective quartermaster sections were expanded accordingly.

Now we shall turn from the structure of staffs to their size. In September 1939 a first class German infantry division had an establishment of 17,885 men. Of these 96, or 0.53 percent formed part of the divisional staff.[10] A Panzer division's staff at this time consisted of 114 men, or some 0.65 percent of establishment strength. Similar figures are available for other types of units at various times during the war.[11]

In 1944-45 a German infantry division's headquarters, including besides the staff also the remaining organs needed to direct and control the unit, consisted of the manpower outlined in table 6.1.

TABLE 6.1
The Structure of a German Infantry Division's Headquarters

UNIT	OFFICERS	BEAMTER[1]	NCOs	ENLISTED MEN	TOTAL
Staff	25	5	35	74	139
Map department	—	—	1	7	8
Military police	1	—	25	7	33
Headquarters troops (quartermaster, signals)	12	1	64	227	304
Total	38[2]	6	125	315	484

[1] "officials" or "clerks"

[2] This represents 7.8 percent of the total number of persons at the infantry division's headquarters.

An armored division's headquarters was somewhat larger, and shown in table 6.2.

For a corps, normally responsible for three divisions plus an unfixed number of corps troops, the figures were as indicated in table 6.3.

The next highest headquarters, that of an army, presents the picture shown in table 6.4.

All these are extremely lean organizations. A division with an establishment strength of some 12,500 men was commanded by a headquarters consisting of 484 men, or 3.87 percent of the total (for an armored division the corresponding figures were 881 and 7.09 percent). A corps with approx-

TABLE 6.2
The Structure of a German Armored Division's Headquarters

UNIT	OFFICERS	BEAMTER	NCOs	ENLISTED MEN	TOTAL
Staff	21	9	37	94	161
Map department	—	—	1	7	8
Military police	3	—	41	18	62
Escort company	3	—	32	152	187
Headquarters troops	13	3	99	348	463
Total	40[1]	12	210	619	881

SOURCE: H. Reinhardt, "Grosse and Zusammenstellung der Kommandobehörden des deutschen Feldheers im II. Weltkriege," U.S. Army Historical Division Study No. P 139, appendix B, p.176.

[1] This represents 4.5 percent of the total number of persons at the armored division's headquarters.

TABLE 6.3
The Structure of a German Corps Headquarters

UNIT	OFFICERS	BEAMTER	NCOs	ENLISTED MEN	TOTAL
Staff	27	11	44	113	195
Map Department	—	—	3	13	16
Military police	2	—	21	10	33
Artillery	6	—	4	12	22
Headquarters troops	31	3	120	584	738
Total	66[1]	14	192	732	1,004

[1] This represents 6.5 percent of the total number of persons at the corps headquarters.

TABLE 6.4
The Structure of a German Army Headquarters

UNIT	OFFICERS	BEAMTER	NCOs	ENLISTED MEN	TOTAL
Staff	80	44	104	270	498
Map department	1	—	12	45	58
Secret military police	2	14	10	78	104
Intelligence/air force	2	—	4	6	12
Liaison/air force	2	1	25	20	48
Higher artillery	6	2	7	20	35
Commander, rear area	14	4	18	36	72
Signals regiment	48	10	317	1,471	1,846

imately 65,000 men was controlled by a headquarters with a strength of 1,004, or 1.52 percent of the total. An army numbering between 200 thousand and 300 thousand men was directed by a headquarters numbering 2,682, or between 1.34 and 0.89 percent of the total. Particularly interesting is the fact that an armored division only had two more officers (but 383 NCOs and enlisted men) in its headquarters than did an infantry division, thus showing that even complete mechanization need not necessarily lead to an increase in "middle management." Yet I am not aware of any historian blaming the German defeat on improper functioning of tactical headquarters.

U.S. Army

Historically, the U.S. Army's General Staff system was taken over by Elihu Root from the German model by way of Spencer Wilkinson's *The Brain of an Army* and Bronsart von Schellendorff's *Generalstabsdienst*. Yet the American system was different from the very beginning in that it put far less emphasis on operations which were, indeed, not even mentioned in the original authorizing bill of 1903. Instead, the staff was supposed to correct the deficiencies brought up during the Spanish-American War and accordingly dealt above all else with planning, mobilization, intelligence and administration. It was not until 1918 that General Pershing, under French influence, created a quintuple division of functions to command his AEF (American Expeditionary Forces): the G 1 (Personnel), G 2 (Intelligence), G 3 (Operations), G 4 (Supply), and G 5 (Instruction and Training). When the functions of G 5 were divided among the G 1 and G 3 in 1921 the present-day structure was substantially complete.[12]

In World War II the structure of a division (duplicated, in essence, at all higher levels) was as shown in figure 6.4.

As even a cursory glance at figure 6.4 shows, American divisional staffs were far less specialized for operations than were their German equivalents. The divisional chief of staff in particular, rather than being an operations officer first and foremost, was a manager whose function was to coordinate and supervise the functioning of the assistant chiefs of staff. These were coequals and thus able to make their plans "independently and objectively"—that is, without the overriding dependence on operational considerations that was the essence of the German system.

Whereas a German unit in combat would be commanded only by Section I, an American staff's forward echelon would include all four assistant chiefs of staff. Not only the staff as a whole, but its forward echelon, too, was therefore less specialized.

According to the Tables of Organization of June 1941, an American infantry division 15,514 men strong was controlled by a staff numbering

FIGURE 6.4
American Staff Organization

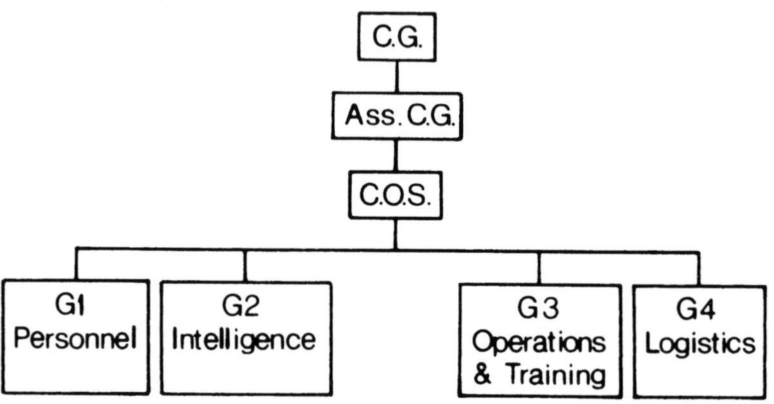

169, or 1.08 percent of the total. The corresponding figures for January 1945 were 14,037, 166 and 1.63 percent respectively.[13]

In March 1942 an American armored division had 14,620 men of whom 185 or 1.26 percent belonged to the staff. The corresponding figures for January 1945 were 10,670, 174 and 1.63 percent.

Since systems of organization differ, it is not easy to compare the size of American headquarters to German ones. Table 6.5, however, will give an idea of the number of men needed to control an American division in January 1945.

TABLE 6.5
The Structure of American Divisional Headquarters

UNIT	INFANTRY DIVISION	ARMORED DIVISION
Staff	166	174
Military police platoon	239	293
Division headquarters company	104	115
Division trains headquarters and headquarters company	—	99
Total	509	681

This means that headquarters formed 4.3 percent of an American infantry division, and 7.19 percent of an armored one. Contrary to the impression given by many historians, therefore, American headquarters were only slightly larger than German ones; however, an infantry division's headquarters contained 79 officers (94, if the divisional artillery commander's staff is included) which is double that of a German infantry division. Officers formed 12.8 percent of headquarters strength in an American infantry division, as against 7.8 percent in a German one. Possibly because of the greater prominence given to logistics and administration over operations, 11.2 percent of the officers of an American infantry division served at divisional headquarters, as against only 7.0 percent in a German one.

An American corps staff was made up as shown in table 6.6.

TABLE 6.6
The Structure of an American Corps Staff

Officers	69
Warrant officers	7
Enlisted men	109
Total	185

SOURCE: K. Greenfield, *The Organization of Ground Combat Troops* (Washington, D.C., 1947), p. 361.

Thus an American corps staff contained 55 percent more officers, but 44 percent fewer other ranks, than did a German one; clearly American officers were employed on numerous tasks which, in the German Army, were carried out by officials, NCOs, and enlisted men. This is an important point to which we shall have occasion to return.

THE STRUCTURE OF DIVISIONS

If an army is like a machine, its divisions are like cogwheels. They should be just strong enough to enable the real working parts, the cogs, to function effectively; anything in excess of this is wasted.

German Army

Though the German Army, like all others, did not escape the gradual growth in the number of trains and services that had been going on since early in the nineteenth century, its divisions nevertheless remained remarkably lean fighting organizations. Table 6.7 gives an idea of combat versus service troops inside two divisions in 1939.

The difference between an infantry and an armored division (which at this time had two armored regiments with approximately 350 tanks between them) was therefore rather small. The favorable teeth to tail ratio was preserved to the end of the war, as the establishment of a Panzer Grenadier Division in 1944-45 indicates in table 6.8.

According to this system of classification, 89.4 percent of all troops were still in combat units. The figure for officers was 89.5 percent; for Beamter, 73.5 percent; for NCOs, 91.6 percent; and for enlisted men, 89.2 percent. Apart from the Beamter, an obvious and necessary exception, the various ranks were therefore distributed almost equally between combat and service units.

TABLE 6.7
The Distribution of Troops inside German Divisions, 1939

UNIT	INFANTRY DIVISION	ARMORED DIVISION
Staffs	1.08%	1.3%
Infantry, including replacement battalion	56.2	27.0
Reconnaissance	3.4	6.4
Artillery	19.0	10.2
Armor	0.0	24.7
Antitank artillery	4.0	6.0
Engineers	4.4	7.0
Signals	2.7	3.6
Total Combat	90.7	86.2
Supply	3.8	7.5
Administration	1.1	1.8
Sanitary services	2.8	3.8
Veterinary services	1.3	0.0
Military police	0.3	0.7
Total Services	9.3	13.8

SOURCE: B. Mueller-Hillebrand, "Statistisches System," U.S. Army Historical Division Study No. PC 011 (Koenigstein Ts., 1949), p. 89.

TABLE 6.8
The Structure of a German Panzer Grenadier Division, 1944-1945

UNIT	OFFICERS	BEAMTER	NCOs	ENLISTED MEN	TOTAL
Divisional staff	26	10	99	120	255
Infantry	150	18	1,056	4,822	6,046
Armored section	21	4	224	308	557
Reconnaissance section	23	3	185	769	980
Antitank section	17	3	145	289	454
Artillery regiment	58	11	770	1,065	1,904
Antiaircraft section	18	3	131	453	605
Engineer battalion	15	5	114	655	789
Signal section	13	3	87	311	414
Depot battalion	17	1	91	850	959
Total Combat	358	61	2,902	9,642	12,963
Supply troops	19	2	101	439	561
Motor repair shops	5	6	40	184	235
Administrative troops	1	7	33	166	207
Sanitary troops	17	4	83	358	462
Field post	—	3	7	8	18
Total Service	42	22	264	1,155	1,483
Grand Total	400	83	3,166	10,797	14,446

SOURCE: H. Reinhardt, "Grosse und Zusammenstellung der Kommandobehörden des deutschen Feldheers im II. Weltkriege," U.S. Army Historical Division Study No. P 139, supplement, p. 12.

U.S. Army

Table 6.9 represents the structure of an American division in January 1945.

TABLE 6.9
The Distribution of Troops inside American Divisions, 1945

UNIT	INFANTRY DIVISION		ARMORED DIVISION	
	Number	Percent	Number	Percent
Staff	166	1.18	360	3.37
Infantry	9,204	65.56	2,985	27.97
Reconnaissance	149	1.06	894	8.37
Artillery	2,111	15.03	1,625	15.22
Armor	—	0.00	2,100	19.68
Antitank artillery[1]	—	0.00	—	0.00
Engineers	620	0.41	660	6.18
Signals	239	1.70	293	2.74
Total Combat	12,489	88.97	8,917	83.57
Service units[2]	1,548	11.03	1,753	16.43
Total	14,037		10,670	

SOURCE: Based on K. Greenfield, *The Organization of Ground Combat Troops* (Washington, D.C., 1947) pp. 306, 320, and adapted to correspond to the German system of classification.

[1] Distributed among other arms.

[2] Including headquarters and service companies, band, trains, military police platoon, maintenance, and military battalions.

As in the German case, officers (4.9 percent of the total in the infantry division) were almost equally distributed between combat and service units. Though this table probably tends to slightly exaggerate the fighting power of American divisions (the U.S. Army, we saw, was less prepared to use specialized troops in roles for which they were not intended, and accordingly classified engineers, for example, not as "combat" but as "auxilliary"), the differences between them and German ones are hardly sufficient to explain anything much. The next step, therefore, will be to turn our attention to the proportion of combat to service troops in the two armies as a whole.

DIVISIONAL SLICES

German Army

Table 6.10 represents the sizes of German divisional slices during various periods in the war.

TABLE 6.10
German Divisional Slices, 1939-1945

Date	9/39	7/41	6/42	12/43	6/44	11/44	4/45
Number of divisions	106	203	239	278	255	260	260
Average establishment	16,626	13,900	13,500	13,000	12,500	12,500	11,500
Average actual strength	16,626	13,800	11,836	10,453	12,155	8,761	9,985
Field army units							
staff, corps, and army troops	4,130	3,800	3,800	3,900	4,100	4,100	4,200
frontier guard	1,075	—	—	—	—	—	—
construction troops	4,028	1,100	1,100	1,000	1,000	1,000	500
Total Field Army	9,233	4,900	4,900	4,900	5,100	5,100	4,700
Replacement army units							
training units	7,027	4,630	4,749	4,495	4,104	4,003	2,292
sanitary personnel and wounded	—	246	1,611	1,979	3,529	2,642	3,248
Total Replacement Army	9,034	6,107	7,531	8,272	9,801	8,983	5,695
Total, Actual	34,873	24,807	24,267	23,625	27,056	22,844	20,308
Total, Establishment	34,873	24,907	25,971	26,172	27,401	26,583	21,895

SOURCE: Mueller-Hillebrand, "Division Slice," U.S. Army Historical Division Study No. P-072 (Koenigstein Ts., 1951), p. 9.

These figures conceal serveral surprises. First, it would appear that the German Army entered World War II as a comparatively flabby force but tended to lose its surplus fat later on. Second, divisional slices (establishment) reached their lowest point in June 1941, at the very time when the army, according to Chief of Staff Halder, reached its "high water mark" in terms of morale, leadership, and combat worthiness.[14] The slowly rising figures after this date reflect a small shift towards an increased number of nondivisional units and, above all, the rapidly increasing number of wounded.

The German Army's divisions comprised 47.6 percent of its strength in September 1939, 55.6 percent in July 1941, 48.7 percent in June 1942, 44.2 percent in December 1943, 44.9 percent in June 1944, 38.3 percent in November 1944, and 49.1 percent in April 1945. The high figure for July 1941 (just after the beginning of the invasion of Russia) and the low one for November 1944 (following a series of heavy defeats in both east and west) are particularly noteworthy.

Turning now to the share of service troops in the Army as a whole, we are handicapped by the fact that German headquarters normally broke down their forces into field and replacement units rather than into combat and service units. The figures in table 6.11, valid for June 1944, are therefore rough approximations only.

TABLE 6.11
Combat and Service Troops in the German Army

Combat Troops	
Division average actual strength	12,155
Staffs, corps, and army troops[1]	2,550
Total Combat	14,705
Service Troops	
Staffs, corps, and army troops	2,550
Construction troops	1,000
Administrative units at home	600
Sanitary personnel in hospitals	392
Guard troops	176
Training units	2,535
Trained replacements in pools	1,569
Recovering personnel	784
Wounded in hospitals	2,745
Total Service	12,351
Grand Total	27,056

SOURCE: Adapted from B. Mueller-Hillebrand, "Division Slice," U.S. Army Historical Divisional Study No. P 072 (Koenigstein Ts., 1951), pp. 7-8.

[1] This assumes that half of all these troops represented combat units (heavy artillery and so forth) and half represented service troops (supply, maintenance, military government).

At this date, therefore, combat troops comprised 54.35 percent of overall strength as against 53.5 percent at the beginning of the war.[15] In spite of growing motorization and the vast number of wounded caused by five years of war, the share of combat troops in the army was maintained and even slightly increased.

To round off this survey of the structure of the German Army, table 6.12 represents a divisional slice in a single theater of war.

TABLE 6.12
Combat and Service Troops in a German Theater of War

Combat troops	
Division average establishment	16,626
50% staffs and corps troops	1,875
Total Combat	18,501
Service Troops	
50% staffs and corps troops	1,875
Construction troops	1,500
Total Service	3,375
Grand Total	21,876

Inside a theater, therefore, combat troops represented 84.5 percent of total strength.

U.S. Army

Remarkably little information about divisional slices is available in the U.S. Army's official history of World War II. All we are told is that there were 89 divisions at the end of 1944. Since the army's overall strength at this time (excluding the Air Force) stood at approximately 5,700,000 the divisional slice must have stood at 64,044.[16]

Unlike their German equivalents, American units were normally kept up to, or near, establishment by means of a continual stream of replacements. Actual divisional strength at this time was accordingly high, averaging 13,400; this means that some 20.8 percent of the army's strength was concentrated in its divisions.

This figure does not stand comparison with the equivalent German one, however. American organization being more centralized, a considerably higher percentage of combat units was kept under the direct control of higher headquarters—army and corps—than was organic to the division. Consequently, a January 1945 theater divisional slice would appear to have looked somewhat like table 6.13.

TABLE 6.13
American Divisional Slices

	NO. OF MEN
Division average actual establishment	13,400
Combat troops in nondivisional units	11,300
Total Combat Troops	24,700
Service troops in nondivisional units	18,700
Total	43,400

SOURCE: K. Greenfield, *The Organization of Ground Combat Troops* (Washington, D.C., 1947) p. 351.

Of the theater total, 56.9 percent were therefore combat troops, though again this figure does not stand an exact comparision with the German one because the U.S. Army operated overseas; that is, as an expeditionary force. Nevertheless, if 21,049 "replacements in training or personnel designated as overheads in the Troop Basis" are added in order to obtain the divisional slice for the army as a whole, then combat troops are found to have formed 38 percent of overall strength. This figure does not, apparently, include wounded.

We shall now trace the evolution of combat versus service units over time. Table 6.14 figures refer to enlisted men only, that is, they do not include officers.

TABLE 6.14
Combat and Service Troops in the U.S. Army in 1942 and 1945

	31 DECEMBER 1942	31 MARCH 1945
Army ground forces combat units	1,917,000	2,041,000
Army ground forces service units	243,000	461,000
Army service forces service units	518,000	1,097,000
Overheads, replacements, unavailables	1,022,000	1,422,000
Total	3,700,000	5,021,000

SOURCE: K. Greenfield, *The Organization of Ground Combat Troops* (Washington, D.C., 1947) and R. R. Palmer, *The Procurement and Training of Ground Combat Troops* (Washington, D.C., 1948).

The share of combat units therefore fell from 51.8 percent to 40.6 percent during the period in question. This was due partly to the fact that combat units were set up first, partly to ever-lengthening lines of communications, but partly also to simple inefficiency. The official history has this to say:

> On 30 June 1944, during the most critical days of the Normandy . . . operation, the number of enlisted men in the US qualified for overseas duty but assigned to Zone of Interior jobs exceeded the number of enlisted infantrymen in the European and Mediterranean Theaters. It exceeded the number of Air Corps person-

> nel, enlisted and commissioned, in the two Theaters. It was 92 percent of the number of enlisted men in the infantry, armoured tank destroyer forces, cavalry, field artillery, coast artillery, and antiaircraft artillery in Europe. Many combat soldiers in the Theaters were physically inferior to men scheduled to remain at home. This situation was not one of which the AGF approved but it was difficult for the War Department to correct in 1944. Since the early days of mobilization many prime physical specimens had been trained as technicians in Zone of the Interior assignments. They now occupied prime positions.[17]

No wonder, therefore, that General Joseph Stilwell in May 1945 wrote of the "disappearing ground combat army."

NOTES

1. There exists an enormous literature showing the close connection between a unit's cohesion and its members' common social background. See, for example, M. Janowitz and R. W. Little, *Militär und Gesellschaft* (Boppard am Rhein, 1965), pp. 263-69; and A. Etzioni *A Comparative Analysis of Complex Organizations* (New York, 1961), p. 189.

2. Fromm, whose chief of staff, Stauffenberg, tried to blow Hitler up on 20 July 1944, subsequently had the main conspirators arrested and shot. This, however, did not save him from subsequent arrest and execution on the charge that he had been involved himself.

3. See picture in K. Macksey, *Guderian, Panzer General* (London, 1975), p. 133.

4. Denkert, "Einsatz der 3. Panzer Grenadier Division in der Ardennen-Offensive," U.S. Army Historical Division Study B 086, 1946, p. 7. Also K. Hesse, *Soldatendienst im neuen Reich* (Berlin, n.d.), pp. 15-16.

5. Bundesarchiv/Militärarchiv (BAMA), Freiburg i. B., file H20/477.

6. E. A. Shils and M. Janowitz, "Cohesion and Disintegration in the Wehrmacht in World War II," *Public Opinion Quarterly* 12 (1948):285, 288.

7. K. Greenfield, *The Organization of Ground Combat Troops* (Washington, D.C., 1947), p. 271.

8. An extreme instance took place in the summer of 1944 when an entire paratroop army sat on its hands in England because no role suitable for its special training could be found.

9. Janowitz and Little, *Militär und Gesellschaft*, p. 113.

10. B. Mueller-Hillebrand, "Statistisches System," U.S. Army Historical Division Study No. PC 011 (Koenigstein Ts., 1949), p. 88.

11. H. Reinhardt, "Grosse und Zusammenstellung der Kommandobehörden des deutschen Feldheers im II. Weltkriege," U.S. Army Historical Division Study No. P 139, appendix B, p. 137.

12. J. D. Hittle, *The General Staff, Its History and Development* (Harrisburg Pa., 1961), p. 201.

13. Greenfield, *Organization of Ground Combat Troops*, pp. 174-75, 320-21.

14. F. Halder, *Kriegstagebuch* (Stuttgart, 1962), 2:214.

15. Based on Mueller-Hillebrand, "Division Slice," U.S. Army Historical Division Study P 072 (Koenigstein Ts., 1951), p. 3 and calculated in a similar way.

16. "Over 60,000 men," according to Greenfield, *Organization of Ground Combat Troops*, p. 213.

17. Ibid., pp. 241-42.

ARMY PERSONNEL ADMINIS-TRATION 7

GENERAL PRINCIPLES

Germany Army

Owing partly to the lingering influence of feudal traditions, but partly als to deliberate choice, the German Army did not employ mechanica methods to administer a force whose size, at its peak, reached 6,550,00 men.[1] This, to modern eyes, astonishing feat was made possible by a extremely decentralized organization; such matters as the distribution o recruits among the various MOS (Military Occupation Specialties), th regulation of leave, the administration of disciplinary measures and th exchange of personnel between units—in short, everything concerning th vital questions of the individual soldier and his personality—were left i the hands of unit (mostly regimental) commanders.

Such a system both postulated mutual trust and helped generate it. Th wide powers over the troops' lives put in the hands of relatively junio officers greatly strengthened the latter's position but at the same time wa supposed to help "keep awake their sense of responsibility for the men i their charge and thereby to reinforce the bonds of mutual confidenc between the soldier and his immediate superiors."[2] This confidence, i turn, was regarded as an indispensable prerequisite for the creation an maintenance of high fighting power.

As one consequence of the decentralized nature of the system, n detailed manpower statistics were kept at the army's Central Personn Office (Heeres-Personal Amt, or HPA). The absence of such informa tion did not greatly matter during the early years of the war but began t make itself felt toward the end of 1941, when mounting casualties on th Russian front made it imperative to put available manpower to the be possible use.

However, a changeover to a mechanized, centralized system was not easy to carry out in wartime. The move also met with considerable opposition by officers who recalled pre-1918 traditions and insisted, not unreasonably, that some means be found to counter the threat to the commander's position and to the principle of unity of command inherent in any centralized system. Finally, the General Staff was reluctant to increase the burden of paperwork resting on the troops and to turn them into collecting agencies for data that would benefit the army as a whole but not them directly. These considerations prevented any important changes from being introduced, and things remained much as they were.

The lengths to which the General Staff was prepared to go in order to avoid "an increase in the burden resting on the troops" (this is a frequently recurring sentence in the literature concerned) were, in fact, quite remarkable.[3] Thus, the organization department did not demand daily reports on actual strength, casualties, and need for replacements; instead, it used establishment strength and losses, reported every ten days, in order to make its own calculations. In so doing it took into account the relative importance of the unit in question; that is, the tactical situation.

Contrary to what moviegoers might be led to expect from a Prussian-German Army, therefore, the system consciously attempted to minimize the amount of paperwork and was quite prepared to take the resulting inaccuracies in stride. Since the army was in any case hopelessly unable to replace its casualties from the winter of 1941-42 on, neither the inaccuracies nor the paucity of the information available mattered very much; in other words, necessity was turned into a virtue.

All this, however, does not mean that the German Army was unable or unwilling to employ sophisticated statistical models where these were called for. This was true above all for the wounded, whose numbers in the later stages of the war were very large. To coordinate the wounded with other replacements, it was necessary to develop accurate models so as to forecast the numbers that would recover, the duration of their recovery, and the resulting degree of physical fitness. This was done.[4]

U.S. Army

From the U.S. Army's official history of World War II, it is possible to glean comparatively little detailed information concerning methods of personnel administration. It is clear, however, that the system was based on frequently sophisticated and almost completely mechanized, very centralized mathematical models.

There existed, it is clear, a strong belief in the virtues of quantification. To make possible a mechanized system of administration, any- and everything was given a number. The official history is clogged with statistics, graphs, and tables; one of which, at any rate, is so complicated as to require ten pages of explanations.[5] Whenever a problem arose, a solution was sought in terms of "engineering," that is, additional organization and paperwork; thus, for example, a crisis in morale in 1940 led to the establishment of a morale branch. In March 1944 a crisis in leadership caused the War Department G 3, General H. L. Twaddle, to institute a procedure under which all unit commanders were required to submit monthly reports on the number of officers regarded as unsuitable or else to state explicitly that there were no such officers under their command.[6]

The use of mathematical methods to determine requirements could not preclude errors in the utilization of manpower. Thus, for example, there had been an acute shortage of officers during the first year of the war; in 1943, however, there already existed such a surplus that 1,000 officers per month had to be transferred away from the antiaircraft artillery units alone.[7]

As an example of the way things were done, the army's Officer Evaluation Report (WD AG PRT 462) will serve. This sixteen-page document was divided into five sections—not counting the one for entering identifying information, itself divided into seven more—and contained over eighty separate questions to be answered according to five different systems while using an electrographic pencil. Performance, a host of personal qualities, judgment, common sense, cooperation, initiative, force, ability to get results, desirability (whether or not the evaluator would like to have the evaluatee under his command) all had to be recorded by means of a point system. Finally an officer could be put into one of four brackets: lowest quarter, below average, above average, and highest quarter, each divided into five grades thus making a scale of twenty.

Filled in twice yearly, the form had to be reviewed by the evaluator's superior—thus doubling the paperwork if properly done. The results were tabulated in digital form for mechanical procession and laid down in the form of a five digit number.

Things were different in the German Army. The form known as Beurteilung (assessment, estimate) had to be filled in every two years. This originally consisted of five pages but, as part of the effort to reduce the administrative burden carried by the troops, was simplified still further in November 1942. The army personnel bureau did not go so far as to require answers to yes/no questions, however. Instead, evaluating officers were asked to estimate their subordinates' character, personality, behavior under fire, professional competence and achievement, physical condition, and fitness for other positions, in that order. Neither point systems nor forced comparisons were employed, thus foregoing objective standards and putting great faith in commanders' ability (and willingness) to differentiate between the unfit and the fit. The purpose of the Beurteilung was to provide "a plastic description of the whole man." The army personnel office, it appears, was especially appreciative of officers who contrived to do this by means of appropriate metaphors, often taken from the equestrian world.[8]

CLASSIFICATION AND ASSIGNMENT OF MANPOWER

To fit round pegs into round holes is a fundamental function of any personnel policy. The following pages will show the different ways in which this problem was handled in Germany and the United States.

German Army

Unless they had already volunteered to serve in one or another of the Services (during the war this also included the Waffen SS), German youths were called into the service upon reaching the age of nineteen. The duration of conscript service after 1935 was two years; during the war, periods of service went on almost indefinitely, though men over 35 or so were constantly being replaced by younger troops in front-line units.

Just what percentage of each age group was actually called up is uncertain. It was put at 75 percent for planning purposes but must have gone higher as the war went on and standards deteriorated.[9] From September 1939 to April 1945 17,893,200 men passed through the Wehrmacht and Waffen SS;[10] taking 90 million (including the Sudetenland, Alsace, and parts of Poland) as the population basis, some 3.6 percent of the entire population must have passed through the armed forces each year. At their peak strength in 1943 the armed forces constituted well over 10 percent of this basis; a figure which in all probability has been exceeded only in Israel, and then during a war lasting days or weeks, not five and a half years.

If the armed forces as a whole thus comprised a fairly representative cross-section of the German population, the share of manpower allocated to the ground forces (Heer) tended to decrease over time, as table 7.1 shows.

The army's share thus went down from 85 percent in 1939 to 67 percent in 1945, whereas Air Force and Navy together increased their's from 14 percent to 24 percent. The Waffen SS, which even in 1942 hardly constituted a serious rival to the army, had turned into a formidable one by the time the war ended. The overall share of the land forces (army plus Waffen SS) also went down steadily; it stood at 86 percent at the beginning of the war, but at only 74 percent when it ended.

The effect of these secular trends on the manpower available to the army cannot be expressed in mere figures, however. As the war went on, the army's status vis-à-vis the other services tended to deteriorate; after

TABLE 7.1
Evolution of Manpower in the German Armed Services, 1939-1945 (strength in thousands)

YEAR	FIELD ARMY	REPLACEMENT ARMY	TOTAL ARMY	AIR FORCE	NAVY	WAFFEN SS	TOTAL
1939	1,400	1,200	2,600	400	50	35	3,085
1940	3,650	900	4,550	1,200	250	50	6,050
1941	3,800	1,200	5,000	1,680	404	150	7,234
1942	4,000	1,800	5,800	1,700	580	230	8,130
1943	4,250	2,300	6,550	1,700	780	450	9,480
1944	4,000	2,510	6,510	1,500	810	600	9,420
1945	3,800	1,500	5,300	1,000	700	830	7,830

SOURCE: B. Mueller-Hillebrand, *Das Heer*, 3 vols. (Frankfurt am Main, 1968).

December 1941 it no longer even had its own commander in chief. Its ability to attract the cream of German youth accordingly declined. Pressed by their Hilter Jugend leaders, more and more youngsters opted for the Air Force, Navy, or Waffen SS rather than enter the "reactionary" army. Another factor working in the same direction was the fact that casualties in the army were, by the nature of things, proportionally much higher.[11]

The German Army's methods for classifying and assigning enlisted men (but not officers) were, by modern standards, extremely crude. The great majority of all recruits were not required to take any kind of written or mechanical test; instead, a physical examination distributed them into six classes, ranking from "fit for war" (Kriegsverwendungsfähig, or Kv) through "fit for garrison-type duty" (Garnisonverwendungsfähig, or Gv) all the way down to "unfit for defense" (Wehrunfähig, or Wu). Examinations were carried out, for the most part, by a chief physician with the aid of an assistant physician whose job it was to supervise the paramilitary personnel that carried out the preliminary tests. Specialists were called on only as the occasion demanded. The organization of examinations on a conveyor belt principle, with a separate physician examining each organ, was explicitly forbidden. The number each physician could see each day was limited to 80.[12]

Even as the physical examination was taking place the physician, together with the Musterung (preliminary review) commander, who had to be present, carried on a conversation with the recruit. Thus men suffering from obvious mental defects could be weeded out; a general picture of the subject's mental condition formed; and his wishes, if he had any, taken into account.[13] While the decision regarding fitness; that is, whether or not a man was to be called up, had to be made on the spot by the commander and imparted to the subject, his assignment to the various arms and services did not take place until the subsequent stage of enrollment (Aushebung).

Enrollment involved a shortened physical examination to determine any recent changes followed by a man's assignment on the basis of physical condition, educational qualifications, professional occupation, paramilitary training (in the Naval Hitler Jugend, for example), as well as their expressed wishes. Regulations explicitly provided for each service to be allocated an equal share of qualified recruits.

The final distribution of the recruits among the various Military Occupation Specialities; for example, a tank company, would take place in the units themselves and was the responsibility of the regimental commander. Thus tests and personal aquaintance during the first four weeks of a twenty-one week training course would determine whether a man was to become a driver, a loader, or a machine-gun operator.[14]

The system as a whole was simple, decentralized, and, above all, personal; it consistently relied on the judgment of physicians and officers rather than on the results of objective tests. In the final stage, as was the case so often in the German Army, the decision lay not with some remote personnel officer but in the hands of the commanders who would subsequently have to train a recruit and, quite possibly, lead him in combat.

All this did not mean that the German Army was uninterested in military psychology; on the contrary, a bibliography of the subject published in 1939 shows German-language works heading the list with 28.4 percent of all titles.[15] An army psychological laboratory was established by the defense minister, General Wilhelm Groener, soon after the resignation of the conservative commander in chief General Hans von Seeckt in 1926. It was led first by Prof. J. B. Riefert and later by Dr. Max Simoneit, a well-known child and school specialist. By 1939 the laboratory employed some 200 psychologists divided between the center in Berlin and the outposts in the various Wehrkreise. Military psychologists were carefully selected from among Ph.D.s in psychology and given three years additional training, culminating in the submission of a thesis, an oral examination, and a test-examination of officer candidates.[16]

The level of effort that went into training military psychologists was thus enormous; nevertheless, Simoneit's establishment throughout the sixteen years of its existence remained a comparatively small scale affair, not to be compared with its sprawling U. S. Army equivalent through which passed millions of men.[17] In 1933–39 the laboratory processed a total of only 478,870 men of whom but a fraction were officer candidates; the largest number examined in a single year before the war was 150,000.[18] Here as elsewhere the German Army concentrated on quality rather than quantity, subjecting specialists (including pilots, drivers of special vehicles, operators of optical and acoustical apparatus, and radio operators) to the most rigorous of tests while leaving everything else in the hands of field commanders.

Since it was believed that the first requirements in war were certain moral attitudes (courage, obedience, loyalty, and independence, among others), the tests administered by Simoneit were designed not so much to establish the presence of certain mechanical talents as to bring out a man's entire personality.[19] Thus, it was possible for a paper on the selection of tank commanders, read in a 1938 symposium of Wehrmacht psychologists, to concentrate almost exclusively on the character traits needed, whereas the problem of testing for mechanical aptitude, such as, spatial and motor coordination, was dismissed in a few sentences. The paper concluded with an appropriate quotation from *Mein Kampf* to the effect that the best, the strongest, and the most determined should step forward to be counted.[20]

Tests for other specialists were designed on similar principles. The one administered to would-be truck drivers, for example, was designed to examine the power of sustained attention in the presence of occasionally introduced distractions, uniformity of reaction, choice behavior, rate of learning, and fatigability. The apparatus used consisted of five lights of differing shape and color; in addition two rattles could be sounded, one from the right and another from the left. The examinee, sitting in front of a screen, had three levers and two foot pedals to operate. The lights were flashed on, and the observer told the examinee which of the three levers was to be pulled with each of the five lights. One of the pedals had to be pressed with the sound of one of the rattles. The subject was given time to work himself in, but was not told the moment at which the test actually started. During a twenty-minute test, six hundred stimuli were presented in predetermined random order and the examinee's responses and reaction times automatically recorded. Not merely his actual performance, however, but his entire behavior was carefully noted by a hidden observer. Security of conduct, efficiency of movements, and facial expressions were all noticed. The final result depended not so much on mechanical performance as on the examinee's overall attitude and his ability to cope.

Thus it was not the measurement of separate qualities, which was regarded as entirely useless, but the assessment of a man's entire personality in which Simoneit was interested. The results obtained in this way were necessarily imprecise, but this was a problem that was deliberately taken in stride and, to some extent, corrected by always having more than one examiner present. As one Army psychologist wrote, the assessment had to be "a work of art."[21] Contemporary (non-German) psychologists regarded the procedure as sound, the more so since little but lip service was paid to racial-biological ideas of the Nazi type.[22]

U.S. Army

The situation of the U.S. land forces in regard to manpower allocation was both more difficult and easier than that facing the German one. It was more difficult in that the land forces never quite reached 50 percent of the entire armed forces (their share at the end of 1944 was 5,575,000 or 48.5 percent out of 11,484,000) and therefore faced stiffer competition by the other services; it was easier in that the pool of available manpower was considerably larger since the armed forces never grew beyond 11,857,000 men or 8.7 percent of a population basis conservatively estimated at 135 million.

The total number of men between 18 and 37 examined for military service in 1940-45 is said to have been 18 million. Of those, no fewer than 5,250,000 or 29.1 percent, were rejected.[23] Though no detailed statistics are available, it seems that a very large proportion of these rejections took place in the first year of the war, when the army, in addition to being short of training personnel, seems to have labored under the delusion that the pool of available manpower was virtually bottomless. After up to 50 percent of all those screened had been rejected during this period, standards had to be drastically lowered in 1943, with the result that men previously regarded as unfit for service were now called up in large numbers whereas others who were perhaps better qualified remained exempt.

Having made its choice, the army proceeded on the assumption that "ground combat in World War II required complex skills, which were in large part technical."[24] Its classification system was accordingly designed to grade men by three criteria; namely, physical fitness, occupational skill, and intellectual capacity.

The system of physical classification was rather simpler than the German one. Instead of six there were only four categories, ranging from A ("fit for duty in combat zones and for any strenuous work"), B ("fit for close combat support duty") and C ("fit for duty in lines of communications, or bases overseas, or in the continental U.S.") to 4 (unfit).[25] Complaints about the system were occasionally voiced, but little was done to correct the matter. Consequently, in the words of the official history, "the question whether . . . a man would engage in hand to hand fighting, march long distances on foot, carry a heavy pack or go without sleep and food counted for very little in his original assignment."

Whereas German physical examinations were carried out by a team of physicians and an officer who, even as the examination was in progress, conversed with the subject, pressure of time dictated that an assembly-line type operation be adopted by the U.S. Army. One physician examined a man's eyes and ears; another his chest and lungs; another his abdomen; another his genital organs; another his legs, feet, and so on. Coming to the end of the line, the man would be confronted by a psychiatrist who, forced to examine hundreds of men per day, would fire rapid questions of the "do you like girls?" type at him.[26]

Much more sophisticated than the physical examination was the system of classification according to occupational skill. A list of 800 numbered Military Occupation Specialities was instituted and was divided into two halves in accordance with whether or not any given speciality had a civilian equivalent. Personnel possessing a skill or trade were assigned, as nearly as possible, to a similar military job; those who did not—normally the young, the not-so-bright or the socially disadvantaged—became fighting men. The system assumed that, the lesser the difference between a man's civilian occupation and his military trade, the better for his morale; this, if true, would have meant that combat units had low morale virtually built-in.[27]

The tests administered to specialists differed considerably from the German ones. Tank drivers, for example, were selected on the basis of a road test in an ordinary motor truck; this lasted ten minutes and involved a checklist with forty-seven separate items such as correct use of clutch, gears, and brakes. Results were registered by means of a point system and mechanically processed. A follow-up study found, not surprisingly, that the test was fairly reliable as a predictor of performance under optimal conditions; under less than optimal ones, however—and when in war are conditions optimal?—its reliability was poor.[28]

Finally, the name of the third examination, the Army General Classification Test (AGCT) is itself a sufficient indication of its importance. Designed to measure "general learning ability," the test consisted of arithmetic, box counting, and vocabulary items. It separated examinees into five classes, that is, I (over 130 points), II (110-129), III (90-109), IV (60-89), and V (59 and down). Of these, the first two were expected to cope with any training program; the third, with most except those requiring mathematical ability; the fourth, with basic and some advanced training; and the fifth—consisting of definitely handicapped men—with basic training only.[29] Results were shown to be fairly reliable and closely related to education. More important still, they were found to be related to combat performance ratings.

The figures in table 7.2, valid for March 1942 (but many similar ones for different periods are available in the documents) give some indication of the results of the system.

Thus, ALL the ground combat arms without exception were in the bottom half of the list. The reason for this sad state of affairs is not hard to find: the operation of the replacement system was in the hands of Army Service Forces, itself one of the three main contenders for the available manpower.[30] Table 7.3, showing the distribution of the various classes between AGF and ASF, bears out this interpretation.

Against this background, the numerous complaints about the low quality of replacements for the various arms which flood the postwar Replacement Board's Report become comprehensible.

TABLE 7.2
Distribution of American Manpower among the Arms and Services (in percent)

	CLASS I & II MEN	CLASS III	CLASSES IV & V
Finance	89.4	10.5	0.5
Chemical warfare	51.2	27.6	21.2
Army air force	44.4	35.3	20.3
Ordnance	41.6	33.0	25.4
Military police	35.3	33.0	31.7
Medical	30.6	29.1	40.3
Quartermaster	28.5	29.4	42.1
Armored force	28.5	29.4	42.1
Branch immaterial	28.5	28.2	43.3
Infantry	27.4	29.0	43.6
Coastal artillery[1]	26.1	31.7	42.2
Cavalry	25.8	31.3	42.9
Field artillery	24.1	29.4	46.5
Engineers	23.4	26.2	50.5

SOURCE: R. R. Palmer, *The Procurement and Training of Ground Combat Troops* (Washington D.C., 1948), p. 17.

[1]Responsible for all fixed artillery, railway artillery, harbor defense, and until 1943, antiaircraft artillery also.

TABLE 7.3
Distribution of American Manpower among AGF and ASF (in percent)

	CLASS I & II MEN	CLASS III	CLASSES IV & V
Arms	29.7	33.3	37.0
Services	36.5	28.5	35.0

SOURCE: R. R. Palmer, *The Procurement and Training of Ground Combat Troops* (Washington, D.C., 1948), p. 3.

TRAINING

While training is undoubtedly of the highest importance for the production of fighting power, very little is available by the way of systematic information on the different methods by which this problem was handled by the German and U.S. Armies. What material can be found consists of impressionistic accounts by individuals that cannot be checked for their representativeness; nor is much to be gained, in this case, from a comparison of training manuals, of which there were endless numbers in both armies. The following account, therefore, will have to be limited, in the main, to a very few fundamental questions. Who did the training, and where did it take place? What were its underlying principles? How long did basic training—the only part that can be compared at all systematically—last?

German Army[31]

The organization of training in the German Army had a threefold purpose; namely, to relieve the Field Army of this task; to simulate, as closely as possible, the actual conditions of the battlefield; and to constantly introduce the most recent combat experiences into training practice.

To achieve the latter two of these aims, very great emphasis was laid on maintaining close connections between the army's two parts: not only were officers constantly being rotated between front-line duty and training units, but each of the latter was in addition tied to one or more divisions. Officers of the training unit and its parent division were expected to know each other personally and to exchange frequent visits and correspondence. Often it was recently wounded personnel, recovering from their wounds, who trained the replacements of their own division.

Fundamentally and in principle, recruits, officer candidates, NCOs, and specialists received their training at the hands of the Replacement Army. However, the Field Army was responsible for merging replacements with their units (for which purpose each division was provided with a Feldersatzbattalion, or Field Replacement Battalion), carrying out additional training during periods of rest, and for supplying advanced training to officers and NCOs. Training aspiring General Staff officers was in the hands of the General Staff.

The longer the war, however, the more difficult it became to maintain the strict separation of functions between the army's two parts. Replacement Army units were moved into the occupied countries, assumed the burden of security operations, were occasionally called on to lend a hand in times of crisis, and were consequently unable to properly carry out their training functions. More and more of the latter were transferred to Field Replacement Battalions, whose importance thus became more pronounced. The separation between the army's two parts thus broke down; however, the administrative difficulties implicit in this may have been more than offset by the fact that the troops were now increasingly trained by their own officers and under conditions closely resembling actual combat.

In the autumn of 1942, an attempt was made to institutionalize these arrangements by setting up the so-called field training divisions.[32] These were assigned the double mission of completing the recruits' basic training and of carrying out current security operations in the occupied countries. In practice, however, they tended to be sucked into the fighting, paid heavily in casualties for their inexperience, and were hastily disbanded.

From early in 1943 down to the end of the war, training was organized as follows:

divisions	completing the training of recruits, NCOs and specialists
armies	training company and battery commanders, as well as giving advanced training to NCOs and specialists
Replacement Army	basic training for recruits, NCOs and specialists; also officer schools
General Staff	courses for General Staff officers, divisional and regimental commanders

Training programs were the responsibility of the Replacement Army's chief of training, who in turn worked closely with the General Staff's Training Department. The latter received a constant stream of current information on combat experience, transformed it into notices for the troops, and from time to time consolidated the latter into new editions of the regulations.

Training aimed at giving a man a thorough mastery of his weapons and teaching him the fundamentals of tactics by making him participate in numerous unit exercises. The bent of training was almost exclusively practical, very little theory being added. Though basic training was carried out separately for each arm of the service, the first parts of all the training manuals were identical—thus ensuring uniformity throughout the army.

The duration of basic training varied. Infantrymen received sixteen weeks in 1938, eight in 1940, sixteen again in 1943, and twelve to fourteen in 1944.[33] Armored personnel received twenty-one weeks' basic training throughout the war, though there did appear a tendency, from 1944 on, to organize things in such a way as to make them able to participate in combat, in a pinch, after a mere sixteen weeks.[34]

In addition, recruits could expect to undergo a further brief period of training in their divisions' field replacement battalions before entering the line, thus getting to know their commanders and benefitting from the most recent local experiences. Whether there were any fixed rules governing the duration of this training phase is not clear; as the war went on and losses mounted, there must have been a tendency to hasten the recruits' integration into their units and standards probably deteriorated.

U.S. Army

Training in the U.S. Army was the responsibility of Army Ground Forces. Its cardinal principles were graduation, from individual to unit training; a strong emphasis on elementary training; maintaining the integrity of tactical units; realism, achieved by the near-as-possible simulation of actual combat conditions.

Enlisted men, NCOs, and specialists received their basic training in Army Training Centers (ATCs) and Replacement Training Centers (RTCs) located in the Zone of the Interior. For officers, Officer Candidate Schools (OCSs) were set up in 1941. Divisional staff officers were trained at the Command and General Staff School opened at Fort Leavenworth in December 1940.

Unlike their German equivalents, the U. S. Army's training units were not tied to specific parent units. Nor did their training personnel possess combat experience during the early years of the war. The War Department, which was responsible for publishing training manuals, followed tactical developments at the front; it was only in the second half of 1944, however, that combat-tried officers began returning home in any numbers to take up jobs as instructors. Even so, ties between training and combat outfits remained, partly owing to sheer geographical distance, tenuous and impersonal and could in no way be compared with the German system.

Training was constructed on the principles of engineering. Tasks were systematically broken down into small components that were first rehearsed and then put into sequence. The goal was to produce men who could serve their weapons automatically, without thought.

The duration of basic training varied. Until 1943 recruits were given only thirteen weeks. This was subsequently increased to seventeen, though special circumstances—for example, the pressure of preparations for "Overlord"—could cause men possessing only thirteen weeks of training to be sent out of the training centers. Armored personnel, trained in separate centers, likewise received seventeen weeks' training, which was further cut down to fifteen in January 1945. On the whole, therefore, American soldiers received a shorter basic training than did their German counterparts, though the picture might of course be modified later by unit training on which no comprehensive figures for either army are available.

Unlike their German equivalents, American divisions did not have a special organization to absorb and retrain newly arrived recruits, and replacements were expected to pick up experience from veterans. On the other hand, newly arriving replacements in the various theaters were often given a few weeks' refreshment training before being sent to join their units.

REPLACEMENTS

Four brave men who do not know each other, wrote Ardant du Picq in his *Etudes de Combat*,[36] will hesitate to attack a lion; four less brave men, but knowing and trusting each other, will do so resolutely. The point of the tale is this: of all the organizational problems an army has to solve, that of how best to merge replacements into existing units so as to ensure the cohesion of the whole is one of the most crucial, since on it depends the unit's fighting power.[37] The sheer size of the problem may be gauged from the fact that, on the average, three months of intensive combat in World War II cost an American infantry regiment a hundred percent of its personnel in casualties.[38]

German Army

We saw that the German Army was built up on a regional basis; that is, units the size of divisions downwards were normally composed exclusively of men originating in the same part of the country and, consequently, speaking the same dialect and sharing something of a common outlook. Naturally this arrangement was not without its disadvantages; in particular, it complicated the problem of bringing up replacements. Since it was believed that unit cohesion depended on the men sharing a common background, however, these complications—both administrative and transport/technical—were deliberately and consciously taken in stride.

The Replacement Army, which gave replacements their initial training, was built up in such a way that each field division had its own replacement battalion in one of the Wehrkreise. This arrangement not only made possible close and personal cooperation between instructors and field commanders, but also meant that replacements, upon completing their training, were sent to join their special units.

Replacements never travelled to their units as individuals, but were put together in 1,000-strong marching battalions (Marschbattalione), armed and equipped to cover long distances on foot and capable, if necessary, of looking after themselves in combat. They were commanded by officers sent by the parent division to pick them up or, alternatively, by personnel that had recovered from wounds and were on their way back to the front. Experience had provided rules for the composition of the marching battalions and for the distribution of the various arms inside them; in any case, since the replacements had only completed their basic training and were supposed to receive further training in the field (and since the Army was hopelessly unable to replace its casualties from early 1942 on) the exact composition of the Marschbattalione by MOS did not matter much.

When earmarked for divisions holding quiet sectors of the front, replacements might travel in marching companies numbering 250 or so men. Specialists alone were allowed to travel individually and then only in exceptional cases.

Upon arrival at their divisions the marching battalions were dissolved. The divisional commander or his representative welcomed the new recruits and decided on their distribution. They were then sent to the divisional field replacement battalion, each of whose three companies was closely tied up with one of the division's three regiments. This arrangement gave the regiments a strong incentive to look after their own replacements' training, made it possible to employ as instructors the very officers and NCOs who would later command the men in battle, and created opportunities for experienced personnel to be temporarily taken out of the line. After a period of training in the field replacement battalion, the replacements would reach the front already knowing both each other and their commanders and forming part of a well-integrated team.

The longer the war went on, the more frequently did difficult circumstances make it impossible to fully carry out these elaborate procedures. The results were strongly negative. Thus, for example, improvised units consisting of men picked out of leave-trains and hurriedly thrown together in a crisis proved to be almost without fighting power.[40] In at least one case—the panic that gripped elements of the 340th division in February 1944, when eighteen-year-old replacements broke in front of a Russian attack, threw away their weapons, and ran—it was possible to trace back these results to the fact that the division, fighting almost continuously, had not found the time to put the new arrivals through its field replacement battalion.[41]

U.S. Army[42]

In the American Army, replacements were first processed through reception centers where they were classified. They were then sent to a Replacement Training Center to receive their basic training. Mathematical models, purporting to forecast the number of casualties, governed the proportion of all men trained for each trade, speciality, and arm.

Their basic training completed, the replacements would be granted ten to twelve days' leave (an arrangement which in itself made it impossible to group them into units on the German model, even if this had been the intention) and then proceeded to replacement depots (popularly known as "repple depples") at the embarkation ports. Travelling individually all the way, they were shipped overseas to a theater depot (in France, for example, this was normally Le Havre). After a night's stay there, they were put aboard trains, each of whose wagons was commanded by a replacement officer; these, however, are said by the official report to have "exercised little control over the transient soldiers placed under their command."

Sometimes the trains would head for a theater depot, where the replacements were given up to five weeks' refreshment training, including squad and platoon training; often, however, they proceeded straight to forward depots and from there on to the divisions. A special divisional organization charged with receiving and absorbing them did not exist, and the new arrivals were simply distributed among the units. Owing no doubt partly to the enormous distances, the time spent in the replacement system normally amounted to four to five months, though nine and even ten months were not uncommon.[43]

Officers went through the replacement system like everybody else, that is, they were assigned to units from pools after graduating from OCS in accordance with T/O vacancies. Whereas German units often asked for specific officer-replacements (that is, men who had previously served in the same units as NCOs) by name, this practice was explicitly discouraged in the U.S. Army.[44]

The effect of such a system on morale, unit cohesion, and fighting power does not have to be imagined, since direct evidence about it is readily available. According to one official account, "some men" complained that they had been "herded like sheep" or "handled like so many sticks of wood." Arriving in the theater after weeks of travel by land and sea, the men "wanted most of all to be identified with a unit," instead of which they might well spend a few more weeks in various depots.[45] In the words of one unit commander,

> Replacements arrived in divisional and regimental areas tired, bewildered and disheartened, after having been shunted from one replacement depot to another, led by officers temporarily appointed for convoy or escort purposes who themselves were more or less bewildered. Field train bivouacs usually were within the sound of guns, and the replacements were acutely and nervously aware that their entry into combat was imminent. They frequently did not know how to take care of themselves.[46]

In fact, such were the effects of the system upon the replacements that medical officers among themselves spoke of a "repple depple syndrome" as a new kind of mental disease.[47]

Replacements were expected to pick up practical know-how from their veteran comrades, who might or might not possess the time and the inclination to assume teaching duties. Consequently, units made up of freshly arrived replacements not infrequently suffered disproportionally heavy casualties.[48]

Another disadvantage of the system of constantly filling in T/O vacancies (rather than having a large number of vacancies always at hand which was, willy-nilly, the case in the German Army) was a pronounced tendency to produce the wrong type of replacements. The mathematical models purporting to predict the number of casualties by MOS were based on the wrong kind of experience and out of date and never came up to expectations.[49] Already, in the spring of 1942, there appeared a large deficit in riflemen, counterbalanced by an even larger surplus of other personnel, including in particular service troops. [50] The MOS produced tended to be more intelligent than the average infantryman; for them to serve in a capacity other than that for which they had been trained, and with the despised infantry at that, constituted a double blow to morale.[51] It was not until early in 1944 that a reorganization of the replacement training centers got underway, but even so, infantry replacements remained in short supply right down to the end of the war.[52]

Voices demanding a change in the system were heard from time to time. In January 1942 General T. J. Christian complained that "unit spirit was lacking in the replacement training centers," and proposed that they be made to turn out complete units, not individual replacements; however, the War Department turned down the proposal on administrative grounds.[53] A system of tying the training centers to specific divisions and making the latter share in the task of training was also proposed. This, however, was rejected on the grounds that "training under the replacement training centers was far superior to the system under which the divisions trained their new recruits"—which may indeed have been true from a purely technical point of view, but failed to take into account the soldier's social and psychological needs as well as the opportunity for raising standards by giving commanders a stake in their own men's training.[54] Some officers wanted to set up an American equivalent of the German field replacement battalions, but nothing came of this proposal either.

Dissatisfied with the system, a few enterprising commanders went ahead and created their own arrangements. In particular, the Seventy-ninth Infantry Division under General Ira T. Wyche set up a well-considered organization for receiving and digesting replacements. The latter would first enter a divisional pool and be given a general orientation talk. Next there were three regimental pools operated by officers and NCOs detached from their regiments and another pool for the special troop section. The system was designed to enable new arrivals "to learn many lessons from old timers" and in addition made it possible for NCOs and officers who needed a break to be temporarily taken out of the line, as was the case in the German Army.[55] In fact, the only important difference between the system and the German one was the use, typical for American lingo, of the word "pool" rather than of some less anonymous, more military-sounding term to describe the institution.

The arrangements instituted by the Seventy-ninth Infantry Division were considered successful enough to be copied, more or less accurately, by several others; even more interesting, the Seventy-ninth is one of the very few combat outfits explicitly commended in the U. S. Army's official history of World War II. "A good combat unit," was Eisenhower's comment in a letter to Marshall.[56]

The conclusions from these facts are inescapable. Beyond a shadow of doubt, the German Army, profitting from the lessons of World War I, possessed an excellent replacement system that only failed, as sometimes happened, when circumstances made it impossible to apply. The U. S. Army by contrast put technical and administrative efficiency at the head of its list of priorities, disregarded other considerations, and produced a system that possessed a strong inherent tendency to turn men into nervous wrecks. Perhaps more than any other single factor, it was this system that was responsible for the weaknesses displayed by the U. S. Army during World War II.

NOTES

1. B. Mueller-Hillebrand, *Das Heer*, 3 vols. (Frankfurt am Main, 1968), 3:254.
2. B. Mueller-Hillebrand, "Statistisches System," U.S. Army Historical Division Study PC 011 (Koenigstein Ts., 1949), p. 68. In the original the passage quoted is underlined twice.
3. "Um die Truppe nicht mit weiteren Meldungen zu belästigen."
4. Mueller-Hillebrand, "Statistisches System," p. 68.
5. K. Greenfield, *The Organization of Ground Combat Troops* (Washington, D. C., 1947), p. 158.
6. R. R. Palmer, *The Procurement and Training of Ground Combat Troops* (Washington, D. C., 1948), p. 126.
7. Ibid., p. 105.
8. See R. R. Hofmann, "Beurteilungen und Beurteilungnotizien im deutschen Heer," U.S. Army Historical Division Study No. P 134 (Koenigstein Ts., 1952), pp. 3, 51-52.
9. Unsigned Note, 8 October 1939 Bundesarchiv/Militärarchiv (hereafter BAMA) H20/482.
10. Mueller-Hillebrand, *Das Heer*, 3:253.
11. Up to the end of 1944, 80.7 percent of all officers killed, missing, and discharged were army men; this was considerably more than the army's relative share in the Wehrmacht (exclusive of Waffen SS) at any time after 1939, when there had been hardly any losses at all. See Mueller-Hillebrand, "Statistisches System," p. 114.
12. See Generalstab, ed., Heeres Dienstvorschrift 81/15, *Wehrmachtersatzbestimmungen bei besonderen Einsatz* (Berlin, 1942), pp. 34-36; and Generalstab, ed., Heeres Dienstvorschrift 252/1, *Vorschrift über militärärtzliche Untersuchungen der Wehrmacht*, part I (Berlin, 1937), p. 6.
13. Schmirigk, "Die psychologische Beurteilungen Dienstpflichtiger bei Musterung und Aushebung," *Soldatentum* 6 (1939):24-27.
14. See Generalstab, ed., Heeres Dienstvorschrift 299/1b, *Ausbildungsvorschrift für die Panzertruppen* (Berlin, 1943), p. 8.
15. See T. W. Harrel and R. D. Churchill, "The Classification of Military Personnel," *Psychological Bulletin* 38 (1941):337-39.
16. H. L. Ansbacher, "German Military Psychology," *Psychological Bulletin* 38 (1941):371-72. Simoneit's assistants often became professors in postwar Germany and, in 1954-55, several among them helped organize the Bundeswehr's psychological service.

17. The laboratory was suddenly closed in the summer of 1942 though some of its parts continued to operate in the service of the Navy and the Air Force. In his preface to M. Simoneit, "Die Anwendung psychologischer Prüfungen in der deutschen Wehrmacht" (U.S. Army Historical Division Study No. P 007 [Koenigstein Ts., 1948]), Halder says that the laboratory was closed because it could not cope with the enormously increased numbers involved. Simoneit, however, suspected that the move had been initiated by the chief of the Armed Forces High Command, Field Marshall Keitel, whose son had failed to qualify for officer training. Keitel himself confirmed as much to the Nüremberg psychiatrist, Dr. Felix Gilbert.

18. "Jahresbericht des psychologischen Laboratorium des Reichskriegsministerium und der psychologischen Prüfstellen der Wehrmacht" (BAMA file RH19/III/494), p. 25.

19. M. Simoneit, *Wehrpsychologie* (Berlin, 1943), p. 55.

20. G. Nass, "Persönlichkeit des Kampfwagenführers," *Beihefte zu angewendete Psychologie* 79 (1938).

21. N. Roth, "Zur Formulierung psychologischer Gutachten bei Wehrpsychologischen Eignungsuntersuchungen," *Soldatentum* 5 (1938):175.

22. Ansbacher, "German Military Psychology," pp. 373, 381-82, 385.

23. Figures from E. Ginzberg, *The Ineffective Solder,* 3 vols. (New York, 1950), 2:26-27, 34-35.

24. Palmer, *Procurement and Training,* p. 3.

25. R. S. Anderson, *Physical Standards in World War II* (Washington, D. C., 1967) p. 71.

26. Owing to the time pressure, American military psychologists were not nearly as well trained as German ones. "A man with psychological training" spent eight weeks at an Army Training Center, then did eight to twelve weeks of "practical work of Army classification." See S. T. Henderson, "Psychology and the War," *Psychological Bulletin* 40 (1942):309, and M. A. Seidenfeld, "The Adjutant General's School and the Training of Psychological Personnel for the Army," ibid., p. 382.

27. Evidence that this was the case comes in the forms of desertions, which were most numerous in combat outfits (infantry, coastal artillery, cavalry, and field artillery) and least so in such places as finance, chemical warfare, ordnance, and signal corps, which presumably included a very high percentage of specialists mobilized straight from civilian life.

28. Personnel Research Section, the Adjutant General's Office, "Personnel Research in the Army: vi. the Selection of Tank Drivers," *Psychological Bulletin,* 41 (1943):499, 508.

29. Ginzberg, *The Ineffective Soldier* 2:45; A. J. Duncan, "Some Comments on the Army General Classification Test," *Journal of Applied Psychology* 31 (1947):143-49; S. A. Stouffer et al., *The American Soldier,* 4 vols. (Princeton, 1949), 2:37.

30. See Report of Replacement Board, Department of the Army, "Replacement System World Wide, World War II" (Washington, D. C., 1947) book 1, part 11. The board recommended the establishment of a "Personnel Command in the Zone of the Interior responsible solely to the Chief of Staff and charged with the administration

and training of all army personnel in the ZI in a casual status," that is, the adoption of the German system.

31. The following remarks are largely based on B. Meuller-Hillebrand, "Personnel and Administration," U. S. Army Historical Division Study No. P 005 (Koenigstein Ts., 1948), p. 77.

32. Feldausbildungsdivisionen.

33. *Ausbildungsvorschrift für die Infanterie,* vol. 1, 1 October 1938; vol. 1E, 21 June 1940; vol. 1E, 16 March 1943; and vol. 1E, 11 December 1943.

34. *Ausbildungsvorschrift für die Panzertruppen,* vol. 1a, 18 October 1943. This one is signed by Guderian as inspector of the "fast" troops.

35. The following remarks are based mainly on Greenfield, *Organization of Ground Combat Troops,* p. 30.

36. *Combat Studies* (Harrisburg, Pa, 1947), p. 110.

37. See K. Lang, *Military Institutions and the Sociology of War* (London, 1972) and its extensive bibliography.

38. R. F. Weigley, *History of the United States Army* (New York, 1967), p. 438.

39. Based on B. Mueller-Hillebrand, "Personnel and Administration," U. S. Army Historical Division Study P 005 (Koenigstein Ts., 1948), p. 16.

40. E. A. Shils and M. Janowitz, "Cohesion and Disintegration in the Wehrmacht in World War II," *Public Opinion Quarterly* 12 (1948):280-315.

41. Beratender Psychiater beim Pz. AOK 4, "Erfahrungsbericht, 1.4-30.6.1944," 14 July 1944, BAMA H20/122.

42. The following is based mainly on Palmer, *Procurement and Training,* p. 170; and on Department of the Army, ed., *The Personnel Replacement System of the US Army* (Pamphlet No. 20-211, Washington, D. C., 1954), p. 359.

43. Replacement Board, Department of the Army, "Replacement System World Wide," bk. 5, part 20.

44. Headquarters Services of Supply, European Theater of Operations, directive APO 887, 13 September 1943, National Archives file RG/332/52/265.

45. Department of the Army, *The Personnel Replacement System,* pp. 379, 464; see also Stouffer, *The American Soldier,* 2:272-74.

46. Department of the Army, *The Personnel Replacement System,* p. 467. The officer in question was Colonel T. J. Cross on the staff of the G 3, 2d Army.

47. Replacement Board, Department of the Army, "Replacement System World Wide," bk. 5, part 19.

48. Palmer, *Procurement and Training,* p. 230. Data from divisions in Italy suggest that one half of all replacements had been with their units for fewer than three days before entering combat; Stouffer, *The American Soldier,* 2:127.

49. Replacement Board, Department of the Army, "Replacement System World Wide," bk. 2, part 45.

50. Ibid., part 60; also Palmer, *Procurement and Training,* p. 395. In March 1942, for example, the Forty-fifth Infantry Division requested 3,217 riflemen but received only 1,082; on the other hand, it did receive 671 servicemen when it had asked for only 50.

51. Replacement Board, Department of the Army, "Replacement System World Wide," bk. 5.

52. According to S. L. A. Marshall, *Soldaten im Feuer* (Frauenfeld, 1951), p. 14 there was on 6 August 1944 exactly ONE rifleman replacement available in the entire European Theater.

53. Christian was Commanding Officer, Camp Roberts, Co, Field Artillery Training Center; see Department of the Army, ed., *The Personnel Replacement System*, p. 359.

54. Ibid., p. 360.

55. Ibid., p. 456. For General Wyche's own postwar testimony, see Replacement Board, Department of the Army, "Replacement System World Wide," bk. 5, part 26.

56. H. M. Cole, *The Lorraine Campaign* (Washington, D. C., 1950), p. 188; and M. Blumenson, *Breakout and Pursuit* (Washington, D. C., 1961), p. 72.

THE MAINTENANCE OF COMBAT EFFICIENCY 8

TROOP INDOCTRINATION

In general, there exists a tendency for the importance of propaganda in wartime to be exaggerated. The propagandists themselves have a clear interest in propagating the importance of their own jobs; their employers may do the same in the hope of deflecting potentially embarrassing questions concerning the nature of the cause;[1] whereas, on the other side, the enemy may use one's own propaganda in order to demonstrate the fundamental wickedness of anyone opposing him.

These interested parties notwithstanding, considerable empirical evidence exists that indoctrination affects troops in much the same way as rain affects a duck: it glances off their backs. A survey among American enlisted men during World War II revealed that only 5 percent fought for what could be called idealistic reasons.[2] A much smaller survey made in 1969 put the figure at five out of thirty-four—which, if true, would lead to the somewhat surprising conclusion that the American soldier who served in Vietnam was actually more idealistic than his World War II counterpart.[3]

On the strength of this evidence, the soldier who fights out of an idealistic commitment to his country's national goals appears to be an exception; the young Hitler, it is said, was such a person.[4] It is not difficult to see why, in the terror that is battle, such thoughts should occupy little place in the soldier's mind. What is hard to see is how educators and propagandists could ever believe otherwise.

To reach the troops' souls, to influence them, to make them move in the desired direction—that is the supreme challenge facing every commander. For an outsider to achieve the same result is an almost impossible task, something granted, if at all, only to a very few truly outstanding men. Except where the propagandists are men of very high calibre and conviction, the dish ladled out by them will be regarded by the recipients as anything between mere entertainment and another load of bullshit.[5] It may even be counterproductive.

To put it in a different way, the contents of propaganda are less important than its organization—it does not matter much what is said, but by whom. The following pages, accordingly, will concentrate on the different ways in which propaganda was organized in the armies under consideration.

German Army

In the German Army before World War I, the concept of "troop indoctrination" was unknown. Instead there was geistige Betreuung, which might be roughly translated as "spiritual strengthening."

Since, according to the regulations, "the officer [was] the leader and educator of his men in every field," a special organization charged with geistige Betreuung did not exist. While attempts at indoctrination—in a conservative-monarchical direction, needless to say, and sometimes assuming ridiculous forms such as organized competitions in plowing and cow-milking—were certainly not lacking either before or during the war, their execution was mostly left to officers and NCOs. It was only in November 1918 that the High Command instituted education officers (Bildungsoffiziere) in a belated attempt to counter the Army's progressive disintegration.[6] But this was to no avail.

While conservative right-wing ideas continued to permeate the army during the Weimar period, no special organization was set up to supervise their propagation. Instead, the "Fundamentals of Education" issued by General von Seeckt in 1920 simply stated that "everybody, officers and men alike, are to regard themselves as representatives of the army at all times," and left it at that.[7]

From 1929 to 1932 the army of the Weimar Republic, confronted with the growing number of Nazi sympathizers in its ranks, tried to combat this menace by sending so called "desk-generals" on the lecture circuit. This was also to no avail.[8]

After the Nazi seizure of power, a conflict rapidly emerged between the army and Goebbels's propaganda ministry concerning responsibility for army propaganda. Commanded by the pro-Nazi minister of war, General von Blomberg, the army was not at all unwilling to allow its men to wear Nazi symbols and insignia, nor to indoctrinate them with Nazi principles.[9] It drew the line, however, at handing over responsibility for the conduct of propaganda, which remained its own exclusive business.

Until 1939, though the Ministry of War might from time to time issue directives for the education of the troops in a Nazi spirit, the situation remained fundamentally unchanged. Shortly before the outbreak of World

War II, however, the Wehrmacht decided to meet the growing Nazi pressure by taking the offensive; it established its own propaganda department and its own propaganda troops.[10]

Geistige Betreuung, however, was not the new organization's task. Instead, it was responsible for—besides censorship—representing the Wehrmacht to the German public and for conducting enemy propaganda, or "psywar." These two functions together were known as "active propaganda."[11]

In July 1939 the following agreement was signed between the Wehrmacht and the Ministry of Propaganda:

> Geistige Betreuung of our own troops is the business of the Wehrmacht alone. The Ministry of Propaganda is limited to supplying suitable material upon request. . . .
>
> It is a fundamental principle that the commander, and he alone, should be responsible for geistige Betreuung. His tasks are as follows:
>
> - preparing the troops before the outbreak of war
> - transmitting military and political news during the first days of the war
> - delivering daily newspapers, later also military newspapers, to the troops
> - supervising radio-listening
> - supervising films, field libraries, front theater.[12]

In practice, of course, the fundamental principle of unity of command was violated to the extent that officers (though many tried hard) could not, and did not, produce most of their own newspapers and broadcasting. Nevertheless, responsibility for maintaining morale continued to rest on the shoulders of the commander and on his alone.

In the autumn of 1940, again in response to the propaganda ministry's pressure, the General Staff thoroughly examined the entire problem of troop indoctrination. The chief of staff, General Halder, insisted that responsibility for morale remain in the hands of commanders alone and carried his point against considerable opposition. The commander in chief, Field Marshal von Brauchitsch, thereupon issued a list of themes to be propagated. These included the German people, the German Reich, German living space, National Socialism as the foundation of various aspects of German national life, and Germany before the Peace of Westphalia.[13]

Not even the Nazi party, it is true, could demand more; and Brauchitsch proceeded to dot the "i's" and cross the "t's" by announcing that "it is absolutely necessary for a UNIFIED [emphasis in the original] conception of National Socialist principles to exist in the army and become the common possession of all soldiers."[14] The even more cardinal principle of unity of command, however, was safeguarded and remained intact.

Meanwhile other Nazi agencies besides Goebbels's propaganda ministry were trying to get a foot in the door. In September 1940 Field Marshal Keitel, chief of the Armed Forces High Command, signed an agreement with Nazi ideologue Alfred Rosenberg under which the latter's office was to supply the Wehrmacht with literature, speakers, and National Socialist training courses for officers. Depsite pressure from Keitel, however, the Army High Command refused to ratify the agreement and in January 1941 flatly stated that it would only turn to Rosenberg to furnish literature and schooling materials as needed.[15]

As the Wehrmacht faced defeat for the first time in the winter of 1941-42, Keitel took the step by ordering all units down to battalion level to appoint Betreuungsoffiziere, or BOs. Working from the office of the intelligence officer, these officers were supposed to carry out propaganda in addition to their normal duties. Not surprisingly, the order caused considerable resistance and even ridicule; commanders appointed their least competent men for the job, and Keitel even had to forbid chaplains from being entrusted with the task of spreading National Socialist propaganda! In any case, the principle that "there can be no division between military and spiritual leadership" was reaffirmed by that model Nazi general, Shoerner, and disseminated throughout the army.[16]

It was only at the end of 1943 that pressure for the establishment of a regular propaganda service within the armed forces started in earnest. The men behind it were Martin Bormann, head of the party chancellery, and an Army colonel by the name of Huebner who had been impressed by the fighting spirit of the Waffen SS but, significantly, had to hide his SS contacts lest they damage his career. Bormann's pressure proved effective, and in December 1943 Hitler signed a directive for the institution of National Socialist leadership officers (Nazionalsozialistische Führungsoffiziere, or NSFOs) in the Wehrmacht.

Things moved quickly from this point on. In February 1944 the "Provisional Regulations for National Socialist Guidance in the Armed Forces" were published; in them the NSFO was invisaged as an ordinary staff officer who, "just like the Intelligence Officer" was to assist the commander in everything pertaining to geistige Betreuung. He was, however, to work through the officers; only in special cases, and then in the presence of the unit commander, was he to address the troops directly. He was not to interfere in the affairs of subordinate commanders, nor to turn into a "wayside preacher"; this, however, was later modified to the extent that the NSFO was permitted to address the troops directly. NSFOs were expected to carry on propaganda in addition to their normal duties, and it was only toward the end of 1944 that special slots for them were provided in the tables of organization.

Two-week courses for NSFOs were held from March 1944 on at Krössinsee, Pomerania, and were attended by officers detailed by the three services. The program consisted of lectures, discussion groups, and, in the evenings, films, concerts, and singing. To organize all this took time; it was not until the second half of 1944 that most units actually got their NSFO.

Even in the eyes of the persons responsible, the NSFO courses were hardly satisfactory, since the students, mostly highly qualified and decorated officers (the possession of a decoration for bravery was made mandatory in order to secure the NSFO a respectful audience) naturally resented party hacks telling THEM about patriotism.[17] As was to happen in the U.S. also, the program's name gave rise to derisive puns and had to be altered several times. Postwar investigators without exception have described the mass of the German troops as indifferent, not to say apathetic, vis-à-vis the great moral, political, and strategic issues arising form the war, and one has even claimed that the NSF program exercised a negative effect on morale.[18] One survey among prisoners of war showed that only 5 percent were concerned with any but their personal problems, while another showed that "fanatical Nazis," apoliticals and anti-Nazis were distributed in an almost regular bell shape with the former constituting only 11 percent of the total.[19] [20] Highly motivated Nazis, however, were considerably more numerous among NCOs and much more so among junior officers—a point that is well worth bearing in mind.

Had Germany won the war, many people who now discount the role played by Nazi propaganda would certainly have changed their tune; on the other hand, a victorious Wehrmacht would hardly have allowed the NSF organization to be set up in the first place. Certainly this organization and the propaganda disseminated by it were a response to defeat rather than a contributor to victory. As an example of the way the party attempted to reassert its slipping hold on the troops in the face of defeat, there were the loyalty oaths and catechisms ("I belong to. . . . I am determined. . . . Never will I. . . . I believe. . . . ") that they were made to repeat from 1943 on.[21] The effect of such formulae on the morale of the German soldier, though impossible to measure, was probably no greater than that of similar nonsense in other armies.

U.S. Army

In the U.S. Army during World War I, efforts at so called "troop indoctrination" were left largely to individual commanders. However, army information in the form of the newspaper *Stars and Stripes* was plentiful and readily available.[22]

In 1940, faced with low morale among conscripts, the army set up a morale branch to deal with the problem. Headed by a civilian, Frederick Osborn, the division became the butt of so much derision on the part of the rank and file that the morale of its own officers suffered and its title had to be changed, first to "Special Services Branch" and then to "Information and Education Division."[23]

Subordinated to the Army Service Forces rather than directly to the General Staff, the division's mission was defined as "assisting officers in all matters pertaining to morale, recreation and welfare." It accordingly prepared lectures, graphic materials, and a series of films entitled *Why We Fight*.[24] (Significantly, the only German equivalent I could find was a 1944 HPA booklet entitled *What Are We Fighting For*). It also employed its officers to disseminate these materials throughout the army.

The program's effect on the army's fighting power is difficult to assess, since it formed only one factor among many. In April 1945 a study concluded that in regard to factual information about the war, attitudes toward the army, treatment of allies, and personnel adjustment to civilian life, there were no "significant and consistent differences" between men who had participated in the program and others who had not.[25] Even where some gains in information could be shown, this was not correlated to any increase in personal commitment to the war. In all, "the orientation program served the useful purpose of reassuring men and reducing somewhat their feeling that the army was not concerned for the welfare of the individual.... But there is little positive evidence that the army succeeded in altering basic orientation toward the war such as to increase personal commitment to the task of winning it." One fact does stand out, however: whereas convinced Nazis were proportionally more numerous among German officers than among enlisted men, only half as many American officers as men reported themselves as fighting for idealistic reasons.[26]

Interestingly, the various information programs were more popular among the higher headquarters—which had ordered them into existence, and to which they represented a way of sharing the burden of maintaining troop morale—than among the rank and file.[27] There exists a simple explanation for this fact; if my own experience is any guide, commanders seldom if ever bothered to attend the information sessions in person, and indeed for them to have done so would have constituted an intolerable admission that they did not know what they were sending their men to die for.

As Table 8.1 shows, the orientation courses were better liked (and therefore, presumably, more effective) when they were directed by personnel who were liked, respected, or admired.

At this point, the fundamental dilemma confronting any centralized organization for troop indoctrination becomes clear: to be effective educa-

TABLE 8.1
Evaluation of Orientation Sessions by American Troops

EVALUATION OF COURSE LEADER	PERCENTAGE OF MEN SAYING THEY GOT A LOT OUT OF THE COURSE
Group's discussion leader is the first choice of the group	39%
Group leader is among top choices of the group, but not first	23%
Group leader is not among top choices of the group	14%

SOURCE: S.A. Stouffer et at., *The American Soldier*, 4 vols. (Princeton, 1949), 1:471.

tion officers must be liked, respected, and admired, but men who possess these prerequisites seldom become education officers.[28] There is, indeed, no reason why they should: such men ought to command others, not to meet them in fleeting orientation sessions. The better at his job an education officer, moreover—the more successful he is in raising and maintaining morale—the more likely he is to undermine the position of the commander whose assistant he is supposed to be. No wonder, therefore, that the morale of morale officers paradoxically became an issue in both the German and the American Armies and that for the former as well as the latter there actually exists evidence showing a negative correlation between troop indoctrination and morale.[29]

We might perhaps conclude that a program of troop indoctrination is unnecessary in victory and is not likely to have much effect in defeat; and that for it to have any effect at all it should not be put into the hands of a separate or centralized organization.

ROTATION

German Army

The German Army had no fixed rules concerning the rotation of units in and out of the line. The problem, indeed, hardly arose during the early years of World War II; blitzkrieg campaigns were by definition brief affairs that did not require rotation. After each campaign, however, the divisions that took part underwent refreshment (Auffrischung)—an operation that required some three weeks, involved considerable logistic and administrative preparations, and was carried out, as far as possible, in one of the occupied countries.[30] Organized by corps headquarters, such an operation involved reorganization and refreshment training for existing units, the merging into them of replacements, and the issuing of new equipment to replace that lost or worn out in battle.

As conditions worsened during the second half of the war, such thorough refreshment of entire divisions became progressively more difficult to carry out. Instead, refreshment more and more often was carried out inside the divisions, which meant that individual regiments or even battalions were taken out of the line for periods varying from days to weeks. The troops thus released were sent to so-called recovery homes (Erholungsheime) behind the front in which they were rested and well looked after, free from every care including even the sudden raids which the General Staff, in times of crisis, carried out among men going on leave.[31] The security thus offered was supremely important; the longer the war, the stronger the tendency to use the recovery homes as a substitute for leave.

U.S. Army

The purpose of the U.S. Army's system of rotation in World War II was not, as in the German case, to restore and preserve fighting power but rather to "equalize the burden" among the troops by having those go home who had served overseas for longer than a certain specified period. The length of this period was fixed by the theater commander and varied between six and twenty-four months. Since the availability of shipping space was the determining factor, it is perhaps not surprising that the lowest figure originates in the North American theater where no fighting took place at all.[32]

Owing to persistent shipping and replacement shortages, in any case, the number of individuals actually sent home in this manner was very small. The policy may even have been harmful, since it gave rise to hopes that, in the vast majority of cases, proved incapable of fulfillment.

On the other hand, the small number of divisions—89 in all—and the policy of keeping them continually up to strength by a steady stream of replacements made unit rotation both impossible and unnecessary. For units operating in the Pacific, the effect of this was mitigated by the pauses between the island-hopping campaigns; in the Mediterranean, France and, above all, in Italy, it meant that the same men had to face combat for day after day, week after week, until, in the words of the army's chief psychiatrist, they either became casualties, deserted, or went beserk.[33]

In November 1944 ETO established a recuperation leave plan, which qualified troops who had been wounded at least twice, decorated twice for bravery, or had spent at least six months at the front for return to the Continental United States. The quota was 2,200 a month, later increased to 5,500. In spite of these very small numbers, the effect on morale is said to have been favorable. The time from France to the U.S. and back was about four months, however, so that only the November contingent returned to Europe in time to take a further part of the war.[34]

PSYCHIATRIC CASUALTIES

German Army[35]

In the German Army during World War I, the concepts of "combat fatigue" and "nonbattle casualty"—both implying that war as such might have a destructive effect on men—were unknown. Men displaying nervous symptoms were divided into mentally ill (Geistkranken) and nervously ill (Nervenkranken). The former averaged 26,070 per twelve month period, which meant that in any given year of war 0.2 percent of all those who passed through the army from 1914 to 1918 (13.3 million in all) became mentally ill or were recognized as such; whereas the latter averaged 613,047 or 4.7 percent of the same figure.

Among the nervously ill, that is nonbattle casualties properly speaking, half were diagnosed as hysterics; between 30 and 40 percent as neurasthenics; and the rest as suffering from shock and other ailments.[36] The problems grew into a serious one toward the end of the war, and interwar authors never tired of repeating how, at the stroke of the armistice, "tens of thousands" of "psychopaths" were cured as if by magic and became "active and noisy revolutionary agitators."[37]

On the treatment of these cases and its success in restoring them to duty, no detailed information is available. It appears, however, that one cardinal lesson was learnt: under no circumstances should men displaying nervous symptoms be allowed to go home, nor should their treatment take place in the Zone of the Interior. The presence of men displaying such symptoms was considered ruinous to civilian morale; on the other hand, the interest and sympathy of the local population might encourage the casualties to retain their symptoms.[38]

During the early years of World War II, in the period of the blitzkrieg campaigns with their inherently limited duration and intensity, few psychiatric casualties appeared. Their numbers rose after the beginning of the invasion of Russia, however. Attempting to generalize, the consulting psychiatrist attached to (formerly Guderian's) Second Panzer Army concluded that "periods without obvious 'results' or 'great events,' periods of waiting and small scale war—also against day-to-day inconveniences—constitute a heavy burden on the troops."[39]

It was typical to the German approach that cases of war-induced neurosis (psychoneurosis) were not regarded as a separate category but rather grouped under the label of "psychiatric cases," which meant simply those cases that required the attention of a psychiatrist. Psychiatric cases were divided as follows. First there were the wounded—men who, in conjunction with physical, visible wounds had received organic damage to the nervous system. Second there were the "neurological" cases—men who, though outwardly intact, were displaying symptoms thought to result from "commotion" or "contusion" received in battle or through accident. Finally there were the "purely" psychiatric cases; pure in the sense that the symptoms did not appear to be related, directly or indirectly, to organic damage.[40]

If the experiences of the consulting psychiatrist attached to Army Group South are any guide, about a third of all psychiatric cases belonged to this third category.[41] They were in turn divided into two subclasses, of which only the first, known as "psychogenics" and comprising 43 percent of all purely psychiatric cases, need concern us here.[42] Of 121 men who were classified as psychogenics during one three month period, only 11 (9.1 percent) were classified as suffering from "primary fear neurosis following enemy action," and the majority of these were said to be "unstable and neuropathic characters."[43] To put it in a different way: among approximately half a million soldiers of Army Group South, 844 came to the psychiatrist's attention during these three months, and of those only 14.3 percent were diagnosed as suffering from what, in American lingo, was known as "psychoneurosis."

The treatment of all kinds of psychiatric casualties not obviously related to organic damage (including cases of paralysis, loss of speech and hearing, blindness, trembling, contractions, and inability to walk) normally took place in a field hospital (Feldlazaret) immediately behind the front. It consisted of calming the patient down, either by talking to him "in a firm but comradely way" or by dosing him with sedatives. After no longer than eight days in bed, patients were put and made to go through a gradually increasing program of "strict military exercises." There followed a period of rest in a convalescent home, from which most went back to their units "completely recovered."[44]

Patients who did not respond to this treatment were evacuated to a military hospital (Kriegslazaret) in their respective theater of war. Here treatment consisted of "Faradization," that is, the application of electric currents weaker than those employed for electroshock but strong enough to cause real pain. Other forms of treatment used, according to circumstances, were cardiozol (a drug causing violent contractions of the body) and hypnosis. Not these means in themselves, however, but rather the suggestion involved—an electrically induced twitch of a paralyzed leg, for example, would persuade a patient that he could indeed walk, while at the same time causing enough pain to make him want to avoid a repetition—were considered effective. To facilitate suggestion, patients were not concentrated in separate wards but distributed among the neurological departments of ordinary military hospitals where their number was not normally supposed to exceed 30 percent.[45]

Whatever the methods used, they were certainly very effective, with up to 85 percent of cases returning to duty from one hospital on which statistics are available.[46] Only the handful who did not were passed on for treatment in the Zone of the Interior, and then only in hospitals remote from their hometowns, where relatives could not visit them. In no case, moreover, were soldiers discharged from the Wehrmacht for such reasons; when all else failed, they were simply locked away in mental institutions.[47]

While detailed statistics on the incidence of psychiatric cases in the Wehrmacht as a whole are not available, it was recognized, even during the war, that German troops in this respect did better than Allied ones.[48] Table 8.2 shows the frequency and distribution of such cases in Rommel's Africa Corps during one four month period of intensive combat followed by a thousand mile retreat.

TABLE 8.2
Psychiatric Casualties in the Africa Corps, by Type

TYPE OF CASUALTY TREATED FOR PSYCHIATRIC ILLNESS	NUMBER OF CASUALTIES
Wounded	68
Nonneurological psychiatric cases	13
Epileptics	10
Schizophrenics	5
Feeble-minded	6
Suspected organic damage to the brain	2
Neurotics and polyneurotics	85
Complaints following damage to the skull	13
Real nervous exhaustion (exogenous)	8
Psychopaths	73
Total	283

SOURCE: Der Beratende Psychiater der Panzergruppe Afrika, "Erster Erfahrungs-bericht, 26.9.1941-17.1.1942," 25 January 1942, BAMA H20/480.

Since the Africa Corps at this time numbered around 43,000 men, psychiatric cases of all kinds must have run at about 2 percent of strength per year. The figure for Army Group South in Russia cannot be precisely calculated, but must have been very much lower.[49] That for Army Group D in France, Belgium, and Holland for the period April-June 1944 (during most of which there was no fighting) was, at 2.7 percent of strength per year, somewhat higher.[50]

From isolated instances of units in which psychiatric casualties were particularly frequent, it is possible to draw conclusions regarding their very low number in the Wehrmacht as a whole. Referring to the first quarter of 1943, a period of heavy defensive fighting which led to a rise in the number of psychiatric cases, the consulting psychiatrist attached to the Second Panzerarmee wrote that they were especially frequent among recently arrived men who had not had the time to form strong comradely ties (Kampfgemeinschaft) with their buddies and among those serving in units where, by the force of circumstances, they were compelled to face danger helplessly and in isolation.[51] Psychiatric cases, the consulting psychiatrist to Army Group D likewise noted, were especially frequent among "Volksdeutsche [ethnic Germans] of List III" who, selected on the basis of "racial" considerations, faced problems of linguistic isolation.[52]

Though comprehensive data are not and probably never will be available, the connection between the Wehrmacht's organization (recruitment by land of origin, replacements on the same basis and in closed groups, the Feldersatzbattalione) and the low number of psychiatric casualties is therefore quite clear. That systems of organization and treatment, and not any native qualities of the German soldier, were behind this fact is also shown by the sharp rise in mental illness following their release from Allied prisoner of war camps.[53]

Summing up the German experience Prof. Panse, consulting psychiatrist to Wehrkreis (Military District) VI (Köln) and one of the most successful practitioners in returning men to duty, wrote early in 1945:

> In my opinion, the systematic attack on psychogenic disturbances is at least partly responsible for the fact that not even in the sixth year of war do such cases constitute a large scale problem. The very fact that the troops know that physicians are not helpless when faced with such cases probably prevents the appearance of many. The danger of a relapse, too, is very small for those who were correctly treated and concerns only constitutionally abnormal types.
>
> As far as Wehrkreis VI is concerned, a rise in the number of cases cannot be shown even in the sixth year of the war. A few more cases were brought to our attention in the last few months, it is true, but in my opinion this is simply the result of better diagnosis by the troops.[54]

U.S. Army

In the U.S. Army, "combat psychiatry" was first developed by Dr. Thomas W. Salmon, director of the National Committee for Mental Hygiene during World War I. Visiting France on a tour of inspection, he noticed that the French and the British had developed different approaches to the treatment of combat neurosis; whereas the former took a hard line and frequently used punishments, the latter evacuated their casualties to mental hospitals in England. The British method was regarded by Salmon as more humane; on the other hand, it resulted in a "quite low" rate of return to duty.[55]

It was thereupon decided to assign a psychiatrist to each division. His job was to examine all cases, treat light ones, control the evacuation of the rest, and investigate suspected cases of self-mutilation. The objective of combat psychiatry was defined as enabling the casualty "to obtain the concurrence of the group and to commit himself to the group and its task." Working by this approach, Salmon is said to have succeeded in returning two-thirds of all cases to their units.[56]

In World War II a different approach was adopted. Instead of concentrating on treatment, the army now introduced preliminary screening procedures intended to probe the unconscious minds of men and eliminate those who were "psychologically incapable of withstanding the stresses of combat duty." Having thus ensured, as it thought, the fitness of the troops, the Army went on to fight World War II, in the words of one critic, "as if World War I had never occurred and Dr. Salmon had never existed."[57]

The results were not late in coming. By mid-1943 admissions to psychiatric hospitals were running at an average of 6.76 percent of strength per year, the lowest figure being 3 percent (which still exceeds that of any German unit I could find) and the highest 120-150 percent.[58] For combat divisions on the European continent between June and November 1944 the figure was 26 percent, or almost ten times that of the opposing German Army Group D.[59] The overall number of soldiers treated for psychiatric disease in World War II was 929,307, or 8.9 percent of all those who passed through the army.[60] Close to 43 million men-days were lost, and 320,000 men had to be discharged as permanently unfit. The number of cases was about equal to that of all battle and nonbattle wounds combined and exceeded the number of those killed by a factor of about three to one. At one time, indeed, more men were being discharged from the army for psychiatric reasons then were added by induction, prompting General Marshall to set up an investigation.[61]

In the German Army "psychogenics" constituted some 43 percent of all purely psychiatric cases; in the American one, 67.7 percent. In the U.S. Army, these were followed by men with character and behavior disorders (12.8 percent), psychotics (7.3 percent), feeble-mindedness (3.1 percent), and "others" (6.9 percent). Over two-thirds of all cases, in other words, were normal men who had failed to make a successful adjustment to army life, including combat—and this in spite of the fact that preliminary screening had already removed 1,686,000 men suspected of emotional or mental disorders.[62]

That the enormous number of psychiatric casualties in the U.S. Army was not due to the intensity of combat seems clear from the German experience; it has instead been attributed to a variety of causes, beginning with the "child oriented" American society and ending with faulty screening procedures which, though they rejected men at a rate exceeding that of

World War I by five to one, somehow failed to catch the right personalities. Unknown to most investigators, however, is documentary evidence from ETO to the effect that American psychiatric casualties fell into two basic types.[63] The first comprised green troops, usually replacements, who went to pieces within five days or so of seeing combat. The other were seasoned troops who cracked after about four months of combat. Everything in our inquiry so far leads us to think that the first kind were the victims of the replacement system and the faulty cohesion of American units; whereas the second kind were brought down by the unlimited tours of duty.[64,65]

Treatment of American psychiatric casualties also differed from that meted out to their German counterparts. Possibly because psychoanalysis was much more influential in the U.S., the symptoms displayed were regarded as manifestations of mental processes buried deep in the unconscious mind and requiring discharge. Psychotherapy, however, was apt to take up a long time, and cases were accordingly evacuated for treatment in the psychiatric (not neurological, as was the German practice) wards of hospitals hundreds of miles to the rear. As a result, only 5 percent of all psychiatric cases during the North African campaign ever returned to their units.[66]

Things, it is true, improved later on. During the later stages of the Italian campaign, army psychiatrists, by concentrating on immediate treatment in "exhaustion centers" close behind the front, succeeded in making some 60 percent of all cases return to duty of one kind or another.[67] The rate fluctuated widely from one unit and hospital to the next, however, and a return rate of 80 percent was regarded as "phenomenal." For the war as a whole, the figure was probably just under 60 percent, though by no means all of those went back to their original duties. Those men who failed to respond to treatment were sent back to the United States, discharged from the army, and put into mental institutions. Here some of them still remained years later receiving such treatments as hydrotherapy, insulin shock, and electroshock.

Although a historian should avoid hasty generalizations, it is hard to avoid the feeling that something was wrong with an army that first allowed nonbattle casualties to reach epidemic proportions and then failed to utilize its own experience in treating them. These evils were compounded by an extremely permissive attitude on the part of the army which, possibly based on the widespread acceptance of Freud's theories, was communicated to the troops by semiofficial channels and caused combat fatigue to be regarded as a legitimate, almost normal complaint.[68] While preventing the army from applying the somewhat harsh methods of treatment used by German physicians, this attitude also built "golden bridges" for men who wanted to escape combat. There even exists evidence that, for some soldiers at any rate, going AWOL, deserting and requesting evacuation on psychiatric grounds constituted alternative courses of action.[69] Patton's method in slapping a soldier who did not fight may not have been so wrong after all.

THE MEDICAL SERVICES

The role played in the life of an army by proper medical services does not require elaboration. It is of the greatest importance to the soldier's morale to know that, if and when wounded, he will be quickly and well taken care of. In a prolonged conflict such as World War II, moreover, wounded personnel returning to duty after convalescence may represent a welcome and significant addition to strength.

German Army

No comprehensive study of the German medical services in World War II is available, and given the state of the evidence, none is likely to become available in the future. The following remarks will therefore necessarily bear a rather general character.

Starting with organization, table 8.3 gives some idea of the extent of Germany's military-medical effort.

The German medical services at their peak, therefore, comprised 341,760 men and women. From 1939 to 1943 the proportion of medical officers (that is, qualified physicians) serving with the troops rose from 48.4 to 54.5 percent of all medical officers; during the same period, that of men and NCOs employed in the same place fell from 73.1 percent to 66.7 percent of the total number of this personnel. Doctors, in other words, were being pushed forward to the front, whereas back in the rear there was a growing tendency to rely on paramedical personnel and, of course, Red Cross auxiliaries, mostly female nurses.

In World War I, men killed in action had formed 13.8 percent of all bloody casualties; this figure rose to 21.9 percent during the French campaign of 1940 and to 22.9 percent during the first year of the Russian campaign. The rise probably reflects both the increased lethality of weapons and the greater difficulty of recovering the wounded during mobile operations.

Between September 1939 and April 1945 approximately 52.4 million wounded and sick were treated in Wehrmacht and SS hospitals.[70] Table 8.4 will give some indication of the results.

Of every 100 wounded who did stay alive during the French campaign, 85 could expect to return to duty (65 to active duty and 20 to garrison duty). This figure fell to 83 (58, 25) during the summer of 1941 in Russia, and went down further to 77 (51, 26) during the winter of the same year. Fifty-eight

TABLE 8.3

Manpower in the German Military Medical Services, 1939–1943

	FIELD ARMY					REPLACEMENT ARMY			TOTAL	
	Troops		Hospitals			Hospitals				
Year	*Officers*	*Enlisted Men*	*Officers*	*Enlisted Men*	*DRK*[1]	*Officers*	*Enlisted Men*	*DRK*	*Officers*	*Enlisted Men*
1939–40	7,798	92,348	1,314	9,731	1,241	7,964	24,179	17,062	16,086	126,258
1940–41	12,127	115,264	3,528	17,951	3,899	7,034	26,153	22,580	22,419	159,368
1941–42	12,757	150,060	4,427	30,472	7,507	8,911	46,047	45,637	26,095	116,579
1942–43	17,034	164,898	4,689	18,737	8,413	9,507	53,438	55,044	31,230	247,037

SOURCE: F. Seidler, *Prostitution, Homosexualität, Selbstverstümmelung, Probleme der deutschen Sanitätsführung 1939-1945* (Neckargemund, 1977) p. 33.

[1]Deutsches Rote Kreuz.

TABLE 8.4
Death and Survival Rates among German Army Wounded (in percent)

	WORLD WAR I	FRANCE, 1940	RUSSIA, SUMMER, 1941	RUSSIA, WINTER, 1941
Died of wounds	6.0	7.9	10.5	12.2
Stayed alive	94.0	92.1	89.5	87.8
Total	100.00	100.00	100.00	100.00

SOURCE: B. Mueller-Hillebrand, "Statistisches System," U.S. Army Historical Division Study No. PC 011 (Koenigstein Ts., 1949), p. 144.

percent of all those who returned to duty did so within three months; 86 percent, within six; 93 percent, within nine; and 96 percent, within a year. The average number of noneffective days for battle casualties was ninety-eight.[71]

Of every 100 men hospitalized for sickness during the war, 98.5 stayed alive; 85.4 returned to duty; 14.6 became unfit. Of those who returned to duty, 48.9 percent did so within a month, 71.7 percent, within two months, 85.9 percent, within three months, 93.8 percent, within four months, 97.2 percent, within five months, and 98.7 percent within six. Not all the sick, however, were treated in hospital; many were looked after in their units. Here a man's chance of staying alive was 99 percent, that of returning to duty 86.7 percent. The average number of noneffective days of these cases was 9.3.

The fact that additional information is not available makes it impossible to add much to these figures. One fact, however, should be noted: it was a cardinal principle, deriving from experience in the field, that wounded personnel, upon their recovery, should be sent to the replacement unit affiliated with their last field unit.[72] Placed in replacement companies to be restored to fitness, they would travel back to their original units in the company of new recruits in the same Marschbattalionen and were frequently commanded by officers who were themselves returning to active duty. Despite growing technical difficulties as the war went on, this principle was rigorously observed.

U.S. Army

The overall strength of the U.S. Army's Medical Department in World War II, according to one source, was 680,438, of whom 48,317 were medical corps; 14,848, dental corps; 2,066, veterinary corps; 19,439, medical administrative corps; 52,128, army nurse corps; and 541,650, enlisted Medical Department personnel.[73] As compared with all army personnel, Medical Department personnel naturally tended to cluster in the rear: this was particularly true for physicians, that is, officers.[74] For example, out of 2,277 neuropsychiatrists who were serving with the army on VE Day, 762 or 33.4 percent were stationed overseas, whereas the remainder served in the Zone of the Interior.[75]

The total number of hospitalizations of all kinds (but excluding psychiatric cases) in World War II is said to have been 16,744,724, of whom 599,724 (3.5 percent) were wounded in battle; 1,800,000 (10.7 percent) were injured from other causes; and 14,345,000 (85.8 percent) were sick. The average number of noneffective days per battle casualty was 117.8; that for all admissions, 23.3.[76] Battle casualties, therefore, were kept in hospitals for somewhat longer periods than was the case in the German Army.

In World War I, 8 percent of all American wounded died; in World War II, only 4.5 percent died. Approximately 64 percent of the wounded returned to some kind of duty, which is considerably below the German figure and may reflect either higher standards or, what amounts to the same thing, the results of the less sophisticated physical classification system employed by the U.S. Army.

Compared with the German medical services, therefore, the American ones—even excluding the Navy—were much larger; treated far fewer cases; were, possibly owing in part to Allied air superiority which facilitated rapid evacuation, considerably more effective in saving lives; and may have been somewhat less effective in returning wounded men to duty, though this is uncertain.

It was, however, not so much in mechanical performance that the difference between the two armies lay as in the way wounded were treated AFTER recovery. "As a result of experience in North Africa," wounded personnel requiring hospitalization were dropped from the rolls following evacuation. Emerging from the hospitals, they entered the replacement system, which treated them like it did everybody else. To prevent "excessive overstrengths" from developing, men were seldom allowed to return to their own units; that was possible only if and when "that unit had an appropriate vacancy and had submitted a requisition."[77] As was so often the case in the U.S. Army, the psychological needs of the soldier were sacrificed to the administrative convenience of higher headquarters.

NOTES

1. The following verse, attributed to Sir Thomas More, might be appropriate here:

> For soldiers have been known to think
> nay colonels to reason.
> And troops who think are (nine cases out of ten)
> on the brink of treason.

2. S. A. Stouffer et al., *The American Soldier*, 4 vols. (Princeton, 1949), 2:108, 110.

3. C. C. Moskos, "Eigeninteresse, Primärgruppen und Ideologie," in *Beiträge zur Militärsoziologie*, ed. R. König (Cologne, 1968), p. 212.

4. See A. Bullock, *Hitler, a Study in Tyranny* (London, 1962 ed.), p. 53. His comrades regarded Hitler as a "white crow."

5. These remarks are based on my own experience and that of my comrades in the service of the Israeli Army's "information department."

6. See R. L. Quinett, "Hitler's Political Officers; the National Socialist Leadership Officers," Ph.D. diss., University of Oklahoma, 1979, p. 4.

7. G. Karldrack, "Offizier und Politische Bildung," Ph.D. diss., Munich University, 1970, p. 15.

8. Ibid., p. 21.

9. See R. J. O'Neill, *The German Army and the Nazi Party* (London, 1966), especially chapter 5.

10. M. Messerschmidt, *Die Wehrmacht im NS Staat* (Hamburg, 1969), pp. 240-41.

11. See O. Buchbender and H. Schuch, *Heil Beil, Flugblattpropaganda im Zweiten Weltkrieg* (Stuttgart, 1974), pp. 14-15.

12. Quoted in H. von Wedel, *Die Propagandatruppen der deutschen Wehrmacht* (Neckargemund, 1962), pp. 28-33; see also O. Buchbender, *Das tonende Erz, Deutsche Propaganda gegen die Rote Armee im Zweiten Weltkrieg* (Stuttgart, 1978), p. 87.

13. The reference to the Peace of Westphalia in 1648 was meant to justify far-reaching territorial demands on France.

14. Quoted in Messerschmidt, *Die Wehrmacht*, p. 252.

15. Quinett, "Hitler's Political Officers," pp. 43-44.

16. Ibid., pp. 45-47.

17. Ibid., p. 190.

18. D. Lerner, *Psychological Warfare against Nazi Germany; the Skywar Campaign, D Day to VE Day* (Cambridge, Mass., 1971), p. 297.

19. E. A. Shils and M. Janowitz, "Cohesion and Disintegration in the Wehrmacht in World War II," *Public Opinion Quarterly* 12 (1948): 303. According to H. L. Ansbacher, "Attitudes of German Prisoners of War: a Study of the Dynamics of National Socialist Fellowship" (*Psychological Monographs* 62, [Washington D.C., 1948]: 21), faith in Hitler stood out like "granite" in a "turgid sea of doubt" about everything else.

20. R. V. Dicks, *Licensed Mass Murder; a Socio-Psychological Study of Some SS Killers* (London, 1972), p. 64.

21. Messerschmidt, *Die Wehrmacht*, pp. 331-32.

22. See A. A. Jordan, "Troop Information and Indoctrination," in *Handbook of Military Institutions*, ed. R. Little (London, 1971), p. 356.

23. Office of the Chief Military Historian, "Study of Information and Education Activities, World War II" (Washington, D.C., 1946), pp. 27, 31.

24. For a history and criticism of the film see R. W. Steele, "'The Greatest Gangster Movie Ever Filmed': *Prelude to War*," *Prologue* 11 (1979): 221-35. From

this it appears that the film's effectiveness was inversely related to its viewers' intelligence.

25. Stouffer, *The American Soldier,* 1:473.

26. Ibid., 2:110.

27. According to Jordan, "Troop Information," there existed "an inverse correlation between rank and enthusiasm for information activities."

28. See A. Haggis, "An Appraisal of the Administration, Scope, Concept and Function of the US Army Troop Information Program," Ph.D. diss., Wayne State University, 1961.

29. Stouffer, *The American Soldier,* 1:467.

30. B. Mueller-Hillebrand, "Personnel and Administration," U.S. Army Historical Division Study P 005, (Koenigstein Ts., 1948), pp. 44-45.

31. Ibid., p. 69. For details about the way things were done, see Merkblatt 18b/31, "Frontsnähe Auffrischung eines Grenadier Regiment," January 1945, Bundesarchiv/Militärachiv (hereafter BAMA) RHD6/18b/31.

32. Replacement Board, Department of the Army, "Replacement System World Wide," (Washington, D.C., 1947), bk. 4, part 5.

33. W. C. Menninger, *Psychiatry in a Troubled World,* pp. 74-75.

34. Historical Division U.S. Forces, European Theater of Operations, "Basic Needs of the ETO Soldier" (n.p, 1946), ch. viii, pp. 80-82.

35. Since no systematic account of this question is available in either published or unpublished form, our remarks are based on archival material and somewhat fragmentary in character.

36. BAMA H20/480. This note is unsigned and undated; it appears to have been part of study intended to serve as a basis for prediction in World War II.

37. E. Zwimmer, "Psychologische Lehren des Weltkrieges," *Soldatentum* 2 (1935):181-85.

38. BAMA H20/481. This is the record of a conference of army doctors and psychiatrists held at the Military Medicinal Academy in Berlin from 30 November to 3 December 1942.

39. Der beratende Psychiater der 2. Panzerarmee, "Seelische Gesundahltung der Truppe," 18 April 1942, BAMA H20/480.

40. BAMA H20/500. These are the records of Dr. Brandt, Beratender Psychiater to Army Group South.

41. Beratender Psychiater Heeresgruppe Süd, "Vierteljährlicher Erfahrungs Bericht, March-June 1943," 10 July 1943, BAMA H200/500.

42. The remaining 57 percent were schizophrenics, depressives, epileptics, drug addicts, and cases of "nervous exhaustion" following illness. In the U.S. Army most of these would be labeled "psychoses."

43. The remaining 90.9 percent comprised men (often slightly retarded) whose symptoms were a reaction to a feeling of inadequacy in their jobs, and a "numerically strong" group of mostly elder men whose "wormly characters" required disciplinary rather than medical measures to help them adapt to the rigors of military life.

44. H20/481; see also Generalstab, ed., Heeres Dienstvorschrift 209/2, Nr. 126, "Richtlinien für die Beurteilung von Soldaten mit seelisch-nervösen Abartigkeiten (Psychopathen) und seelisch-nervösen Reaktionen sowie für

die Ubersweisung in Sonderabteilungen," (Berlin, 1 August 1942).

45. Zimmer, ed., *Wehrmedizin, Kriegserfahrungen 1939-1943* (Vienna, 1944), 3:606-14. "Faradization" apparently involved work with currents 100 milliamperes strong applied for 2 to 3 minutes.

46. Beratender Psychiater beim Heeres-Sanitätsinspekteur, "Sammelbericht No. 8," June 1944, p. 16, BAMA H20/90. This was Professor Wuth.

47. Beratender Psychiater beim Heeres-Sanitätsinspekteur, "Sammelbericht No. 4," July 1943, pp. 4, 6, BAMA H20/574.

48. Canadian Brigadier General B. Chisholm as quoted in *Newsweek*, 1 November 1943.

49. From October 1943 to the end of March 1944, a period of continuous fighting, 1,188 cases were brought to Dr. Brandt's attention; BAMA H20/500.

50. Beratender Psychiater beim Heeresgruppe D, "Vierteljährlicher Erfahrungsbericht," April-June 1944, BAMA H20/122.

51. Beratender Psychiater der 2. Panzerarmee, "Erfahrungsbericht 1.1-31.3. 1943," 9 April 1943, p. 9, BAMA H20/485.

52. Beratender Psychiater beim Heeresgruppe D, "Tagesbuch-Auszug für die Zeit v. 1.11.1942-30.1.1943," BAMA H20/502.

53. M. Janowitz and R. W. Little, *Militär und Gesellschaft* (Boppard am Rhein, 1968), p. 128.

54. Beratender Psychiater beim Wehrkreisarzt VI to Berichtsammelstelle der Militärärztliche Akademie," 1 February 1945, BAMA H20/502.

55. On Dr. Salmon see B. J. Wiest and D. A. Davis, "Psychiatric and Social Work Services," in *Handbook of Military Institutions*, ed. R. Little (London, 1971), p. 322.

56. P. Watson, *War on the Mind* (London, 1978), p. 235.

57. Stouffer, *The American Soldier*, 2: 207. Procedures used are vividly outlined in the *Saturday Evening Post*, 8 January 1944, p. 19.

58. Wiest and Davis, "Psychiatric and Social Work Services," p. 322; also R. R. Palmer, *The Procurement and Training of Ground Combat Troops* (Washington, D. C., 1948) pp. 227-78.

59. Menninger, *Psychiatry in a Troubled World* (New York, 1948), p. 345.

60. The U.S. Army, Medical Department, *Medical Statistics in World War II* (Washington, D. C., 1975), p. 43.

61. E. D. Cooke, *All but Me and Thee, Psychiatry at the Foxhole Level* (Washington, D. C., 1946), p. 11.

62. E. Ginzberg, *The Ineffective Soldier*, 3 vols. (New York, 1949-), 2:36.

63. Replacement Board, Department of the Army, "Replacement System World Wide," bk. 5, part 12.

64. Empirical evidence that group cohesion is positively related to mental health is presented in S. E. Seashore, *Group Cohesiveness in the Industrial Work Group* (Ann Arbor, 1954), p. 98.

65. British troops, who were frequently rested, lasted twice as long.

66. Menninger, *Psychiatry*, p. 305.

67. U.S. Army Medical Department, *Medical Statistics*, p. 43; Ginzberg, *Ineffective Soldier*, 1:94; R. S. Anderson, *Neuropsychiatry in World War II*, 2 vols. (Washington, D. C., 1966) 2:153-54.

68. K. Lang, *Military Institutions and the Sociology of War* (London, 1972), p. 77; Stouffer, *The American Soldier,* 2:196-200; for the evils of such an approach see also F. M. Richardson, *Fighting Spirit* (London, 1978), p. 62.

69. A. M. Rose, "The Social Psychology of Desertion from Combat," *American Sociological Review* 16 (1951):614-29.

70. F. Seidler, *Prostitution, Homosexualität, Selbstverstümmelung, Probleme der deutschen Sanitätsführung 1939-1945* (Neckargemund, 1977), p. 53.

71. Heeres-Sanitätsinspekteur, ed., *Die Wiedereinsatzfähigkeit nach Verwundungen, Erfrierungen, Erkrankungen* (Berlin, 1944), p. 21.

72. See E. Weniger, *Wehrmachtserziehung und Kriegserfahrung* (Berlin, 1938).

73. Menninger, *Psychiatry,* p. 599.

74. As of 30 September 1944, 33.7 percent of all European Theater Operations (ETO) personnel were in the Communications Zone, as against 51.9 percent of all medical personnel. Thirty-eight percent of all ETO officers were in Communications Zones, as against 64.1 percent of all medical officers. See U. S. Army, Medical Department, *Personnel in World War II* (Washington, D.C., 1963), pp. 310-11.

75. Menninger, *Psychiatry,* p. 600.

76. U. S. Army, Medical Department, *Medical Statistics,* p. 13.

77. Department of the Army, ed., *The Personnel Replacement System of the US Army* (Pamphlet No. 20-211, Washington, D. C., 1954), p. 460.

REWARDS AND PUNISHMENTS ______ 9

To ensure smooth functioning, no social system, however well organized, can do without a system of rewards and punishments. To meet its task, such a system should be powerful, pervasive, and fast in action; above all, it should be just.

PAY

German Army

Pay in the German armed forces went with rank and seniority; apart from the Air Force, no distinctions were made between the various arms and services. Thus a corporal, for example, received the same basic pay regardless of whether he was serving as a rifleman in Russia or as a waiter in the comfort of General Staff headquarters.

Starting in October 1912, when scales of pay were substantially raised, a common soldier received 9 marks, a corporal, 10.50 marks, and an NCO candidate, 15 marks per month. These, to modern eyes ridiculously low sums, were in fact much higher than those paid to any other European conscripts. The professional armies of Britain and the United States, of course, were a different matter entirely.[1]

Before and during World War II, basic pay varied from just under 200 marks per year for a raw recruit to 2,064 marks for an NCO with 14 years service, 7,700 for a major, and as much as 26,500 for a colonel general.[2] Not only were differentials large, but a colonel general's pay was approximately 25 times per capita gross national product, which stood at just over 1,000 marks in 1938.

An entirely different picture obtains, however, when the various allowances (Zulagen) are taken into account. Allowances were paid for housing, families, and service in "particularly difficult" places or conditions. For men serving in some especially expensive country or region, there were also cost-of-living allowances.

Allowances for service in difficult areas are, for obvious reasons, especially interesting. For service in North Africa, for example, the enlisted men received an allowance of 2.00 marks per day; NCOs, 3.00 marks; and officers, 4.00 marks. In other words, by joining Rommel, a private could increase his basic pay 400 percent, an NCO (assuming he had 14 years' service), 53 percent, and a major, only 19 percent.

The scales governing the pay of specialists in the Wehrmacht's employ are also significant. Fundamentally there were three different scales of pay, that is, one for Beamter, one for various specialists, and one for soldiers. Men on the two former scales could not rise above 12,600 marks basic pay a year, which was the equivalent of a colonel's salary. The only exception to this rule was formed by the highest rank of physicians (Generalstabärtze), who could earn 19,000 marks a year, that is, as much as a lieutenant general. The system as a whole, therefore, was so designed as to make soldiers receive the most pay.[3]

A final noteworthy point: personnel working for the Reich Labor Service (Reichs Arbeits Dienst, or RAD) were on a scale of pay only slightly lower than that of soldiers. Like generals, the service's leaders received pay that was far higher than that of either Beamter or specialists.

U.S. Army

In the U.S. Armed Forces, too, pay went by rank and length of service and was (except for the Marine Corps, whose men were on a separate and higher scale) equal for all arms and services. A detailed examination, however, reveals significant differences between the American and German systems.

A U. S. private in World War I received $30 basic pay a month; this was reduced to $21 in 1923, where it remained throughout the interwar years. It was not until June 1942 that pay scales were again revised, this time upwards. A private's basic pay was now $50 a month, that of a staff sergeant with 15 years service, $120; that of a major, $250; and that of a general of the army, $666.67.[4] Differences among the ranks were therefore much smaller than in the German Wehrmacht and were further cut down by the existence of a whole series of allowances to which enlisted men but not officers were entitled.[5] The highest pay, that of a general of the army, exceeded the per capita gross national product ($500 in 1939) by a factor of sixteen to one.

Like their German counterparts, American soldiers could receive family, rental, and subsistence allowances. There also existed an allowance for foreign service, constituting 20 percent of basic pay in the case of enlisted men and NCOs and 10 percent in the case of officers. American troops in general, but the rank and file above all, were thus given a far smaller inducement for service outside the homeland than were their German counterparts.

Unlike the Wehrmacht, the U. S. Army did not have a separate scale of pay for specialists; instead, these were normally given a commission and paid in accordance with their rank. The strict separation between officers and experts, crucial to the German system, was unknown.

LEAVE

German Army

In principle all German soldiers, regardless of rank or arm, were entitled to the same amount of leave. Its distribution was the responsibility of company commanders in whose hands it could form, when well administered, a powerful weapon for maintaining discipline and morale. The company commander's authority was not unlimited, however: to maintain secrecy on the eve of some major operational movement, or else in times of crisis, higher headquarters could and did block all leave.

Soldiers serving in the Field or Replacement Armies were entitled to fourteen days' ordinary leave a year, exclusive of two days' travel. Special periods of leave lasting from ten to twenty days could be granted in case of important family events, special hardship (including a bombing attack on a soldier's house), and following a stay in the hospital. Married men, especially those with problems at home, were normally given priority over unmarried, usually younger, personnel. The regulations stated that the number of troops on leave from the Field Army at any one time was not to exceed 10 percent of overall actual strength.[6]

The way in which these regulations were implemented is, by the nature of things, difficult if not impossible to investigate. A spot-check in the papers of one army, however—Model's Ninth—brought to light some interesting information. The Army seems to have sent approximately 10 percent of its personnel on leave every month. Soldiers, during their first year at the front, could look forward to one period of leave in twelve months; during the second year, to one in nine months; and during the third, to one in six. Front-line troops—those serving forward of regimental headquarters—were given priority over the rest. For the army as a whole, the distribution of leave went on as usual even during periods of heavy fighting, though exceptions might be made in the case of individual divisions holding some particularly important section of the front.[7] Here, as in regard to the question of rotation, the large number of divisions thus had a favorable effect.

Though the overall amount of leave granted was sparing indeed (in August 1942, the Ninth Army had 123,760 men who had not been home for a year or more; this was one-third of its strength), its distribution among the ranks seems to have been equitable.[8] Thus, in May 1942 out of 179,997 men who had not been home for at least a year, 32,064 or 17.8 percent were NCOs and 5,489 or 3 percent officers.[9] These figures correspond very well with those of these ranks throughout the army as a whole.

Side by side with these general arrangements, Ninth Army Headquarters systematically used leave as a reward for troops—both officers and enlisted men, but mainly for the latter—who had distinguished themselves in some particularly dangerous job such as sniping, antitank warfare, and the like. Printed accounts of the men's deeds, together with the announcement that they were going on immediate leave, were distributed throughout the Army after being signed by Model in person.[10]

U.S. Army

According to a regulation of 1876 that remained in force for seventy years, officers in the U.S. Army were entitled to leave; enlisted men received furlough. The former amounted to thirty days a year and could be accumulated and redeemed for cash; the latter was unspecified in duration, went unrecorded, and could not therefore be either accrued or redeemed. All this did not perhaps matter much in times of peace, but it did mean that officers—not enlisted men—were able to accumulate considerable sums of money during the war when much leave, by the nature of things, went unused.

In addition to these general arrangements, special provisions existed for sending home soldiers in case of an emergency. Distances during the war were so large, however, and bureaucratic arrangements so cumbersome, that such leave was normally approved only six months following request.[11]

To gain an impression of how things actually worked, I carried out another spot-check in the papers of the European theater of war, which was the largest single container of manpower by far. It turned out that Eisenhower's troops during their stay in England were granted seven days' leave every three months or so, which meant that some 7 percent of all men were absent from duty at any one time.[12] There is no direct evidence of leave being used as a tool for leadership, the reason apparently being that divisional commanders were not authorized to grant it to the recipients of decorations and so forth.[13]

ETO troops in France did not, it seems, receive any leave during the summer and autumn of 1944. Once the front had been stabilized along the German border, however, forty-eight-hour passes began to be issued for large cities such as Paris and Brussels. Typical groups enjoying this privilege consisted of, for example, 12,307 men in January 1945, of whom 2,097 or 17 percent—almost twice their proportion in the army—were officers.[14] In early March 1945 one group of 560 (!) officers and 56 enlisted men was enjoying a vacation in the Riviera.[15] The problem was sufficiently serious to require the personal intervention of General Marshall in a letter to General Eisenhower.[16]

DECORATIONS

In any army, but in large and impersonal ones above all, the importance of decorations cannot be overestimated; as Napoleon said, it is with colored ribbons that men are led.

German Army

In the German Army during World War I, the entire problem of decorations had been grossly mismanaged. The number of different medals that could be awarded was too small, so that repeated deeds and services could not be properly rewarded. For the same reason, the distinction between bravery and other front and rear services could not be maintained; decorations were much easier to obtain in the second half of the war than in the first, leading to widespread dissatisfaction. Confusion was created by the many different decorations awarded by the various states and the privileges often pertaining thereto. Separate awards existed for officers and enlisted men, so that the latter could not attain the highest decoration of all, the Pour le Merite.[17]

Though these shortcomings were recognized, little seems to have been done to correct them during the interwar years. When World War II broke out, Germany's most important decoration—the Iron Cross, founded during the Napoleonic Wars—was "revived" as it had been in every previous conflict. Its two classes could be awarded only to members of the armed forces, and only for wartime service.

Soon after the Polish campaign, the need was felt to institute additional decorations for men who already possessed both classes of the Iron Cross and who continued to perform deeds of exceptional valor. Between 1940 and 1944 there accordingly came into being the five classes of the Knight's Cross to the Iron Cross, that is, the Knight's Cross, the Oak Leaves, the Swords, the Diamonds, and the Knight's Cross of the Iron Cross with Golden Oak Leaves, Swords, and Diamonds. The last and highest of these was, typically, reserved to individual warriors (Einzelkämpfer) and the number of recipients limited to twelve. In any event, only one was ever awarded.[18]

These decorations were cumulative; that is, a man could be recommended for each grade only if he already possessed all the previous ones.

This meant that equal deeds could not always be equally rewarded but at the same time created a strong incentive for repeated deeds of bravery. While the number of decorations awarded each year grew steadily from 1941 on, this reflected not so much the relaxation of requirements as the intensity of the fighting as measured in the number of casualties. Requirements were, if anything, tightened up—for example, the number of aircraft a pilot had to shoot down, increased.

Though all ranks could be recommended for all classes of the Iron Cross, the prerequisites for an award were not the same for all. To be decorated with one of the higher classes (Knight's Cross and up) an enlisted man or NCO either had to perform some outstanding deed of valor (often in antitank defense) or else take some independent decision.[19] For commanding officers, several instances of independent action constituted an unconditional prerequisite; mere bravery, however exceptional, was not enough. Asked to recommend one Lieutenant Colonel Mokros for the Oak Leaves of the Knight's Cross, Field Marshall Schoerner wrote that for a regimental commander to personally lead his men in a successful counterattack with machine gun and hand-grenades constituted "a self evident duty."[20]

To become the recipient of one of these higher decorations, a regimental commander, for example, had to be recommended by his direct superior. Provided the recommendation received the endorsement of the corps and army commanders, the completed forms, including a brief autobiographical sketch (often used by the candidates to emphasize their service in the Hitler Jugend and so forth) and a photograph, was submitted for Hitler to decide. The entire procedure normally lasted anywhere between three and five weeks, though in some cases only a fortnight or even less was required. Once a recommendation was approved the newspapers and broadcasting services were informed that, for example, Major X had been the nth soldier of the German Wehrmacht to be awarded the Oak Leaves.

The decorations awarded from September 1939 to May 1945 are shown in table 9.1.

TABLE 9.1
Distribution of Iron Crosses in the German Army

DECORATION	DISTRIBUTION
Iron Cross, 2d Class	2,300,000
Iron Cross, 1st Class	300,000
Knight's Cross	5,070
Oak Leaves	569
Swords	87
Diamonds	13
Golden Oak Leaves, Swords, and Diamonds	1

SOURCE: R. Absalon, *Wehrgesetz und Wehrdienst, 1939-1945* (Boppard am Rhein, 1960).

The holders of the five highest awards formed a tiny elite, constituting no more than 0.033 percent of all those who passed through the Wehrmacht in five-and-a-half years of war, and approximately 0.3 percent of those killed in action. To preserve this exclusiveness, a special series of decorations—the German Cross in Silver and Gold—was instituted in September 1941 for personnel already in possession of the Iron Cross First Class, whose repeated deeds of valor or sterling service (not accompanied by independent action) did not entitle them to the Knight's Cross. The German Cross, however, was neither part of the Order of the Iron Cross nor a prerequisite for the award of its higher classes; the two orders were kept strictly apart.

To gain an impression of how things worked out in practice, I carried out a random spot-check among recommendations and awards in various units at various times during the war. One is immediately struck by the large number of cases in which the higher decorations (upwards of the Iron Cross First Class) were awarded for independent action by men and officers of all ranks; these constituted approximately 40 percent of the total.[21] The system continued to function right down to the end of the war, and Hitler, himself, a mere twenty-four hours before he put an end to his life, still took the trouble to reject a recommendation.[22] More remarkably still, the system went on working even after VE Day, when there was no longer either a war, a Fuehrer or a Reich.

U.S. Army

In World War I, according to General Marshall, the U.S. Army had been extremely niggardly in the distribution of decorations. Not only had few awards been made, but time intervals were such that most recipients only got their medals after hostilities were over. This was a state of things that Marshall was determined to correct, even in the face of accusations that the medals would thereby be cheapened.[23]

As it operated in World War II, the American system of awards and decorations differed considerably from its German equivalent. Having been established at different times and with differing prerequisites, the various medals were not interconnected and not cumulative. Some could be awarded to soldiers alone, but others went to civilians also. Not a single American decoration included the demand for independent action among the provisions for its award; on the other hand, far greater importance was attached to meritorious service in noncombat duties. Whereas in Germany it was more difficult for officers than for other ranks to earn the higher decorations, this was not the case in the U.S. Army.[24]

Good intentions notwithstanding, Marshall did not succeed in greatly cutting down the interval between a man's deed and his being awarded a medal; the average waiting time for the higher classes was probably between five and six months, though it must have been less than that for the lower ones.[25]

The highest decoration, the Medal of Honor, was awarded for conspicuous gallantry in action above and beyond the call of duty; 289 of these decorations were distributed during and after the war. The next highest award, the Distinguished Service Cross, likewise involved "extraordinary heroism in connection with military operations against an armed enemy," and 4,434 of these were distributed. The third highest medal was the Distinguished Service Medal, which went for exceptionally meritorious service in positions of great responsibility; the number of recipients in 1940-45 was 1,439.[26]

Below these, the Silver Star (73,651 awarded) went for gallantry in action not warranting one of the two highest decorations, and the Legion of Merit was awarded for exceptionally meritorious conduct in the performance of extraordinary service (20,273 awarded). The five highest classes together were thus awarded 100,086 times, constituting a number equal to some 33 percent of the number of men killed in action. This exceeds the German equivalent figure by a factor of 100 to 1.

Other medals included the USAF's air medal, awarded more or less indiscriminately to anyone who flew combat missions; its equivalent for the land forces, the Bronze Star, was not awarded nearly as freely, and this gave rise to widespread envy. Down at the bottom of the scale was the Purple Heart, awarded freely by the hundreds of thousands for battle and, frequently, nonbattle injuries.

The heavy emphasis placed by the U.S. Army on meritorious service in responsible positions as opposed to actual leadership in combat tended to favor officers, who received close to one-half of all medals awarded.[27] A breakdown of the recipients of the five highest decorations according to rank presents the picture shown in table 9.2.

TABLE 9.2
Recipients of American Decorations, by Rank

TYPE OF DECORATION	NUMBER AWARDED	TO OFFICERS	PERCENT TO OFFICERS
Medal of Honor	289	94	32.5
Distinguished Service Cross	4,434	2,071	46.7
Silver Star	73,651	23,877	32.4
Total Combat	78,374	26,042	33.2
Distinguished Service Medal	1,439	1,438	99.9
Legion of Merit	20,273	17,159	84.6
Total Noncombat	21,712	18,597	85.6
Total	100,086	44,639	44.6

SOURCE: War Department, ed., *Decorations and Awards* (Washington, D. C., 1947).

Thus, the greater the demand for bravery in the requirements for any one medal, the smaller the percentage of officers who received it.

MILITARY JUSTICE

Command, it has been said, consists of a mixture of example and persuasion; where these two fail, coercion may have to be used. Without a proper system of justice, capable of quickly and effectively enforcing the law, no social organization, let alone an army, can function.

German Army

During World War I, possibly as a result of favorable experiences during the Wars of Unification, the German Army gave the lie to its reputation for "militarism" and displayed an extraordinary reluctance to pass capital sentences and carry them out.[28] This is shown by the figures in table 9.3.

TABLE 9.3
Death Sentences in the German Army in World War I

TYPE OF OFFENSE FOR WHICH DEATH SENTENCE WAS PASSED	CARRIED OUT	NOT CARRIED OUT	TOTAL
Refusal to obey orders in face of enemy	4	21	25
Treason	10	17	27
Desertion in face of enemy	18	31	49
Rebellion and calling for rebellion	2	7	9
Attack on superiors in the field	3	5	8
Murder	11	21	32
Total	48	102	150

SOURCE: Volkmann, *Soziale Heeresmisstände als Mitursache des deutschen Zusammenbruchs* (Berlin, 1929) p. 63.

Thus, 78.6 percent of all death sentences passed and 77 percent of those carried out were for military rather than for civilian offenses. The surprisingly low figures are open to conflicting interpretations: either discipline in the Imperial Army was so good that no drastic disciplinary measures were called for, or else the military justice system—possibly also with political considerations in mind—was reluctant both to impose the death sentence and to carry it out.[29] Among those who took the latter view was Adolf Hitler.

In 1935 the code of military law was altered. A new and typically Nazi capital offense, Zersetzung der Wehrkraft (literally: undermining fighting power) was added to the existing ones of treason, mutiny and incitement thereto, desertion, attack on a superior in the field, and plunder. Among civilian offenses, murder, unnatural sex, and robbery were also punishable by death.

Throughout World War II desertion and Zersetzung der Wehrkraft (which included self-mutilation) were the principal offenses for which capital sentences were passed, as shown by the figures in table 9.4.

TABLE 9.4
Offenses Leading to Death Sentences in the Germany Army, World War II

	OCTOBER TO DECEMBER 1943	APRIL TO JUNE 1944
Total Number of Death Sentences	1,455	1,906
For Zersetzung[1]	309	343
For desertion	728	1,033
For all other offenses	418	530

SOURCE: BAMA file H20/481.
[1]undermining fighting power.

On the strength of this and other evidence, Zersetzung and desertion together made up about 70 percent of all capital sentences passed, followed at a great distance by all the rest.[30] Table 9.5, though inaccurate and incomplete, will give some idea of the absolute figures involved.[31]

TABLE 9.5
Death Sentences and Executions in the German Army, World War II

YEAR	SENTENCED TO DEATH FOR DESERTION	NO. EXECUTED FOR ALL OFFENSES
1940	312	559
1941	470*	425
1942	1,551	1,560(?)
1943	1,364*	2,880
1944 (Jan.-Sept.)	1,605*	3,829
1945 (Jan.-April)	n.d.	2,400*
Total	5,302	11,753

SOURCE: OKH ed., "Krieg-Kriminalitätstatistik für die Wehrmacht," 1 January 1940-31 March 1942, BAMA W-05-165 and 166; F. W. Seidler, "Die Fahnenflucht in der deutschen Wehrmacht während des Zweiten Weltkrieg," *Militärgeschichtliche Mitteilungen* 22 (1977): 27, 36.
* My own guesstimate

Though these figures lay no claim to accuracy, they are probably a good indication of the order of magnitude involved, and show how much more draconian the military justice system had become since World War I.[32]

That these measures had some effect in preserving the Wehrmacht's cohesion in face of the very heavy odds it confronted is shown by the following estimate of the overall number of deserters and AWOLs.[33] This rose from 9,778 in 1941 to 16,550 in 1942, to 66,861 in 1943, and to 202,422 in 1944. The overall ratio per thousand strength works out at about 7.9 per year, with the highest figure—that for 1944—standing at 21.5.

From January 1940 to June 1941, 2,251 officers, 17,107 NCOs, and 87,188 enlisted men—a total of 106,546—stood trial. Thus officers, with 2.1 percent of all offenses, were somewhat underrepresented in relation to their numbers, whereas NCOs with 16 percent were present in exact proportion to their share in the army as a whole. The overall number convicted was 95,230, or 89.4 percent of those accused. The system appears to have been biased insofar as officers stood a 22.6 percent chance of being acquitted, and NCOs a 15.5 percent chance, but enlisted men only a 9.3 percent chance.

Nevertheless, in other ways the system was quite as capable of protecting subordinates against their superiors as it was of enforcing the latter's authority. Punishments for both kinds of offenses were similar: up to two years in jail for insulting a superior (article 91 of the Code of Military Justice), the same for insulting a subordinate (article 121). Assaulting a superior (article 97) carried a sentence of not less than three years in prison, but so did mishandling a subordinate (article 122). Article 122a, moreover, defined mishandling as "deliberately or unnecessarily making life difficult for a subordinate, or tormenting him in other ways, or tolerating such actions on the part of other soldiers." That these were not empty words is shown by figures in table 9.6.

For the period as a whole, the differential is 26.2 percent.

TABLE 9.6
Cases of Attacks on Superiors versus Mishandling of Subordinates in the German Army

PERIOD	JAN.-JUNE 1940	JUNE-DEC. 1940	JAN.-JUNE 1941	JUNE-DEC. 1941	JAN.-MAR. 1942
Cases of attacks on superiors	746	738	1,246	920	515
Cases of mishandling subordinates	434	603	893	939	431
Differential	71.8%	22.3%	39.5%	-2.1%	19.4%

SOURCE: BAMA W-05-165 and W-05-166.

U.S. Army

Whereas the American code of military justice, like that of any other army, contained numerous articles designed to enforce discipline (Article of War [AW] 63, "disrespect towards superior officer"; AW 64, "assaulting or willfully disobeying superior officer"; AW 65, "insubordinate conduct towards NCOs," and others), it differed from the German one in that it contained no explicit provisions for the protection of the troops against their superiors. Instead, "cruelty to soldiers" was mentioned in AW 95, which dealt with "conduct unbecoming an officer and a gentleman" and put this offense on a par with such things as drunkenness, giving a bad check, and the like. A proper attitude toward one's subordinates, in other words, was made a question of the officer's honor.

As compared with the German Army, the enforcement of the law in the American one was decidedly lax; of close to four million men who passed through ETO (the only theater on which detailed statistics are available) between 1942 and 1945, only 22,214, or around 0.5 percent, ever stood trial before a court of military justice. Of these 1,737, or 7.8 percent were officers who were thus represented in accordance with their numbers. On the other hand, the system resembled the German one in that officers, once brought before a courtmartial, were twice as likely to be acquitted as were enlisted men.[34]

Though desertion in the U.S. Army, as in the German one, was punishable by death (AW 58), a study of the capital sentences passed in both armies brings out some very deep differences in their respective philosophies. The figures in table 9.7 (ETO only) tell their own story.

Thus, not only did capital sentences for civilian offenses outnumber military ones, but the chances of a man sentenced to death for a civilian offense of actually being executed were 54 (!) times as large as those of a man sentenced for a military one. Possibly as a result, desertion rates reached 45.2 per thousand in 1944 and 63 per thousand in 1945, exceeding the German figure several times over.[35] In the end, only 2,854 of hundreds of thousands who deserted or went AWOL were ever tried; of these a single one was executed, and his relatives are currently suing the government for damages.[36]

SOLDIERS' COMPLAINTS

Launching a complaint is a risky business in any army. The authority to whom the complaint is addressed is far away; whereas the one against whom it is directed is likely to be near at hand and, what is more, capable of giving a man hell. Unless the plaintiff can be reasonably sure about the ability and willingness of an authority to deal with his complaint, therefore, he is likely to keep his grievance to himself.

TABLE 9.7
Death Sentences and Executions in ETO, 1942-1945

OFFENSE	DEATH SENTENCES		AFTER REVIEW		CARRIED OUT	
	No.	As % of Total	No.	As % of Total	No.	As % of Total
Total	441	100.00	108	24.3	70	15.8
Murder	82	18.7			28	
Murder and rape	18	4.1			12	
Murder and desertion	2	0.4			—	
Rape	151	34.1			29	
Total Civilian	253	57.5			69	27.4
Desertion	73	16.8			—	
Desertion to avoid hazardous duty	57	12.9			1	0.5
Misbehavior in front of the enemy	24	5.7			—	
Sentinel offenses	3	0.7			—	
Assault on officer	24	5.4			—	
Mutiny	7	1.6			—	
Total military	188	42.5			1	0.5

SOURCE: Historical Brigade, Office of the Judge Advocate General with the U. S. Forces, ETO, "Statistical Survey—General Courts Martial in the European Theater of Operations," MS 8-3.5 AA, vol. 1, NA file 204-58 (87).

German Army

A unitary procedure for soldiers' complaints was instituted by the German Army in 1895 and modified in 1921 and 1936.[37] Soldiers, normally with the aid of an older comrade, could complain orally or in writing during the period commencing one day after the supposed injury and ending seven days (for officers, three days) thereafter. Complaints by privates and NCOs were made to their immediate superiors or, in case that the immediate superior was himself the object of the complaint, to the next highest commander who had the decision in his hands. In case a negative reply was given, the complaint could be repeated to the next highest commander and so, in theory at any rate, on to the highest instances (first the Kaiser, then the president of the Republic, and later, Adolf Hitler). Unfounded complaints were not, again in theory, supposed to lead to penalties provided the plaintiff had acted with good intentions and in accordance with the regulations.

The system, typical of the decentralized way in which the German Army did things, thus placed remarkable confidence in the willingness of commanding officers to support plaintiffs even against their own subcommanders; on the other hand, once a complaint was recognized as just, the recipient was in a position to deal with it promptly and effectively.

U.S. Army

In the matter of soldiers' complaints, as in so much else, the U.S. Army relied on centralization in order to try and achieve fairness. Grievances, accordingly, had to be addressed to the inspector general of each arm and service. However, the latter's powers were purely advisory: according to AR 20-30 of 1937, the inspector general's department "could reach conclusions from developed facts and make recommendations believed to be supported thereby, but it has no power to reach findings or to impose punishment." Whether, under such a system, a plaintiff could expect swift and reliable justice may well be questioned.

NOTES

1. In Austria-Hungary conscripts were paid 4.05 marks per month, in France, 2.40 marks; and in Russia, 1.20 marks. A British private got 30 marks; and an American one, 63 marks per month. Figures from Militärgeschichtliches Forschungsamt, ed. (hereafter MGFA, ed.), *Handbuch zur deutschen Militärgeschichte,* 7 vols. (Frankfurt am Main, 1965-), 5:102.

2. R. Absalon, *Wehrgesetz und Wehrdienst 1939-1945* (Boppard am Rhein, 1960), p. 302.

3. M. Schreiber, *Heereseverwaltungs-Taschenbuch 1941/42* (Grimmen, 1941), p. 61.

4. War Department, ed., *Technical Manual TM 14-509, Army Pay Tables* (Washington, D.C., 1945).

5. *Report of the Secretary of War's Board on Officer-Enlisted Men Relationships* (The Doolittle Report) (Washington, D.C., 1946), pp. 12-13.

6. B. Mueller-Hillebrand, "Personnel and Administration," U.S. Army Historical Division Study P 005 (Koenigstein Ts., 1948), pp. 73-76.

7. AOK9/IIa/b, "Tätigkeitsbericht 18.8.-31.12.1943," Bundesarchiv/Militärarchiv (hereafter BAMA) 52535/18.

8. AOK9/IIa/b, "Beilage zum Kriegstagebuch, 1.7-30.9.1942," ibid.

9. AOK9/IIa/b, "Beilage zum Kriegstagebuch, 1.4-30.6.1942," Model order of 6 May 1942, ibid., 29234/2.

10. See, for example, Model order of 6 November 1942, ibid., 29234/11; and another of 17 January 1943 in ibid., 32878/26.

11. Historical Division, U.S. Forces, European Theater of Operations (hereafter ETO), "Basic Needs of the ETO Soldier" (n.p., 1946), ch. viii, p. 45.

12. Ibid., p. 5.

13. General Arnold's Testimony, Replacement Board, Department of the Army, "Replacement System World Wide," bk. 5, part 32.

14. Historical Division, U.S. Forces, "Basic Needs of the ETO Soldier," ch. viii, p. 38. Here several more examples of this kind are mentioned.

15. Ibid., p. 24.

16. Ibid., p. 22.

17. E. Weniger, *Wehrmachtserziehung und Kriegserfahrung* (Berlin, 1938), pp. 91-93; see also Blecher, "Gedanken zur Erneuerung des Eisernen Kreuzes vor 25 Jahren," *Soldatentum* 6 (1939):245.

18. See Absalon, *Wehrgesetz und Wehrdienst,* p. 258.

19. Since enlisted men who received this decoration could expect to be taken on as officer candidates on the basis of Bewahrung vor den Feind (sterling service in front of the enemy), almost all of their higher classes went to the officers.

20. Schoerner note of 10 March 1945, BAMA Rh7 v 299.

21. See BAMA 29234/9.

22. BAMA Rh7 v 298.

23. Marshall to King, National Archives (hereafter NA) file No. 204-58-90 (22-819).

24. That this be changed was one of the main recommendations of the 1946 Doolittle Report on officer-enlisted men relationships.

25. Figures based on a survey of ETO files (Box 322/Admin. File ETO 7/38 and 38/183 at the NA.

26. All figures from War Department, ed., *Decorations and Awards* (Washington, D. C., 1947), p. 10.

27. 804,533 out of 1,800,739, or 44.6 percent. Exclusive of Purple Heart.

28. E. Schwinge, *Die Entwicklung der Manneszucht in der deutschen, britischen und französischen Wehrmacht seit 1914* (Berlin, 1941), p. 48.

29. From 4 August 1914 to 31 March 1920 British courtmartials passed 3,080 death sentences of which 346 were carried out. See War Office, ed., *Statistics of the Military Effort of the British Empire during the Great War* (London, 1922), p. 648.

30. Oberkommando des Heer, ed., "Krieg-Kriminalitätstatistik für die Wehrmacht," 1 January 1940-31 March 1942, BAMA W-05-165 and 166.

31. For another estimate based on different sources but arriving at substantially similar figures, see O. Hennicke, "Auszüge aus der Wehrmachtkriminalstatistik," *Zeitschrift für Militärgeschichte* 5 (1966):444, table 4.

32. Under Nazi pressure, the penalties for the various kinds of desertion were made more draconian still as the war went on. The military judges countered this, however, by convicting a growing proportion of offenders for going AWOL rather than for desertion.

33. F. W. Seidler, "Die Fahnenflucht in der deutschen Wehrmacht während des Zweiten Weltkrieg," *Militärgeschichtliche Mitteilungen* 22 (1977):30.

34. Historical Brigade, Office of the Judge Advocate General with the U.S. Forces, ETO, "Statistical Survey—General Courts Martial in the European Theater of Operations," Ms. 8-3.5-AA, vol. 1, NA file 204-58 (87).

35 R. A. Gabriel and P. L. Savage, *Crisis in Command; Mismanagement in the Army* (New York, 1978), p. 180, table 1. Absolute figures on desertion are unavailable.

36. *International Herald Tribune,* 8-9 September 1979, p. 5. According to his biographer, this man had hoped to escape combat by trading it for a prison sentence

which would be commuted after the war; thousands of others did so successfully, but in his particular case the arithmetic failed to work. See W. B. Huie, *The Execution of Private Slovik* (New York, 1954), p. 107.

37. H. Frahm, *Wehrbeschwerdeordnung* (Berlin, 1957), p. 13.

The Non-Commissioned Officers 10

GERMAN ARMY

Selection and Training

In the old Imperial Army, there existed a clear social dividing line between officers and enlisted men, but the same was not true in regard to NCOs. The latter were mostly drawn from small peasant and lower-middle-class stock. Few possessed any education beyond elementary school.[1]

The selection of future NCOs took place after a year's service. The same company and battery officers who, acting in accordance with guidelines issued by the General Staff, carried out the selection, were later responsible for accepting or rejecting a man for service in their unit. A leftover from feudal times, this extremely decentralized system helped forge strong links between NCOs and their units and was retained right down to 1945.

The training of NCO candidates took place in a special battalion of the regiment; not until 1936 was a Central Army School for NCOs established.[2] Training lasted two years and was in the hands of regimental officers and senior NCOs. Contacts with the latter, both on and off duty, were extremely close, with the result that there grew up a kind of NCO esprit de corps. The frequent meetings held between NCOs of various units in the regiment, as well as their comparatively high status in society, combined to create that class of tough professionals on which the structure of any army must ultimately rest.

During the Weimar period, the long period of service imposed by the Allies (12 years) made it possible to make the training of NCOs even more thorough than before. Three-and-a-half years' training were followed by another seven to eight months' regimental duty, during which a strong emphasis was placed on leadership, practical knowledge of weapons, and sport. Acting on the principle that every man should be able to perform the duties pertaining to a post two grades above his own, the Reichswehr built up an NCO corps which, during the early thirties, was able without difficulty both to train the rapidly expanding army and to supply leaders to the Nazi party's armed formations.

Though the duration of training was cut back to two years in 1933, the exceptionally thorough work done by the Reichswehr enabled the demand for NCOs to be met without a significant drop in quality down to the outbreak of World War II. Indeed, the reverse may well have been true; whereas the intelligent, thinking NCO had been an exception in 1914, he became the rule twenty-five years later.[3]

An aspect of the NCO selection system that deserves special mention is the way in which the regulations, which were identical for all arms in peacetime, discriminated in favor of those who had seen front-line service once war broke out. Thus, promotion to NCO in the Field Army could take place after six months' service and might take place, in especially deserving cases, even when no suitable T/O vacancy was available. In the Replacement Army, by contrast, a soldier could only be promoted to NCO after a year's service (including two months at the front) and then only if a suitable slot was available for him.[4]

Conditions of Service

In the German Army until 1939 the NCO career (Laufbahn) was separate from and parallel to that of the officer. Men signing on as professional NCOs did not therefore aspire to become officers, nor was such promotion possible in any but the rarest of cases. The reason for this, it appears, was not so much perceived lack of ability as the fact that the NCOs, unlike their commissioned superiors, were not regarded as perfectly reliable politically in the pre-Nazi years.[5]

During World War I, this system gave rise to widespread dissatisfaction and criticism. At the front NCOs, often tried and proved men, saw themselves put under the command of the so-called Einjährige, middle-class youths who, after receiving a high school diploma, served for a year, received four to six weeks' officer training, and were then commissioned as second lieutenants. Consequently milksops of nineteen or twenty frequently found themselves in command of men far more senior and experienced than themselves.[6] Besides causing much justified bitterness, the system also adversely affected the Army's performance in the field.[7]

In 1919, accordingly, the institution of the Einjährige was abolished. Acting through Minister of Defense Gustav Noske, and First Quartermaster General Groener, the Social Democratic government proceeded to select 1,000 deserving NCOs and promoted them to commissioned rank.[8] Subsequently the hurdle separating noncommissioned from commissioned rank, though still high, was at any rate no longer insuperable. It broke down further during World War II, when tens of thousands of NCOs received their commissions, in some exceptional cases even without going through officer school first. By 1945 the land-bound components of the armed forces alone included eleven officers of general rank who had started their careers as NCOs; significantly, three of these—including the notorious Sepp Dietrich, onetime commander of Hitler's bodyguards and the man responsible for the Malmedy massacre—were serving in the ranks of the Waffen SS.[9]

In addition, opportunites for NCOs to earn promotions within their own Laufbahn were extended during the Weimar years. After two years' training, an NCO candidate could become a Gefreiter; another four years, and most would be promoted to Feldwebel, though exceptionally qualified men could skip this rank. Promotion to Oberfeldwebel depended on taking a special examination and could take place after seven (in exceptional cases, five) years from promotion to Gefreiter. In 1935 another rank, that of Hauptfeldwebel, was added, while those who elected to stay on beyond the normal period of service for NCOs (12 years) could be promoted to Stabsfeldwebel.

Such men, however, were the exception. The army's high social standing and its comparatively small size made it fairly easy to attract a sufficient number of suitable candidates during the Imperial and Weimar periods. Still, in 1936 it became necessary to institute side by side with the normal twelve-year Laufbahn a truncated one lasting five years only. Men approaching the end of their two years' conscript service were thus given the opportunity of signing on for another three years.

Upon signing on for an extension of service, future NCOs from 1900 on received the sum of 100 marks as well as additional pay during their period of training. To help guarantee the political reliability of the corps, a retirement grant of 1,000 (later raised to 1,500) marks had been introduced in 1890. Men thus discharged could look forward to careers in officialdom to which they had a priority claim and where their qualities of conscientiousness and utter reliability were much sought after. Some of these men subsequently rose to the medium ranks of the hierarchy.[10] Others, aided by generous loans and grants instituted by a Nazi government that regarded NCOs among the most valuable of all social types, bought farms and settled on the land.

Position and Performance

In the old Imperial Army, the NCOs formed the lowest rung of the military hierarchy. This in itself sufficed to give them a certain esteem as representatives of the state's power and numbers of its cherished instrument of war.

Partly for this reason, but partly also because of the substantial rewards—both material and nonmaterial—which NCOs enjoyed over and above those of enlisted men, there never arose a shortage of suitable candidates.[11] Indeed, the opposite was the case: even in 1900 there had been 1,200 NCOs in excess of establishment in the Prussian Army alone, and the number of applicants continued growing thereafter.[12] To cope with the demand, the number of NCO T/O positions in the Army had to be increased by 719 in 1904.[13]

During the Weimer period, securing NCOs for the 100,000-man army constituted hardly any problem. The situation began changing during the years of hectic expansion during the years preceding World War II, however, and this led to the institution of the five-year Laufbahn side by side with the traditional twelve-year one. At the outbreak of World War II in 1939, nevertheless, the Wehrmacht possessed only 75 percent as many NCOs as had the Imperial Army in 1914, though the two forces were of approximately equal size.[14] During the war itself only one of six of all NCOs was a professional; as late as 1943, however, over one-half of all NCOs captured by the Western Allies stemmed from the prewar Army. They were tough, highly trained men who did their duty out of a deeply felt commitment to the soldierly profession.[15]

The position of NCOs differed from that of their comrades in most other Continental Armies. They did not possess disciplinary powers and worked under the close supervision of their officers rather than in the latter's stead. Possibly for the same reason, it was the NCOs who, when in command of troops, tended to make the most frequent use of punishments.[16]

In World War I, 110,618 NCOs (both active and reserve) were killed whereas another 190,205 went missing, presumed dead, and another 477,734 NCOs were wounded.[17] Prussian, Bavarian, and Saxonian NCOs together earned 2,544 medals of the kind that served as the NCOs' equivalent of the officers' Pour le Merite.[18]

How many NCOs were killed in World War II is unknown. It is known, however, that out of a total of 5,740 Knight's Crosses (of all grades) awarded during the war approximately 1,300 went to NCOs.

U.S. ARMY

In the U.S. Army, NCOs were enlisted men who had been promoted on the basis of ability or seniority. Since they were denied an officer's privileges and were in any case the scions of a different social environment, they tended to identify with the enlisted men. An NCO esprit de corps, "the backbone of an army" as the saying goes, is said not to have existed.[19]

Given the low pay and scant esteem in which it was held, the interwar Army had some difficulty in attracting high quality manpower to serve as NCOs. The result was that during the great influx of much better educated men in 1940 and 1941, NCOs tended to be the least educated, least capable men in the unit.[20] As selectees won their stripes later on, this problem largely solved itself.

Promotion to NCO went mainly by seniority. Schools were provided—and this is again typical of the entire U. S. Army approach to things—for men requiring technical skills, such as radio operators or motor technicians, but not for those in leadership positions such as, for example, rifle platoon sergeants, first sergeants, or tank commanders. The latter were supposed to develop their leadership abilities simply by service with the troops and to require no special training.[21] Suggestions for altering this system were voiced from time to time, but all were shot down by Army Ground Forces Command with its persistent fight for a "simple" Army.[22]

The number of men who became NCOs is astonishing. During World War II only one in every six German soldiers had worn the stripe, but in the U.S. Army at the time of VE Day approximately 50 percent of all enlisted men were NCOs.[23] In particular, the influx of NCOs from the Zone of the Interior via the replacement system had an unfortunate effect on the morale of old timers who saw their own prospects for promotion blocked by new arrivals. On the other hand, for the latter to enter the line as riflemen, often under the command of men with fewer stripes, was equally ruinous to morale. The net result, according to the official history, was that NCOs—theoretically the army's toughest and best trained men—were one type of replacement that was not welcomed by the divisions.[24]

NOTES

1. Based on Militärgeschichtliches Forschungsamt, ed. (hereafter MGFA, ed.), *Handbuch zur deutschen Militärgeschichte,* 7 vols. (Frankfurt am Main, 1965–), 5:91-92, 7:375-76.

2. In July 1944 the number of NCO schools had risen to twenty-one. The training personnel, mostly wounded officers and NCOs who had served with great distinction, numbered 5,250. The number of trainees in all schools was 13,400. See W. Lahne, *Unteroffiziere* (Munich, 1965), p. 487.

3. MGFA, ed., *Handbuch,* 7:378.

4. Generalstab, ed., Heeres Dienstvorschrift 29/a, *Bestimmungen über die Beförderungen und Ernennungen der Unteroffizieren und Mannschaften bei besonderen Einsatz* (Berlin, 1939) p. 7.

5. MGFA, ed., *Handbuch,* 5:93.

6. Exceptionally experienced NCOs, usually indispensable specialists such as experts on weapons, fortifications and so forth, could on rare occasions be promoted to commissioned rank. They remained a separate body, however, and did not merge with the officer corps.

7. See M. Hobohm, *Soziale Heeresmisstände als Teilursache des deutschen Zusammenbruchs von 1918* (Berlin, 1929). This is one volume in a great many officially sponsored ones designed to ascertain the causes of defeat.

8. K. Demeter, *Das deutsche Offizierkorps* (Berlin, 1965), p. 49.

9. In the ranks of the Navy and Air Force, the numbers were larger.

10. MGFA, ed., *Handbuch,* 7:377.

11. These included better pay, improved medical services, night leave, and the right not to carry a pack during exercises and maneuvers.

12. MGFA, ed., *Handbuch,* 5:97.

13. Lahne, *Unteroffiziere,* p. 321.

14. MGFA, ed., *Handbuch,* 7:378.

15. E. A. Shils and M. Janowitz, "Cohesion and Disintegration in the Wehrmacht in World War II," *Public Opinion Quarterly* 12 (1948):280-315.

16. G. Blumentritt, "Das alte deutsche Heer von 1914 und das neue deutsche Heer von 1939," U. S. Army Historical Division Study B 296 (Allendorf, 1947), ch. 1.

17. Figures from Lahne, *Unteroffiziere,* pp. 379-80.

18. MGFA, ed., *Handbuch,* 5:94. The medals in question were: the Golden Military Merit Cross (Prussia), the Golden Medal for Bravery (Bavaria) and the St. Heinrich Medal (Saxony).

19. S. A. Stouffer et al., *The American Soldier,* 4 vols. (Princeton, 1949), 1:401-03.

20. Ibid., pp. 60-63.

21. Command and General Staff College, Fort Leavenworth, "History of the Army Personnel Replacement System," 1948, p. 280.

22. R. R. Palmer, *The Procurement and Training of Ground Combat Troops* (Washington, D. C., 1948), pp. 477-78.

23. Stouffer, *The American Soldier,* 1:237-38. That a higher degree of technological sophistication was not responsible for this fact is shown by the present-day Bundeswehr in which every third soldier is an NCO.

24. Ibid., 2:279; also Palmer, *Procurement and Training,* p. 249.

LEADERSHIP AND THE OFFICER CORPS 11

The time has now come to examine a constituent of fighting power that, perhaps more than any other, decides the outcome of wars: leadership. An enormous literature exists to show that, in the words of Kurt Lang, "it is what the leader does that counts."[1] Everything connected with him—from the way he is selected to the system used for his promotion—is therefore of quite extraordinary, indeed decisive, importance.

Before starting the discussion, a warning may be in place. Unlike troops and machines, which may be produced relatively quickly, an officer corps requires long tradition and broad experience in order to function effectively. The American officer corps, expanded fortyfold during the war, did not and could not have this tradition and this experience. A systematic comparison between it and the German officer corps cannot ignore this basic fact.

IMAGE AND POSITION

German Army

In the old Imperial Army, a vast gulf separated officers and enlisted men. The former's privileges regarding pay, uniform, food, lodging and other comforts were very large, probably contributing to the army's disintegration in the last month of the war and also to the outbreak of mutiny in the Navy.[2] The subject of a lively debate during the Weimar years, these privileges had been very substantially cut down by the time World War II broke out.

To gain an impression of the qualities that the German Army demanded and presumably got from its officers, we again quote from the *Truppenführung* of 1936:

6. Leadership in war[3] demands leaders possessed of judgment, a clear understanding, and foresight. They must be independent and firm in making a decision, determined and energetic while carrying it out, insensible to the changing fortunes of war, and possessed of a strong consciousness of the high responsibility resting on them.
7. The officer is leader and educator in every field. Besides a knowledge of men and a sense of justice, he must distinguish himself by superior knowledge and experience, moral excellence, self-control and high courage.
8. The example of officers and men in commanding positions has a crucial effect on the troops. The officer who demonstrates cold-bloodedness, determination and courage in front of the enemy pulls the troops along with himself. He must, however, also find his way to his subordinates' hearts and gain their confidence by understanding their feelings and their thoughts. His care for them must never cease.

   Mutual confidence is the secure basis for discipline in times of need and danger.
9. Every commander is to commit his entire personality in any situation without fearing responsibility. A readiness to assume responsibility[4] is the most important of all qualities of leadership. It must not, however, go so far as to lead to headstrong decisions without regard for the whole, or to the imprecise execution of orders, or to an I-know-better-than-you attitude. Independence should not turn into arbitrariness. But independence which knows its limits is the foundation for great successes. . . .
12. Commanders are to live with the troops and to share with them danger and deprivation, happiness and suffering. Only thus can they gain a real insight into their troops' fighting power (Kampfkraft) and requirements.

    The individual man is responsible not merely for himself but for his comrades also. Whoever possesses more ability, is stronger, must aid and lead the inexperienced and the weak.

    On such foundations does the feeling of real comradeship grow. Its importance in relations between commanders and men is as great as among the men themselves.
13. . . . It is every commander's duty to proceed against breaches of discipline, to prevent excesses, plundering, panic and other harmful effects by using every means at his disposal, including even the most drastic ones.

    Discipline is the central pillar on which the army is built. Its strict maintenance is a blessing for all.
14. The troops' forces must be conserved so that the highest demands can be made on them at the decisive moment. Whoever demands unnecessary chores sins against the prospect of success.

    The use of force in combat must be proportionate to the purpose at hand. Demands that are incapable of fulfillment are as harmful to the troops' confidence in their leaders as they are to their morale.

THE LOCATION OF THE CO AND HIS STAFF

109. Personal influence by the Commanding Officer on his troops is of the greatest importance. He must be near the fighting troops.

110. The selection of a location for a corps headquarters is determined above all by the need to keep in close and constant touch with both the divisions and the rear. A corps commander is not to rely on technical means of communication alone.

In spite of the availability of advanced technological apparatus, staying far away from the front extends the way orders and reports must travel, endangers communications and may cause reports and orders to arrive belatedly or not at all. It also puts difficulties in the way of obtaining a personal view of the country and of the state of combat.

On the other hand, the location of a corps headquarters should be fixed in such a way as to make possible the orderly activity of the various services.

111. A divisional commander's place is with his troops. . . . During encounters with the enemy seeing for oneself is best.

These are pretty authoritative words to which little if anything can be added. Passing now from theory to practice, it is worth mentioning that the road from noncommissioned to commissioned rank was an open one in World War II, traversed by tens of thousands of men. The bond between officers and men was emphasized more strongly still by the use of a comprehensive term, "soldiers," to describe them both, and by the regulations that required the men to salute not merely their officers but each other too. Having spent much of their training period in the company of enlisted men, officers were freely permitted to fraternize with them off duty and even encouraged to do so by the tenets of National Socialism. Possibly as a result of all this, in interviews with prisoners of war, "nearly all NCOs and officers of the company grade level were regarded by the German soldier throughout the Western campaign as brave, efficient, and considerate."[5]

U.S. Army

The following are the sections of FM 100-5 dealing with leadership and command:

102. Leading troops in combat, regardless of the echelon of command, calls for cool and thoughtful leaders with a strong feeling of the great responsibility imposed upon them. They must be resolute and self-reliant in their decisions, energetic and insistent in execution, and unperturbed by the fluctuations of combat.

103. Troops are strongly influenced by the example and conduct of their leaders. A leader must have superior knowledge, willpower, self-confidence, initiative and disregard of self. Any show of fear or unwillingness to share danger is fatal to leadership. On the other hand, a bold and determined leader will carry his troops with him no matter how difficult the enterprise. Mutual confidence between the leader and his men is the surest basis of discipline. To gain this confidence the leader must find the way to the hearts of his men. This he will do by acquiring an understanding of their thoughts and feelings and by showing a constant concern for their comfort and welfare.

104. A good commander avoids subjecting his troops to useless hardships; he guards against dissipating their combat strength in inconsequential actions or harassing them through faulty staff management. He keeps in close touch with all his subordinate units by means of personal visits and observation. It is essential that he know from personal contact the mental, moral, and physical state of his troops, the conditions with which they are confronted, their accomplishments, their desires, and their needs.

105. The commander should promptly extend recognition for services well done, lend help wherever help is needed, and give encouragement in adversity. Considerate to those whom he commands, he must be faithful and loyal to those who command him. A commander must live with his troops and share their dangers and privations as well as their joys and sorrows. By personal observation and experience he will then be able to judge their needs and combat value. When necessary to the execution of the mission, the commander requires and receives from his unit the complete measure of sacrifice.

106. A spirit of unselfish cooperation with their fellows is to be fostered among officers and men. The strong and the capable must encourage and lead the weak and the less experienced. On such a foundation the feeling of true comradeship will become firmly established and the full combat value of the troops will be made available to the higher commander....

109. ...A wise and capable commander...will so regulate the interior administration of the unit that all groups perform the same amount of work and enjoy the same amount of leisure. He will see that demonstrated efficiency is promptly recognized and rewarded. He will set before all a high standard of military conduct and apply to all the same rules of discipline....

119. ...Command and leadership are inseparable. Whether the force is large or small, whether the functions of command are complex or simple, the commander must be the controlling head; his must be the master mind, and from him must flow the energy and the impulse which are to animate all under him....

121. A willingness to accept responsibility is the foremost trait of leadership. Every individual from the highest commander to the lowest private must always remember that inaction and neglect of opportunities will warrant more severe censure than an error of judgment in the action taken. The criterion by which a commander judges the soundness of his own

decision is whether it will further the intentions of the higher commander. Willingness to accept responsibility must not manifest itself in a disregard of orders on the basis of a mere probability of having a better knowledge of the situation than the higher commander. The subordinate unit is part of a tactical team employed by the higher commander to accomplish a certain mission, and any independence on the part of a subordinate commander must conform to the general plan for the unit as a whole.

CONDUCT IN BATTLE

140. After providing for the issuance of orders, the commander places himself where he can best control the course of action and exert his leadership. His command post affords the advantage of established signal communications. When opportunity offers and when his presence at the command post is not urgently required, he visits his subordinate commander and his troops in order to inspire confidence and to assure himself that his orders are understood and properly executed. . . .

142. During the decisive phase of the battle, the place of the commander is near the critical point of action.

Thus, though entire sentences have again been lifted straight out of the German regulations, the general effect remains slightly different. There is more emphasis on knowledge as the first of the commander's attributes. Loyalty to one's superiors ("the criterion by which a commander judges the soundness of his own decision is whether it will further the intentions of the higher commander") is given a more prominent place, independent action, a lesser one. Though the American paragraph 106 is a literal translation from the German no. 12, the words concerning comradeship between officers and men are, significantly, omitted. Discipline—"the central pillar on which the army is built" according to the German regulations—is hardly mentioned in the American regulations, which may explain something about the operation of the military justice system. Instead of being told to keep his troops well in hand, like the German officer, the American one is exhorted to treat them justly.

The hurdle separating non-commissioned from commissioned rank in America's World War II Army was considerably higher than in the German one. This is confirmed by the regulations concerning the salute and also by the absence of a comprehensive term to embrace all service personnel, something which the recommendations of the Doolittle Report failed to change. The gulf between the two groups is illustrated by the fact that, to gain a commission, a man first had to be formally discharged from the army and then reenlisted. Off-duty fraternization between American officers and enlisted men was forbidden, one curious result being that Women's Army

Corps (WAC) officers were off limits to the latter. It was with some surprise that an official War Department publication, signed by General Marshall in person, noted that German company commanders were expected to congratulate their men on the occasion of their birthdays.[6] Possibly as a result of all these factors, 70 to 80 percent of all American enlisted men questioned during the war thought that officers put their own welfare above that of their troops.[7]

SELECTION

German Army[8]

In the years before 1914, one could become an officer either by enlisting in one of the ten cadets' schools (first established by Frederick the Great in order to give the sons of officers and other impoverished nobles a cheap education) or else by applying to the commander of some regiment.[9] The decision as to whether or not a man should be accepted as an officer candidate lay in the hands of the regimental commander, who first checked social origins, education, and religion (Jews found it almost impossible to become officers) and then conducted extensive interviews in order to determine general suitability. The same commander also decided whether a candidate, when his training had been completed, should be given a commission; his decision did require the endorsement of the sovereign, but this was normally a mere formality.

In sifting applicants, regimental commanders looked for willpower and a sense of responsibility above all—in short, it was character that counted. Character, needless to say, was often equated with social origins; no men coming from unsuitable families (anything below middle class was definitely unsuitable) need apply.

Though education was deliberately and consciously put behind character, the general level of schooling tended to rise during the quarter century before World War I, as table 11.1 shows.[10]

Of the various German states, only Bavaria demanded the Abitur as a sine qua non; the remainder were content if a Reifeprüfung (a diploma received after six years of gymnasium) had been obtained, and even here exceptions were made in favor of families regarded as particularly deserving. On the whole, however, the trend toward more and more education was both irresistible and officially sanctioned. Not only were Abiturienten upon commissioning given a two year head start in seniority, but acceptance for General Staff training—the shining goal toward which the vast majority of officers aspired—depended on it.[11]

Such was the prestige surrounding the officer's profession that, even in comparatively bourgeois Bavaria, Abiturienten flocked into the army,

TABLE 11.1
The Education of Prussian Cadets, 1890 to 1914

YEAR	1890	1900	1905	1910
Abiturienten[1] among Prussian cadets	35%	44%	48%	63%

YEAR	1895-1899	1900-1904	1905-1909	1910-1914
Abiturienten among naval cadets	31.1%	43.5%	65.0%	77.8%

SOURCE: D. Bald, E. Lippert, and R. Zabel, *Zur Sozialen Herkunft des Offiziers* (Bonn, 1977), p. 42.

[1]Men possessing an Abitur, that is, a diploma granted after nine years at a gymnasium, and which was necessary to enter the university.

some going so far as to apply to thirty regiments simultaneously. In an average year the authorities could expect a flood of 3,000 aspirants who competed for 154 vacancies; one could really choose![12]

World War I, by generating a hugely increased demand for officers, radically altered this favorable situation, forced a sharp drop in social and educational standards, and enabled anyone only halfway acceptable to obtain a commission. As casualties among the regular officer corps mounted, elderly reservists and young Einjährige took their places. From 1916 on Supreme Headquarters, as part of a deliberate policy aimed at preserving what was left of the old officer corps, began withdrawing its members from the front into General Staff service, thus causing a further dilution of front-line leadership. The results may certainly be regarded as one reason behind Germany's defeat in World War I.

In 1919, forced to radically cut down the number of officers in order to conform to the limits set by the Treaty of Versailles, Noske and Groener selected 3,000 out of 200,000 men. They also promoted 1,000 deserving NCOs, thus helping to remove one of the principal sources of dissatisfaction that had marred the last years of World War I. Selected among those who had served in combat units, been decorated for bravery, and performed the duties of a sergeant lieutenant (Offizierstellvertreter) for at least six months, these men in most cases were only given their commissions after completing their education and passing through officer school.[13]

It was, however, the next chief of the Truppenamt—the disguised General Staff of the Reichswehr—who took on the task of reforming the officer corps in earnest. General von Seeckt closed the cadet schools and abolished the institution of the Einjährige. Official doctrine now had it that "from knowledge to competence it is a big step; from ignorance to competence, an even bigger one."[14] Officer candidates were accordingly expected to possess an education that would have earned them the right to enter a university, though the Abitur itself was not made into a formal requirement. Its lack could be made up for by taking examinations (the Vor- and Nachprüfung), a system which left the way open to enlisted men to become officers and thus presented them with an incentive to study.[15]

Seeckt also did much to improve the education of his officers in other ways. Thursday lectures were instituted, and sitting for the General Staff Candidacy Exam (Wehrkreis Prüfung) was made obligatory for all officers instead of voluntary, as it had previously been.[16] A considerable number of officers were detailed to technical schools, the reasoning being that lack of technical education had been a cardinal reason behind the defeat in World War I.[17] These measures had their effect, and by 1930 no fewer than 77.5 percent of newly commissioned officers were Abiturienten.[18]

In other things, Seeckt was a restorer rather than an innovator. The demand for character remained decisive, and to help guarantee it, he insisted that candidates be graduates of a sports or youth movement. More important still, the decision as to who was to become an officer remained in the hands of regimental commanders, and it was only after Seeckt's retirement in 1926 that Groener prevailed upon the army to set up a psychological testing office.

The road to becoming a cadet was now as follows: Candidates continued to present themselves to the regiments of their choice, were screened in regard to background (age, education, police record, political activities) and, if found acceptable by the regimental commander, were called for a series of examinations held in their local Wehrkreis, all expenses paid.[19] Here the candidates, in groups of five or six, would remain for two to three days. They underwent extensive interviews with officers and psychologists of Simoneit's laboratory and were subjected to strenuous bodily exercises (for example, repeatedly climbing a smooth wall in full pack, or flexing an extender through which a gradually increasing electrical current was passed) designed to test willpower; meanwhile, a hidden movie camera recorded gestures and facial expressions for subsequent study. Technical aptitude was tested by means of a variety of instruments, including a children's construction set. To determine pedagogic ability, the candidate was required to teach a group of soldiers—always kept on hand—how to make, for example, a coat hanger out of a piece of wire. He might be asked to describe a picture, paraphrase a poem, or explain—in writing—how he would set about leading his class on an excursion to Berlin. "The height of the characterological examination" (Simoneit) was reached when the candidate was asked to enthuse his fellow candidates by talking about a subject of his own choice; it being assumed, again quoting Simoneit, that "men can influence men only when they show themselves adequate and free."

The entire lengthy procedure was brought to a close by an interview with a board made up of one officer, one psychiatrically trained physician, and one psychologist.[20] The results were first summed up separately by the three men, who then met to reach a final decision. This was put in writing—there was no point system—and sent to the regimental commander on whom, however, it was not formally binding. The final decision continued to rest in his hands alone.

Not the least remarkable feature of the system was that it did not systematically attempt to study intelligence—it being assumed, as the Truppenführung put it, that war is a matter of character above all. The nearest thing to a straightforward intelligence test was a series of thirty-two objects of various sizes, colors, and shapes that could be arranged in accordance with various principles, but even here the way in which the candidate went about his task was adjudged more important than his actual performance. Willpower and the inclination toward an outdoor life, technical competence and a warlike nature (manifested, among other things, by rebelliousness at school; to have repeated a class or two was accordingly taken as a point in favor), the capacity to represent and the ability to lead; these, and not cerebral excellence per se, were presumed to be the prime qualities needed in an officer.

The effectiveness of these methods is hard to assess except indirectly. The scope of the examination being so broad, its results were impossible to quantify and difficult to follow up, the more so since it was recognized that men possessing very different personalities might make equally good officers. Being a practical man above all, Simoneit was little concerned with theoretical justification for his methods so long as they produced results; he himself claimed a success rate of well over 80 percent (one source even claims a 98 percent correlation between the laboratory's assessments and the trainees' subsequent ratings) and no evidence to contradict this has ever come to light. American psychologists reporting on the system for the benefit of the U.S. Army in 1940-41 were unanimous in their opinion that it was likely to prove effective. So were subsequent observers who, without exception, commented on the high quality of German officers before and during World War II. It may be, as one of Simoneit's critics wrote, that his ideas on the qualities of an officer were preconceived and unsupported by empirical evidence; even this critic, however, calls his methods "exemplary."[21]

If the psychological testing of officer candidates during the Nazi years was thorough, indeed, the hugely increased demand soon made it necessary to lower standards in other ways. Above all, social and educational requirements were relaxed—something which accorded well with Nazi ideology and which, in the eyes of some, goes a long way to explain why the officer corps, now for the first time in its history made up of men of all classes, fought a lost war down to the bitter end.[22]

Though the army that invaded Poland on 1 September 1939 also included considerable numbers of elderly reserve officers trained in the Reichswehr and even the old Imperial Army, as well as ex-Austrian officers, the majority, especially among junior ranks, were graduates of Simoneit's laboratory. The latter, nevertheless, was and remained a mere technical organ; it could make suggestions, but the decision in regard both to the acceptance of a man for officer training and his commissioning stayed firmly in the hands of regimental commanders. Only through this decentralized system, it was thought, could the indispensable mutual confidence among officers in the same unit be created and maintained.

U.S. Army

In the U.S. Army during World War II, the "paramount requirement" of an officer was the ability to lead men in battle. Administrative positions, it is true, had to be filled; since it was necessary for one officer to be able to step into the shoes of another, however, an excess of specialization among junior officers was regarded as undesirable.[23]

For officers of the ground arms, "the ability to direct the performance of enlisted men and to cooperate with other officers amid the hazards and uncertainties of battle" were major prerequisites. These were summed up in the ideas of "responsibility and leadership" in that order.

Though the army's doctrine was thus quite well defined, no clear procedure existed to determine a man's intangible "potential as a fighter or combat leader."[24] Direct means being unavailable (or, at any rate, extremely time-consuming to devise, prepare and apply), reliance was placed on "more or less indirect indications" among which the Army General Classification Test was paramount.[25] Since this test discriminated in favor of the well educated, but also because the American draft swept up men of all age groups between eighteen and thirty-seven and not merely nineteen-year-olds, American officers tended to be better educated than German ones, 86.5 percent of them having completed high school and no fewer than 51.8 percent having spent at least some time in college.[26]

Aspiring officers, after being tested, would travel to an officer candidate school, of which there were many throughout the country; travel and lodging were at their own expense. The actual selection was in the hands of the school commandant and his staff who interviewed applicants.[27] Standards varied, but always involved age, physical condition, military service, capacity for leadership, learning ability, citizenship, character, and education.

Again, however, the practical tools available did not match the ideal put forward by official doctrine. For a school Commandant to determine qualities of leadership was anything but easy; on the other hand, the results of the written AGCT were readily available. Hence, in the words of the official history, they "remained the principal instrument for selection."[28]

The differences between the German and American systems are worth summing up as they are entirely typical of the way things were managed in the two armies. Both recognized leadership as the paramount prerequisite in officers, but whereas the German Army took very great pains to determine its presence, the U. S. Army, no doubt partly because of the pressure of time, did not. The Germans looked for character, the Americans, for intelligence. Though the Germans did make very extensive use of psychological testing, the selection of officers ultimately lay in the hands of the very men who were later to train the cadets and lead them in battle—whereas the selection of American officers was split between a psychological office and school commanders who, though responsible for training, were unlikely to again meet a man once he had been commissioned.[29] The German system was thus personal and decentralized; the American one, impersonal and centralized.

Behind these differences, of course, there lurked diverging ideas as to the nature of leadership and, indeed, that of war. German officers were combat leaders above all; the main problem, in Simoneit's view, was to reconcile this requirement with the need for educators during long periods of peace.[30] Though the identification of character and the prediction of its future development were enormously difficult tasks that must sometimes have led to errors (not to mention the influence of political considerations which, prior to 1933, denied character not merely to anybody tinted slightly red but also to scions of the wrong families), it cannot be denied that the Germans tried hard and, in so doing, pioneered methods that are still in use in many armies. The U.S. Army, by contrast, was mainly interested in intelligence; though its officers were also supposed to lead men in combat, this was regarded essentially as a problem in "human engineering." To become a qualified "personnel technician," an officer had to acquire the tricks of the trade.[31] The differences between the two armies are therefore clear.

TRAINING

German Army

In the old Imperial Army, officer candidates (that is, those enlisted at nineteen years of age who had not passed through one of the cadet schools) received eighteen months' training before being commissioned. Of these, nine were spent in basic and advanced training and nine at officers' school.[32]

As World War I progressed and the demand for officers grew, these periods had to be progressively cut down. In 1918 active officers received three months' basic training in the Replacement Army, served for three months with a unit of the Field Army, were sent for a three months' officer training course, took an exam, returned for another period with the Field

Army, and were finally given their commissions.[33] A reserve officer's training was similar, except that the period spent with the fighting troops (fechtende Truppe) was much longer.

In the Reichswehr, thanks to the very long period of service imposed by the Allies, it was possible to extend officer training and make it more thorough than ever before. Candidates now spent a full two years with the troops (whose quarters they shared) before being taken into officer school, which lasted ten-and-a-half months. Then there followed another ten-and-a-half months at the officers' specialized arm school; overall time from enlistment to commissioning thus was close to four years.[34]

Under the guiding hand of Seeckt, the contents of training were also revised. Though the German Army's tradition of putting personality before knowledge and character before intellect was reaffirmed, considerably more attention was now devoted to the so-called "scientific" (wissenschaftliche) subjects.[35] In officer school the cirriculum was as follows: tactics, six hours a week; weapon technology, three hours; engineering service, three hours; topography, army organization, and citizenship, two hours each; antiaircraft defense, signals, and motor vehicle technology, one hour each; sport theory, one hour; sanitary service, two-thirds hour; and military administration, one-third hour. Later on, when an officer continued his training in one of the specialized arm schools, some of the theoretical subjects (including citizenship) were dropped; on the other hand, two to three hours of military history—based on independent work by the students, and regarded as second in importance only to tactics—were added. Also added were such specialized subjects as mathematics, physics, and chemistry.

On the whole, this system stayed in force until 1937. Training remained divided into three parts, that is, one consisting of basic training with the troops, one at officer school, and one at an arm school. A further period of service with the troops followed, and a cadet could expect to be commissioned approximately two years after enlistment. The contents of instruction at officer school were made more practical; tactics now occupied nine hours a week, and an hour's indoctrination in National Socialist principles took the place of citizenship. The Reifezeugniss remained the minimum standard of education required, although late in 1942 this had to be dropped.[36]

Following the outbreak of World War II, there was a growing tendency to replace formal training in officer school by periods of active service at the front. Thus, until the end of 1942, prospective officers were first given six months' training in the Replacement Army, did a spell of three months at the front, returned for three months in officer school, served another two to four months at the front, and were finally commissioned after fourteen to sixteen months' service. Losses among the cadets during their periods at the front were so heavy, however, that the system had to be changed once again. From the fall of 1942 to the end of the war, the road to becoming an officer was normally marked by the following stages:

	MONTHS
basic training in the Replacement Army	3-4
NCO training in the Replacement Army	2-4
platoon-leader training in the Replacement Army	2
promotion to NCO	
service at the front	2
promotion to cadet (Fahnenjunker)	
officer school	3-4
promotion to senior cadet (Oberfahnrich)	
advanced officer training	2
total[37]	14-18

In addition, men not originally destined for officer training, but who had given a good account of themselves while on active service, could now be recommended by their regimental commanders for officer training after a minimum of six months if they possessed the Abitur and after twelve if they did not. Selected on the basis of "demonstrated leadership . . . personality, soldierly behavior and achievements," such men would be sent to officer school and then, under normal circumstances, return to their own units in order to receive their commissions at the hands of the regimental commander.[38] This arrangement, which made sterling service in front of the enemy (Bewahrung vor den Feind) into the predominant criterion for officer selection, enabled tens of thousands of NCOs and enlisted men to gain their commissions during the war.

Whatever a man's road to becoming an officer, it is thus clear that active service at the front was regarded as the best training he could receive. Though circumstances did not make it possible to retain the five to seven months instituted at the beginning of the war, no candidate was commissioned without having first fired quite a number of shots in anger.

U.S. Army

During the years before World War II, as today, officer training in American service academies lasted four years. For various reasons, however, the proportion of all training time devoted to professional subjects tended to decline; at Annapolis, for example, a midshipman spent 31.6 percent of his time on cultural subjects of the kind that could be learnt at any college, 31.2 percent on technical subjects, and only 37.2 percent on professional training.[39]

At West Point—which then as now served as a model for others to imitate—the system instituted by Superintendent General Thayer over a century ago tended to turn out men who were excellent managers above all. Great emphasis was placed on getting things done quickly and effectively, even under pressure.[40]

Since the army was small and, moreover, scattered in small groups all over the vast country, opportunities for practical training were few. American officers accordingly spent much of their careers in schools, either teaching or being taught, and were seldom put in command of any sizeable body of troops. The one exception was formed by the inevitable tour of duty in the Philippines, where the presence of a considerable garrison enabled officers to gain at least some practical experience.

When rearmament got under way in 1940 the U.S. Army, then numbering a mere 20,000 regular officers, was faced with the Herculean task of finding officers to command and administer a force which, though its ultimate size was still unknown, would certainly number millions of men. Early in 1943 this task had been accomplished; within two years, the officer corps had expanded over thirtyfold, and the shortage of commissioned personnel turned into a surplus that continued right down to the end of the war. Since the fighting had by this time hardly begun, scant possibility existed for commissioning enlisted men on the basis of service at the front. Worse still, the surplus meant that personnel inducted after the early months of 1943 stood little chance of earning a commission, regardless of ability. Instead, the best of them tended to become NCOs—with unfortunate results for everybody concerned.[41]

Like all enlisted men, future officers in the U.S. Army first received thirteen (later seventeen) weeks of basic training. Next came four weeks at an officer candidate preparatory school, where weapons, small unit tactics, map reading, and drill were taught. Officer Candidate School itself lasted about seventeen weeks and was specialized by arm. In this respect the system differed from the German one. The total time a man spent in the army from enlistment to commissioning was between eight and nine months, though in some cases men were commissioned after a mere seven months.[42]

The curriculum of one OCS, responsible for the training of armored branch officers, is outlined in table 11.2.

Besides being examined on these subjects, officer candidates were constantly rated on attitude in class, force, initiative, leadership, and so forth.[43] Performance was recorded by means of point scales, though there existed no uniform standards throughout the army.

A dearth of detailed information makes it impossible to compare the contents of American officer training with its German equivalent. It can be noted, however, that an American officer candidate received a total of eight

TABLE 11.2
The Training of American Officers, by Subject

SUBJECT	NUMBER OF HOURS	
	Common Training	Branch Training
drill and discipline	99	—
general subjects	52.5	—
tactics	129	108
communications	42	—
motors, wheeled	50	—
motors, full track	—	46
gunnery	136	94
instructor training	33	—
orientation	17	—
reserved time	9.5	—
total	568	248

SOURCE: R.R. Palmer, *The Procurement and Training of Ground Combat Troops* (Washington, D.C., 1948), p. 363.

to nine months' training, whereas a German one, depending on the period in the war in which he was drafted, received nine to sixteen months of training, in addition to a period of front-line service varying from two to as many as seven months. An American cadet, upon graduation, would enter a pool (the very word was unknown in the German Service, "reserve" being used instead) and was then assigned to any one of the army's ninety-one divisions in accordance with T/O vacancies. A German one, by contrast, would be commissioned into a regiment in whose ranks he had seen previous service and whose commander would indeed often ask for him by name.

PROMOTION

German Army

Promotion in the old Imperial Army went by seniority and was, by modern standards, excruciatingly slow. For a lieutenant to become a captain took fifteen years. For a captain to be promoted to major took another ten. The vast majority of active officers ended their career as majors.[44]

To qualify for preferred promotion, an officer had to possess General Staff training as a virtual sine qua non—a fact that tended to cancel out the comparatively low educational standards of the lower ranks. General Staff officers, selected by competitive examinations and numbering 3 to 4 percent of the total, could expect comparatively rapid promotion, even in peacetime.

Though the system did ensure that there would be no Colonel Blimps in the army (a blimp would be discharged before attaining the rank of colonel), it also meant that company and battalion commanders were often elderly gentlemen of doubtful competence. During World War I, therefore, these ranks were repeatedly combed out: twice in 1914, twice in 1915, three times in 1916, seven times (!) in 1917, and twice again in 1918.

The essentials of this system were retained during the Weimar period, although the restricted size of the army meant that promotion was now even slower than before. Seeckt, however, did reform the Evaluation Forms by which superiors of every rank judged their subordinates and which constituted the main instrument for selection; in 1920 these were redrafted to put an even heavier emphasis on character, that is, honesty, selflessness, readiness to commit oneself, and a sense of responsibility. Careerism was frowned upon, whereas the ability to generate and maintain trust was counted as the single most important virtue.

To prevent the system of evaluations from developing into a free-for-all, commanding officers were warned that they would be judged, among other things, by the quality of their reports. The latter had to be kept brief but to contain everything essential: personality, character, professional competence, and achievements.

On the basis of this system, officers in the normal course of service could expect to end up, at most, as regimental commanders—a post which, in the German service, carried considerable responsibilities and prestige. To advance further in the ranks, however, one normally had to serve as the chief of staff (Ia) of a division and thus have General Staff training. The next highest post, that of divisional commander, depended on the completion of this training in virtually all cases.

One problem that Reichswehr personnel planners faced and tried to solve was that of preventing the limited opportunities for promotion in a small professional army from adversely affecting the spirit of the officer corps. This was done by adding ability to seniority and entering exceptionally qualified officers—on the average, perhaps 15 percent of the total—on special lists. Selected on the basis of their ability to fill the next highest position, most of these officers were general staff men; others, however, could also be considered in exceptional cases, and a sine qua non for the preferred promotion of a General Staff officer was the completion of a tour of duty with a field unit. Once granted, preferred promotion meant a real boost (worth 200-275 places on the Army Lists) to a man's career. The dismal opportunities for promotion created by the Treaty of Versailles were thus to some extent corrected, at the cost, it is true, of considerable mobility in and out of the officer corps.[45]

Apart from the fact that the army's expansion led to a rapid and welcome rejuvenation of the officer corps, this system also was retained during the thirties. General Staff officers continued to receive preferred promotion, as did a small number of exceptionally competent troop officers, who could be promoted ahead of the rest.[46] The officer corps' rapid expansion, together with the opportunities that this created, were not without disadvantages; this was, indeed, the time for "careers."

The system of evaluations, too, was retained in its entirety. Troop officers were now judged in even years, members of the General Staff and generals, in uneven ones—a division which enabled the latter to receive attention out of all proportion to their number. In addition to marking the next two higher positions for which a subordinate was suited, superiors were asked to rate their men as "above average," "average" or "below average"; in time of peace, those rated below average were automatically eliminated. Neither forced comparisons nor point systems were used. In 1938 a suggestion for the introduction of a point system was raised but rejected by the great majority of officers on the grounds that the much desired picture of "the whole man" would thereby be lost.[47]

Drawing on the evaluations, each division kept lists of officers divided into seven parts. These were those suitable for service at the Army High Command, those suitable for General Staff duty, those suitable for the adjudantur, those with a special aptitude for training or research, those temporarily deserving consideration on grounds of ill health, those considered unsuitable for the next highest position, and those who where not properly carrying out their present duties.

In these lists, together with the evaluations, the Army Personnel Office possessed an admirable instrument for deciding on promotions and assignments. The office's officers, moreover, were frequent participators in maneuvers and exercises; they personally knew virtually every general and General Staff officer and could shape their policy accordingly.[48]

During the first half of the war this system, the product of centuries of development, was retained even though growing losses inevitably tended to make seniority count for less and competence for more. In November 1942, acting upon Hitler's direct orders, HPA embarked on a series of reforms which institutionalized the situation thus created:

> The Fuehrer orders that any officer who successfully leads a unit against the enemy and has given proof of the necessary qualities be promoted to the rank corresponding with his position.
>
> The Fuehrer demands, in addition, that officers possessed of exceptional personal qualities and achievements be put into commanding positions and promoted.
>
> A system of equal promotion for all [that is, by seniority] is contrary to the leadership and Fuehrer principle to which the Wehrmacht, for the sake of victory, must commit itself....
>
> The present order applies to front-line officers above all. They are nearest death and should be rewarded accordingly.[49]

Under this system, promotion for front-line officers, especially those who stepped into their fallen comrades' shoes, was radically sped up. A second lieutenant, for example, commanding a company could become a first lieutenant after a mere two months in that position, and a first lieutenant commanding a battalion could be made a captain after only six months. The ranks thus attained were, moreover, permanent.[50]

The longer the war, the heavier the pressure on officers to earn promotion by means of front-line service. From July 1944 on, General Staff officers could only qualify for promotion by doing a tour at the front. A new character attribute—Krisenfest, or "crisis proof"—made its appearance in the evaluations. Constantly urged on by Hitler, HPA more and more downgraded seniority and upgraded character, the latter often being equated with outstanding service at the front. The system's advantages in bringing to the fore men of proven ability cannot be denied; on the other hand, it did contribute in breaking up the officer corps' traditional homogeneity and esprit de corps, which may indeed have been Hitler's intention.[51]

That the measures thus taken did not fail to have their effect is shown by table 11.3, comparing planned versus preferred promotion during the first half of 1943.

The number of officers in each arm who received retroactive promotion (that is, were given a rank corresponding with the actual position they were holding) was directly related to that arm's losses, as the figures in table 11.4 show.

Dangerous service, it is clear, was well rewarded.

TABLE 11.3

Planned versus Preferred Promotion in the German Army, 1943

PROMOTED TO	TOTAL NO.	PREFERRED PROMOTION		PLANNED PROMOTION	
		No.	%	No.	%
colonel general	3	3	100.0	—	0.0
general	26	25	96.1	1	3.9
lieut. general	86	67	77.9	19	22.1
major general	154	58	37.7	96	62.3
colonel	328	198	60.4	130	39.6
lieut. colonel	309	206	67.7	103	33.3
major	384	245	96.0	39	4.0
total	1,290	902	69.2	368	30.8

SOURCE: W. Keilig, *Truppe und Verbände der deutsche Wehrmacht*, 7 vols. (Wiesbaden, 1950–), 3:203-04.

TABLE 11.4
Retroactive Promotion in the German Army, by Arm

ARM	RETROACTIVE PROMOTIONS (percent of total)	ARM'S LOSSES (percent of total)
Infantry	57	53
Armor	19	20
Artillery	16	18
Engineers	6	7
Signals	1	2
General Staff[1]	1	—

SOURCE: W. Keilig, *Truppe und Verbände der deutsche Wehrmacht,* 7 vols. (Wiesbaden, 1950–), 3:204-05. Figures valid for the period to 31 May 1945.

[1] General Staff losses are included in those of the various arms.

U.S. Army

In the U.S. Army during the interwar period, promotion went strictly by seniority. In 1920, it is true, a plan had been proposed for preferred promotion to be given to a small number of exceptionally able men; it was rejected, however, on the grounds that "it was impossible in peacetime to predict which junior officers would make good higher commanders in wartime," and that the army consequently had to "rely upon the general competence of the officer corps rather than upon a relatively small number of brilliant individuals."[52]

As the army began its expansion in 1941, a shortage of officers developed, and it became necessary to decide which junior officers should be promoted to field ranks. Selection accordingly replaced seniority, with 60 percent of all recommendations tendered by field commanders and 40 percent reserved to the War Department.[53] This policy caused each part of the army to go its own way and created considerable confusion. In a directive of July 1943, therefore, the War Department ordered that promotion again be tied to "the rate prevalent throughout the Army," which in turn was based on the number of months spent in each rank.[54]

By this time, a large surplus of officers had replaced the shortage of 1941. Any officers who became casualties could easily be replaced from T/O overstrengths (which all units had been authorized to carry) or from pools of OCS graduates in the Zone of the Interior. Furthermore, replacements arriving from the United States often carried ranks higher than those of the men whom they were meant to replace.[55] The result was a double blow to morale: whereas the men in combat units saw themselves robbed of a chance for promotion, the new arrivals were forced into positions below those to which they were entitled by rank.

In 1944, the average monthly number of promotions per 1,000 officers was 36 in the Quartermaster Corps, 31 in the Corps of Engineers, 28 in the field artillery, but only 25 in the infantry.[56] Since promotion continued to be tied to the number of months spent in each rank, there is only one possible explanation for these differentials: in the infantry, officers were becoming casualties before they could attain the necessary seniority, and a stream of replacements stepped into their shoes. A greater contrast with the German system cannot be imagined.

Amidst all this, the system of efficiency ratings continued to operate. The form did contain a rubric earmarking an officer as belonging to the "lowest quarter," but in practice it was almost impossible to get rid of an inefficient officer except by having him transferred elsewhere.[57] There existed a strong tendency, moreover, to enter the majority of all officers as belonging to the "highest quarter." This obviously ruined the entire system and was, indeed, a major reason why a new form relying on forced comparisons between all officers in a unit was introduced soon after the war in an attempt, so typical of the entire American approach, to compensate for human frailties by employing a piece of social engineering.[58]

DIGRESSION: THE GENERAL STAFF SYSTEM

German Army

In the German Army until the middle of World War II, membership in the General Staff corps constituted virtually the sole way by which a man could qualify for preferred promotion or attain general rank. The corps' officers formed an exclusive club, an elite within an elite; their prestige in the eyes of the people was unrivalled, their influence on national life, out of all proportion to their numbers. The impact of the General Staff on the army's fighting power cannot be overestimated.[59]

In the Imperial Army before World War I selection for the War Academy (Kriegsakademie) was by means of annual competitive examinations. Subjects included tactics, fieldcraft, engineer service, weapons, languages, geography, and history, with a strong emphasis on tactics. After 1920 sitting for the examination was made obligatory for all officers, and the subjects were extended to include mathematics, physics, chemistry, and physical exercises as well. The seriousness of the examination can be gauged from the fact that it normally took five months' preparation. As always under Seeckt, the results were used not only to assess knowledge and competence, but also in an attempt to gain insight into the personality and character of the examinees; the difficulty of the preparation (which had to take place in an officer's spare time) and the excitement surrounding the examination proper were, accordingly, regarded as one of their principal advantages and something of a substitute for the stress of war.[60]

Expanded during the Nazi years, the system of examinations was retained with little modification (except that the natural sciences were made optional and reserved for officers aspiring to a career in one of the technical branches) until the outbreak of World War II. From this time, future General Staff officers, mostly captains who had given proof of outstanding ability on active service and were often the holders of high decorations, were detailed for attendance at staff courses by their corps commanders. The latter had to evaluate the candidates' character, performance, professional achievements and health, in that order. All evaluations had to end with the explicit statement: "X is fit for service with the General Staff."

Candidates before 1914 were normally between thirty and thirty-five years old; this went down to between twenty-five and thirty in the Weimar period, but rose again to between twenty-eight and thirty-two after 1933. Most students entering the War Academy were thus officers of several years' experience, yet they were not too old to learn something new. Standards being extremely high, the number of successful candidates was always very small; between 150 and 160 each year before 1914, 70 during the Weimar years (of whom only between 10 and 15 could hope to complete the full course and 5 to 10 could be accepted as permanent members of the staff), and 150 out of 1,000 for example even in 1936, in the face of a growing shortage. During World War II itself 17 courses (Lehrgänge) for General Staff officers were held, attended by between 60 and 80 officers and, after 1943, by between 100 and 150 officers each.

Training in the War Academy lasted three years.[61] Its purpose was to produce operational experts qualified, above all else, to occupy the post of chief of staff cum operations officer (Ia) in a division. Tactics and military history accordingly formed the principal subjects, followed at quite a distance by all the rest; staff work and army organization, intelligence, supply, transport, weapons-technology, and interservice cooperation, all taught in such a way as to emphasize the overriding importance of tactics. Nonmilitary subjects included foreign languages and, during the third year of study (which always took place in Berlin) international affairs, politics, and economics, which were lectured upon by visiting experts. A number of students each year were sent to attend courses at technical universities. Sport was always given a prominent place.

Training methods were graduated. Groups of ten to fifteen students attended lectures during their first year, then progressed to exercises, seminars, independent presentations (often on subjects of military history), the planning of maneuvers and operations, plan games and war games. Exercises in class alternated with outdoor ones, and staff rides and excursions to historical battlefields and military installations were held several times a year. During the summer, kept free of formal teaching, the students were detailed to the various arms in order to gain insight into the possibilities and limitations of each. The three-year course was crowned by a two-week staff ride during which a major operation would be simulated and worked out in meticulous detail. This exercise was also decisive for the final grading of the students.

Selection at the end of the course was carried out by the supervising staff (though in some particularly difficult cases the students might be asked to rate each other) on the basis of their intimate knowledge of the students gained by informal social visits also; there were no written examinations. Intelligence and logical thought; speed in decision and an eye for essentials; creativity and the ability to work long hours, intensively and reliably, without fatigue; these were the main qualities looked for.

Graduates of the War Academy were taken on the General Staff for a probationary period lasting from one to two years. Only then were they taken on as full members, entitled to wear the coveted crimson stripes and silver collar insignia, and to add "i.G" (im Generalstab) after their rank. They had arrived.

When World War II broke out in 1939, the shortage of staff officers and the expectation of a short conflict caused the War Academy to be closed. Its three years were replaced by eight-week courses designed to enable graduates "to perform usefully at the lower echelons of the General Staff in accordance with their superiors' directives and under their supervision." Character and the capacity for independent thought and inner force remained decisive for selection. The subject matter was kept strictly practical, with a strong emphasis on tactics, supply, transport, staff work, intelligence, and counterintelligence. Methods of teaching were, as far as possible, kept similar to those employed in peacetime, though the number of excursions and so on naturally suffered. Normally some 80 percent of the graduates were evaluated as "suitable for being detailed to the general staff"; the rest were either "not yet suitable" or "unsuitable."

In March 1942, as casualties mounted and the need for General Staff officers became desperate, another reorganization gave the system its final form. Aspiring General Staff officers were first to receive six months' practical training on the staff of a division; to follow this with three months' work on a higher staff, for example, that of an army; to spend eight weeks at a General Staff Lehrgang; and to undergo another six-month probationary period before finally being taken into the General Staff. Training therefore lasted approximately a year and a half in all and, since it included much practical work at the front in accordance with the usual German idea that war is the best teacher of war, frequently involved not inconsiderable casualties among the trainees.

A remarkable aspect of the German system was the absence of an interservice academy, explicable on the grounds that the land army was, after all, by far the most important of the three services and possessed of the longest history. An interservice (OKW) academy was in fact set up in 1939 but quickly closed at the outbreak of war; its first course is said not to have been a success. During the Norwegian and Mediterranean campaigns, interservice cooperation on the tactical and operational levels nevertheless functioned admirably (in both cases, interestingly, it was Air Force officers who were put in supreme command). Germany's war effort being essentially continental by character, the country did not perhaps require an interservice academy to the same extent that Britain and the United States did.

While all authorities are unanimous that the training given before 1939 was, on the whole, excellent, opinions about that dished out during the war differ and cannot be reconciled here. Instead it is worth repeating a few points which to a large extent gave the system its unique character. The existence of a single, all-embracing academy; the enormous emphasis put on tactical and operational expertise to the neglect, some would say, of strategy, and the higher conduct of war; the very great importance attributed to the students' character as opposed to their knowledge and competence per se; the reliance on intimate knowledge of the students by their instructors rather than on written examinations, much less point scales; the emphasis on practical work as well as formal teaching in both peace and war; the long probationary period; the use of the academy, at any rate until 1943, as almost the sole vehicle for promotion to higher rank; and finally the exclusiveness and separateness of the General Staff corps—these were the distinguishing features of an institution which generations of historians since the Franco-Prussian War have never tired of describing.

U.S. Army

The U.S. War Department General Staff, founded in 1903 by Elihu Root and in many ways deliberately modelled on the German system, nevertheless bore a different character right from the beginning. It was, as the name implies, both a War Department and a General Staff. To a degree far greater than the German organization, it combined general administration with the command of armies in war, and its members were trained accordingly. As a result, Pershing, for example, when he went to war in 1917, found himself without a body of staff officers capable of running operations at the highest level and had to train his own.[62]

Preparation for service on the General Staff proceeded in two stages. In 1901, the infantry and cavalry school at Fort Leavenworth was expanded and turned into the Command and General Staff School offering one year courses in staff work to officers (normally lieutenants) recommended for proficiency. The graduates were employed in staff positions throughout the army, thus constituting in effect a much diluted counterpart of the German Truppengeneralstab (general staff with the troops).

To prepare officers for service in the General Staff proper, the War College was founded in 1904, though it was not until 1922 that graduation from this institution was made into a sine qua non. Selection for the War College depended on graduating from Fort Leavenworth first, though officers with outstanding efficiency ratings could sometimes skip this stage. Highly prestigious lists of officers eligible for the college were kept and published to encourage others. In 1928, for example, the list carried the names of 1,400 regulars and 125 National Guard officers. How many attended the college each year is not clear. Courses lasted one year.

The mission of the college, according to a lecture given by its assistant commander to new students in 1928, was to prepare officers for the conduct of field operations at the higher echelons, including the political, economic, and social matters pertaining to the conduct of war; to instruct them in War Department General Staff duties; to train them for joint operations with the Navy; and to give instruction in the strategy, tactics, and logistics of past conflicts, including especially the World War.[63] In practice, the curriculum was weighted on the side of international relations, economics, industry, and interservice problems, since its purpose was not so much to train officers for command in the field as to prepare them for the general administrative duties of the War Department.

Learning was mainly by doing. Committees, conferences and guest lectures were supervised by the students themselves. Relations between faculty and students are said to have been informal, freedom of expression was encouraged.[64]

The War College, to sum up, differed considerably from the Kriegsakademie; whereas the latter trained staff officers for service in field units as well as with the General Staff proper, the former prepared senior administrators for War Department duties, as shown also by the upper age limit for admission, which was fifty-two. It could not therefore be employed as the principal vehicle for selection, or perhaps one should rather say that selection started later than it did under the German system. The General Staff corps itself was less exclusive than its German equivalent; on the one hand, there was no probationary period, and on the other, service in the General Staff was limited to four years after which the officer would return to his own arm or service. The American fear of elitism may have played a role in this and also in the fact that not until 1933 were the corps given their own insignia.

Given its organization and purpose, the War College could not, of course, turn out the large numbers of staff officers needed during World

War II. Instead, these were trained in eight-week courses opened at Fort Leavenworth from 1940 on.

NUMBERS AND DISTRIBUTION

German Army

In the days before World War I, the Imperial Army was 751,000 men strong; of these 29,000 (3.8 percent) were active officers. Mobilization brought in another 81,000 reserve officers, so that total mobilized officer strength reached 120,000 (3 percent) in an army numbering 4 million.[65]

The overall number of officers (both active and reserve) who saw service in World War I is put at 272,053.[66] This figure, if correct, constitutes approximately 2.1 percent of the number of men who went through the army during four years of war. It serves to demonstrate the German Army's readiness to accept a shortage of officers rather than to compromise in regard to their quality.

Little information is available on the distribution of these officers among the various arms and services. It appears that, in 1914, the infantry, as the least technical arm, had proportionally fewer officers than the army as a whole: it constituted 65 percent of total strength, but accounted for only 53 percent of all officers. In peacetime, an infantry battalion counted between 2.64 percent and (in a Jaeger battalion) 3 percent of its strength in officers.[67] The difference between the proportion of officers in the army as a whole and their number inside an infantry battalion of the line was therefore quite small.

The Treaty of Versailles authorized 4,000 officers (4 percent of strength); in spite of this and the favorable situation in regard to recruitment, however, the actual number in 1933 is said to have been just 3,600. In the same year, the Reichswehr had forty-seven officers of general rank, so that their ratio to overall strength was 1 to 2,100. No details are available on the officers' distribution among the arms and services.

In 1934, when rearmament started, the army lost 500 officers to the newly established Air Force. Some 1,100 officers were added in 1934, and a similar number, in 1935, so that the total was now close to 5,000. In the same period, the army as a whole grew by 150 percent, so that the proportion of officers fell by one-half.

Though more officers were lost to the Air Force in 1935, the promotion of NCOs, reactivation of reserve officers, incorporation of police officers, and new commissionings enabled the army to register a net gain of 2,400 officers. By 1936, out of approximately 10,800 officers, more than half had received their commissions since 1933. The fall in the proportion of officers continued, however; it was not until the autumn of 1937 that their percentage in the army—now counting 590,000 men—again reached half the Weimar figure.[68]

In 1938, the incorporation of the Austrian Army brought a welcome addition to strength. Officers in the Austrian Army were proportionally more numerous than in the German one (2,128 or 3.6 percent in a force of 58,000) but many of these were elderly men. In the end, only 1,600 were transferred to the Wehrmacht; no fewer than 55 percent of the generals had to go.[69]

On 1 September 1939, upon mobilization, the situation was as shown in table 11.5.

TABLE 11.5
The Distribution of Officers in the German Army

	TOTAL STRENGTH	OFFICERS
Field Army	2,741,064	81,314 (2.98%)
Replacement Army	996,040	24,080 (2.41%)
Inside the Infantry Division		
combat elements	13,462	457 (3.34%)
service elements[1]	4,293	83 (1.93%)
Total Infantry Division	19,895	540 (3.01%)

SOURCE: B. Mueller-Hillebrand, *Das Heer*, 3 vols. (Frankfurt am Main, 1969–), 3:255. For the number of officers in the infantry division, see table 6.9, p. 55.
[1]Including the Field Replacement Battalion.

In July 1944, Field Army officers forward of the regimental level formed 3.7 percent, rearward, 3.2 percent of total actual strength.[70] Though differentials are not large, officers clearly became more numerous, the closer a unit was to the front.

In 1944, the officers of the Wehrmacht were distributed as shown in table 11.6.

TABLE 11.6
The Distribution of German Officers, by Type

OFFICER	TOTAL	ACTIVE	RESERVE
Troop	245,000	55,000 (22.4%)	190,000 (77.5%)
Sanitary	28,000	3,000 (10.7%)	25,000 (89.3%)
Veterinary	9,000	1,000 (11.1%)	8,000 (88.9%)
Home guard	5,800	2,800 (40.7%)	3,000 (59.3%)
Administrative	61,000	11,000 (18.0%)	50,000 (82.0%)
Transport	4,800	1,000 (20.8%)	3,800 (79.2%)
Judges	1,200	400 (33.3%)	800 (66.6%)
Total	345,800	74,200 (21.5%)	280,600 (78.5%)

SOURCE: D. Bachlin, "Deckung des Offiziersbedarf in deutschen Heer während des 2. Weltkrieg," U. S. Army Historical Division Study D 110 (n.p., n.d.) p. 22.

Seventy percent of all officers, therefore, were with the troops, whereas administrative officers by contrast formed only 17.4 percent of the total. Of all active officers, 74.2 percent were with the troops, as opposed to only 67.7 percent of all reserve officers. Active officers were proportionally most numerous in the home guard—which by this time was made up largely of disabled personnel—and among military judges; apart from these exceptions, however, they were fairly equally distributed.

The distribution of active officers among the ranks at various times before and during the war was as shown in table 11.7.

TABLE 11.7
Rank Structure of the German Officer Corps (Active) 1932-1943

RANK	MAY 1932	OCTOBER 1936	OCTOBER 1938	MAY 1943
Field marshals	—	1	—	15
Colonel generals	—	1	3	18
Generals	3	16	31	141
Lieutenant generals	14	41	87	369
Major generals	27	91	140	501
Total General Officers	44 (1.18%)	150 (1.77%)	261 (1.59%)	1,044 (2.44%)
Colonels	105	328	472	325
Lieutenant colonels	191	421	872	448
Majors	374	1,139	1,303	4,304
Captains	1,097	2,466	3,161	7,794
First lieutenants	1,275	1,584	2.006	11,126
Second lieutenants	638	2,366	8,283	11,418
TOTAL	3,724	8,454	16,358	42,709

SOURCE: Figures for 1932-38 from Militärgeschichtliches Forschungsamt, ed., *Handbuch zur deutschen Militärgeschichte,* 7 vols. (Frankfurt am Main, 1965–), 5:373; those for 1943 from W. Keilig, *Truppe und Verbände der deutsche Wehrmacht,* 7 vols. (Wiesbaden, 1950–), 3:203/21.

Though the column on the extreme right of table 11.7 only comprises some 20 percent of all officers, the decline in the number of generals within the army as a whole (from 1 to 2,100 in 1932 to 1 to 4,600 in 1944) makes it clear that there was no inflation of ranks.[71] Indeed, the opposite may have been the case: in 1944, the Wehrmacht had hundreds of battalions commanded by majors, captains, and even first lieutenants.[72]

In May 1944, the German land army was short of 5,157 infantry officers, 1,407 armored corps officers, 1,827 artillery officers, 551 engineering officers, 429 signals officers, 516 supply officers, and 3,000 officers in army troops, security divisions, and so on; the total shortages amounted to 12,887.[73] Under such conditions, the question as to what was to be done with an officer did not arise.

U.S. Army

At the end of 1943, the U. S. Army (inclusive of the Air Force) had around 600,000 officers. Of those, 15,000 (2.5 percent) were Regulars of the pre-Pearl Harbor army; 19,000 were National Guards; 180,000 came from the officers' Reserve Corps; 100,000, mostly specialists such as physicians, administrators, and chaplains, had been commissioned directly from civilian life; and 300,000 had passed through either OCS or flying school.[74]

The percentage of officers in the U. S. Army had always been much higher than in the German one. In 1940 officers numbered 14,000 (5.75 percent) in a strength of 243,095, and at the time of VE Day this had risen to 885,645 (9.6 percent) out of 8,290,993.[75] This figure includes approximately 57,000 warrant and flight officers.

Officers were distributed among the ranks as shown in table 11.8.

TABLE 11.8
Rank Structure of the American Officer Corps in 1928 and 1944

RANK	1928	JANUARY 1944
Generals	Not available	5
Lieutenant generals	"	28
Major generals	"	303
Brigadier generals	"	860
Total general officers	"	1,196 (0.17%)
Colonels	531	7,854
Lieutenant colonels	660	19,568
Majors	2,172	48,280
Captains	4,142	130,422
First lieutenants	2,774	182,294
Second lieutenants	1,464	283,081
TOTAL	11,743	672,695

SOURCE: Nineteen-twenty-eight data from Hearings before Subcommittee 1 of the Committee on Military Affairs, House of Representatives, 25 January 1924; 1944 data from War Department, ed., *World Wide Strength Index* (n.p., n.d.) p. 4.

With majors outnumbering second lieutenants, the 1928 officer corps was clearly top heavy; whereas the 1944 army had a surplus of junior officers (second lieutenant to captain) recently graduated from OCS.

In the land army in December 1944, officers numbered 485,185 or 8.8 percent in an overall strength of 5,506,197.[76] Since officers were supposed to number 54 per 1,000 in AGF, and 97 per 1,000 in ASF, it is possible to calculate that there existed a surplus of approximately 50,000 officers.[77] To reduce it, units had already been authorized to take on officer overstrengths, that is, 25 percent in the Zone of the Interior and 15 percent overseas. In December 1944, divisions were even authorized to set up special companies of lieutenants up to 200 strong.[78] All these measures proved unavailing, however, and the army—with the highly significant exception of the infantry, which just happened to suffer 70 percent of all casualties—retained a surplus of officers right down to the end of the war.[79]

Table 11.9 shows the share of officers as a percentage of all personnel in the various units, theaters, arms, and services.

TABLE 11.9
The Distribution of Officers as a Percentage of All Personnel in the U.S. Army

RIFLE COMPANIES[a]	INFANTRY REGIMENTS[b]	INFANTRY DIVISIONS[c]	SIXTH ARMY[d]	OVERSEAS THEATERS[e]	ZONE OF INTERIOR[f]
3.5	5.0	5.7	6.2	8.5	9.1

SOURCE: S. A. Stouffer et al., *The American Soldier*, 4 vols. (Princeton, 1949), 2:8; Replacement Board, Department of the Army, "The Replacement System World Wide, World War II" (Washington, D. C., 1947), bk. 6, parts 83 and 81; U. S. War Department, ed., *World Wide Strength Index* (n.p., n.d.), p. 11.

[a]Actual strength, 6 June 1944.
[b]T/O strength, 10 April 1945.
[c]Average actual strength, six infantry divisions, Sixth Army, autumn 1944.
[d]Actual strength, autumn 1944.
[e]Actual strength, exclusive of the Army Air Force.
[f]Calculated by subtracting Zone of Interior strength from total strength.

Within the Zone of the Interior itself, officers formed 9.3 percent of all ASF personnel but only 7.0 percent of all AGF personnel.[80] These figures make it perfectly clear that the further away any unit was from the actual fighting, the higher the percentage of officers it contained.[81]

CASUALTIES

The German Army's casualties (dead) in World War I can be broken down as shown in table 11.10.

TABLE 11.10
German Dead in World War I, by Rank

Active officers	11,357	=	24.7% of total
Reserve officers	35,494	=	15.7% " "
NCOs and men	1,751,809	=	13.3% " "

SOURCE: Volkmann, *Soziale Heeresmisstände als Mitursache des deutschen Zusammenbruchs* (Berlin, 1929), p. 35
NOTE: For more detailed figures see C. von Altrock, *Vom sterben des deutschen Offizierkorps* (Berlin, 1922) p. 57.

For the period from 1 September 1939 to 31 December 1944 the figures, again referring to dead only, are as shown in table 11.11.

TABLE 11.11
German Dead in World War II, by Rank and Year

YEAR	TOTAL NUMBER	OFFICERS
1939-40	73,829	4,357 = 5.9%
1940-41	138,301	7,831 = 5.6%
1941-42	445,036	16,960 = 3.8%
1942-43	418,276	16,484 = 3.9%
1943-44	534,112	20,696 = 3.9%
1944-45 to Dec. 1944	167,335	5,304 = 3.2%
Total	1,776,889	71,632 = 4.0%

SOURCE: Heeres Personal Amt file, "Verluste der Wehrmacht," Bundesarchiv/Militärarchiv HG/737.

Early in the war, therefore, an officer's chance of getting himself killed was twice as good as that of all military personnel; by 1944, since the proportion of officers in the army as a whole had fallen to just under 2.5 percent, it still stood at over 150 percent.[82] This relative predominance of officers among the dead holds true for every single campaign that could be examined, and also for individual units.[83]

Proceeding now to break down officer casualties according to type, the picture outlined in table 11.12 emerges.

TABLE 11.12
German Officer Casualties in World War II, by Type and Campaign

CAMPAIGN	OFFICER LOSSES AS % OF TOTAL LOSSES		
	Killed	Wounded	Missing
Poland 1939	4.60	1.95	1.35
France 1940	4.85	3.10	2.00
Russia to 3 August 1941	5.45	3.65	1.90
Russia to 1 October 1941	4.37	3.25	1.74
Russia to 31 December 1941	4.27	3.16	1.75
Russia to 10 September 1942	3.82	2.89	1.40
Russia to 31 July 1944	3.40	2.85	2.62
Russia to 31 December 1944	3.20	2.86	3.01
Total Field Army to 31 December 1944	4.07	n.d	1.68

SOURCE: B. Mueller-Hillebrand, "Statistisches System," U. S. Army Historical Division Study PC 011 (Koenigstein Ts., 1949), pp. 119-20.

Officers, in other words, were excessively numerous among the dead; more or less met their quota among the wounded; and were conspicuously absent (apart from the second half of 1944, when vast battles of encirclement were fought both in Russia and in France) from the ranks of the missing. Again, the same is true for every individual unit checked.[84]

Finally, it is possible to compare the number of noncombat dead among officers with similar figures for enlisted men and NCOs. The results are shown in table 11.13. This may not be a bad measure of the extra strain on officers.

TABLE 11.13
Noncombat Dead in the German Army, World War II, by Year, Type, and Rank

YEAR	ACCIDENT, SUICIDE, ILLNESS		DEATH SENTENCES	
	Total	Officers	Total	Officers
1939-40	14,138	986 = 6.9%	519	3 = 0.6%
1940-41	21,296	1,601 7.5%	447	— 0.0%
1941-42	38,252	2,333 6.0%	1,637	10 0.6%
1942-43	44,117	2,501 5.6%	2,769	30 1.6%
1943-44	45,312	2,447 5.9%	4,118	51 1.2%
1944-45 (to 31 December 1945)	15,186	529 3.9%	206	9 4.3%
total	178,301	10,397 5.9%	9,696	103 1.0%

SOURCE: Bundesarchiv/Militärarchiv, HG 737.

U.S. Army

According to one source,[85] the overall number of U.S. Army battle casualties in World War II (killed, wounded, missing, captured, and interned) was 948,574 of whom 99,954 or 10.5 percent were officers. Officers formed 24,546 or 13.9 percent of 175,407 killed in action; 39,936 or 6.6 percent of 598,528 wounded (including those who later died of their wounds); and 34,487 or 19.7 percent of 174,639 missing, captured, and interned. Officers were therefore overrepresented among the dead, considerably underrepresented among the wounded, and even more strongly overrepresented among the missing, captured, and interned. Their share among all casualties was somewhat though not much in excess of their numbers in the army as a whole.

These figures thus present a pattern very different from the German one and are only explicable by the fact that the U.S. Army included the Air Force also. In the Air Force one man in six was an officer, and the proportion among flying crew was much higher still. This largely explains the disproportionate numbers of missing, captured, and interned.

In the land forces alone, battle casualties numbered 829,760 of whom 48,216 or 5.8 percent were officers. Officers constituted 6.6 percent of those killed in action, 5.5 percent of the wounded, and 5.3 percent of those who were missing, captured, or interned. These figures are considerably below the proportion of officers in the land forces; on the other hand, they correspond very well with the share of officers in the Army Ground Forces, which is said to have been 54 to 1,000.

Officers in AGF units, in other words, took their share in casualties, though not much more than that. On the other hand, the vast numbers sheltering in ASF clearly did not. While officers formed a 97 to 1,000 ratio in ASF units, they comprised only 7.2 percent of all casualties in the Signal Corps and 5.3 percent in the Quartermaster Corps. For the remaining services, similar figures can be adduced.

An examination of ETO casualty reports supports this interpretation. Between D Day and D plus ninety (6 September 1944), 82.9 percent of all ETO losses consisted of infantry, whereas the services (engineer corps, medical corps, signal corps, quartermaster corps, military police, chemical warfare, and transportation corps totalled) took only 9.4 percent of all losses. As of 21 December 1944, however, only 19.2 percent of all (land-bound) ETO officers were in the infantry; whereas 40.7 percent were to be found in the above named services, so that service officers actually outnumbered infantry ones by better than two to one.[86]

Passing now to nonbattle casualties, the picture in table 11.14 presents itself.

TABLE 11.14
Noncombat Hospital Admissions in the U.S. Army, by Type and Rank

CAUSE AND AREA OF ADMISSION	HOSPITAL ADMISSION RATE PER 1,000 (MALE) STRENGTH, 1942-45	
	Officers	Enlisted Men
Nonbattle admissions, all areas	507	680
Continental U.S.	480	678
All Overseas Theaters	554	683
Disease admissions	454	601
Continental U.S.	434	611
All Overseas Theaters	490	588
Nonbattle injury admissions	53	79
Continental U.S.	46	67
All Overseas Theaters	64	95

SOURCE: U.S. Army, Medical Department, *Medical Statistics in World War II* (Washington, D. C., 1975), p. 27.

These data are open to at least two interpretations. One is that officers were only hospitalized for serious illnesses and injuries, which would explain both their smaller numbers as compared to enlisted men and the longer periods spent convalescing. If the rate of disease and nonbattle injuries is taken as a measurement of stress, however, the figures may well mean that U.S. Army officers lived so much better than the rank and file that they were less liable to be hospitalized—and that, once taken in, they were pampered. In view of the lack of evidence, the reader is invited to form his own conclusions.

NOTES

1. K. Lang, *Military Institutions and the Sociology of War* (London, 1972), p. 68. On this and the following pages a very extensive bibliography concerning various aspects of leadership and its effect on the men is included.

2. D. Horn, *Mutiny on the High Seas, the Imperial German Naval Mutinies of World War I* (London, 1969), ch. 2.

3. German: Heer-wie Truppenführung.

4. German: Verantwortungsfreudigkeit, or "joy in responsibility."

5. E. A. Shils and M. Janowitz, "Cohesion and Disintegration in the Wehrmacht in World War II," *Public Opinion Quarterly* 12 (1948):280-315.

6. War Department, ed., *Absence without Leave* (Washington, D. C., 1944), p. 14.

7. S. A. Stouffer et al., *The American Soldier*, 4 vols. (Princeton, 1949), 1:227.

8. Based on Militärgeschichtliches Forschungsamt, (hereafter MGFA, ed.,) *Handbuch zur deutschen Militärgeschichte*, 7 vols. (Frankfurt am Main, 1965–), 5:88.

9. For a very sharp criticism of these schools, see Ein Stabsoffizier, *Das alte Heer* (Charlottenburg, 1920), ch. 1.

10. In 1835 the Saxonian adjutant general, writing to his king, put forward a classic justification for this policy. While the need for a general education could not be denied, it should not be allowed to become the cardinal factor. The growing sophistication of war required professional knowledge even in junior officers, and if the result should be occasional distraction from day-to-day duties, this was the fault not of the knowledge but of the way in which it was imparted. For a practical officer, knowledge was not enough; competence was what he needed. But competence could only be acquired through knowledge. See K. Demeter, *Das deutsche Offizierkorps* (Berlin, 1965), p. 102.

11. K. Hesse, "Militärisches Erziehungs-und Bildungswesen in Deutschland," in *Die deutsche Wehrmacht*, ed. Wezell (Berlin, 1939), p. 472.

12. H. Rumschöttel, "Bildung und Herkunft der Bayerischen Offiziere 1866 bis 1914," *Militärgeschichtliche Mitteilungen* 2 (1970):131, fn. 131.

13. W. A. Robertson, "Officer Selection in the Reichswehr 1918-1926" (Ph. D. diss., University of Oklahoma, 1978), p. 143.

14. Quoted in Demeter, *Das deutsche Offizierkorps*, p. 103.

15. Robertson, "Officer Selection," pp. 218-20.

16. MGFA, ed., *Handbuch*, 7:367. Officers who failed this examination (which could be repeated) stood scant chance of ever reaching general rank.

17. Demeter, *Das deutsche Offizierkorps*, p. 104.

18. F. Doepner, "Zur Auswahl der Offizieranwärter im 100,000 Mann Heer," *Wehrkunde* 22 (1973):261.

19. The present account is based on T. W. Harrell and R. D. Churchill, "The Classification of Military Personnel," *Psychological Bulletin* 38 (1941):331-53;

H. L. Ansbacher, "German Military Psychology," *Psychological Bulletin* 38 (1941):370-92; and A. H. Martin, "Examination of Applicants for Commissioned Rank" in *German Psychological Warfare*, ed. L. Farago (New York, 1941), pp. 171-78.

20. See M. Simoneit, *Leitgedanken über die psychologische Untersuchung des Offizier-Nachwuchs in der Wehrmacht* (Berlin, 1939), pp. 24-25; also H. Masuhr, "Zur Unterstützung militärischer Menschenauslese durch soziologische Statistiken," *Soldatentum* 1 (1934):145-61.

21. R. F. Bigler, *Der einsame Soldat* (Frauenfeld, 1963), p. 30.

22. G. Blumentritt, "Warum hat der deutsche Soldat in aussichtlosser Lage bis zum Schluss des Krieges 1939-1945 gekämpft?" U.S. Army Historical Division Study B 338 (Allendorf, 1947), pp. 18-20.

23. R. R. Palmer, *The Procurement and Training of Ground Combat Troops* (Washington, D. C.: 1948), pp. 93-94.

24. Ibid., pp. 10, 11.

25. No information on the IQ required of officer candidates is available in the official history. From L. A. Pennington, *The Psychology of Military Leadership* (New York, 1943), p. 166, we learn that class I men "make excellent material . . . for officer training schools." Since they numbered only seven in one hundred, however, it is clear that many class II men also became officers.

26. W. C. Menninger, *Psychiatry in a Troubled World*, p. 110.

27. How long these interviews took is unclear. In one officer candidate school, however, a committee of four to five officers interviewed cadets already in training. This lasted fifteen minutes. Answers were recorded on a point scale.

28. Palmer, *Procurement and Training*, p. 329. A follow-up later established that there was little correlation between pen and paper performance and combat ratings of officers; see J. W. Eaton, "Experiments in Testing for Leadership," *American Journal of Sociology* 52 (1947):523-35.

29. The number of German publications on the selection of military personnel exceeded that in all other languages combined; Harrell and Churchill, "The Classification of Military Personnel," p. 331.

30. Simoneit, *Leitgedanken*, p. 27.

31. Pennington, *Psychology of Military Leadership*, pp. 1, 167.

32. See Hesse, "Militärische Erziehung," p. 487.

33. The length of this period is unknown and may not have been fixed.

34. M. Messerschmidt et al., "Verhältniss von algemeinbildenden und fachlichen Inhalten in der Ausbildung zum Offizier," unpublished paper, MGFA (Freiburg, i. B., 1971), pp. 9-10.

35. Seeckt order of 1 January 1921 quoted in Hesse, "Militärische Erziehung," p. 481.

36. Messerschmidt et al., "Verhältniss von algemeinbildenden," pp. 13-15.

37. G. Bachlin, "Deckung des Offiziersbedarf im deutschen Heer während des 2. Weltkrieg," U.S. Army Historical Division Study D 110 (n.p., n.d.) p. 110.

38. Generalstab, Heeres Dienstvorschrift g 151, *Mobilmachungsplan für das Heer: E. Erhaltung des Heeres im Kriegszustand* (Berlin, 1939), article 553 ff.

39. S. P. Huntington, *The Soldier and the State*, p. 295. No equivalent figures for West Point are available, but here too general cultural subjects tended to grow in importance.

40. For an excellent discussion of the West Point system see G. Ellis and R. Moore, *School for Soldiers, West Point and the Profession of Arms* (New York, 1974).

41. See p. 125.

42. Palmer, *Procurement and Training,* pp. 264, 353.

43. Ibid. pp. 330-34. According to this source, the system tended to produce candidates who were afraid of asking questions, taking responsibility, and showing initiative. Evidence is also said to exist that they took these qualities along into combat.

44. Based on MGFA, ed., *Handbuch,* 5:89, and Hofmann, "Beurteilungen und Beurteilungnotizien im deutschen Heer," U.S. Army Historical Division Study P 134 (Koenigstein Ts, 1952), p. 3.

45. D. N. Spires, "The Career of the Reichswehr Officer," Ph. D. diss., University of Washington, 1979, p. 218.

46. Hofmann, "Beurteilungen," p. 57.

47. Ibid., p. 45.

48. No system existed for evaluating the Beurteilungen, but Heeres Personal Amt officers nevertheless tried to check on their reliability by means of personal acquaintances.

49. Quoted in H. Meir-Welcker, *Untersuchungen zur Geschichte des Offizier-Korps* (Stuttgart, 1962), p. 205.

50. Hofmann, "Beurteilungen," p. 56.

51. Meier-Welcker, *Untersuchungen zur Geschichte,* p. 206.

52. Huntington, *The Soldier and the State,* p. 297.

53. War Department Press Release, 12 June 1941, National Archives (NA) file 407/14103/12/B.

54. War Department/Hq ASF/Adjutant General, Memorandum No. S 605-17-43, 21 July 1943, NA file 204/58/106-253.

55. This complaint occurs dozens of times in the Replacement Board's Report, Department of the Army, "Replacement System World Wide," bk. 6.

56. S. A. Stouffer, et al., *The American Soldier,* 4 vols. (Princeton, 1949), 2:271. Only in the coastal artillery was the rate lower still; 20 per 1,000.

57. Out of 872,000 officers who passed through the army from September 1940 to April 1946 only 6,700 or 0.77 percent were brought before reclassification boards. Three hundred and twenty-seven were demoted, 2,593 honorably separated, 1,500 separated other than honorably, and 253 reassigned. Menninger, *Psychiatry in a Troubled World,* p. 16.

58. E. D. Sissoh, "The New Army Rating," *Personnel Psychology* 1 (1948):365-81.

59. The number of works on the German General Staff is legion. See W. Goerlitz, *History of the German General Staff, 1657-1945* (New York, 1953); W. Erfurth, *Die Geschichte des deutschen Generalstab von 1918 bis 1945* (Göttingen, 1957); and above all, H-G Model, *Der deutsche Generalstabsoffizier* (Frankfurt am Main, 1968) on which the present account is mainly based.

60. Spires, "The Career of the Reichswehr Officer," p. 102.

61. During the Weimar years, owing to the Treaty of Versailles, the first two years had to take place at the various Wehrkreise and only during the third were the survivors of the selection process concentrated in Berlin.

62. Pershing Report, *Infantry Journal* 15 (1919):691, 692.

63. Col. J. L. de Witt, Lecture, 4 September 1928, Center of Military History files, unnumbered, pp. 19-20.

64. G. S. Pappas, *Prudens Futuri; the US Army War College 1901-1967* (Carlisle, Pa., n.d.) ch. 6.

65. MGFA, ed., *Handbuch*, 5:90-91, 7:353.

66. Demeter, *Das deutsche Offizierkorps*, p. 47.

67. H. Metz, "Die deutsche Infanterie," in *Die deutsche Wehrmacht*, ed. Wezell (Berlin, 1939), p. 169.

68. MGFA, ed., *Handbuch*, 7:308.

69. Ibid., p. 310.

70. Tagesbuch Heerespersonal Amt, 19 July 1944, Bundesarchiv/Militärarchiv (hereafter BAMA), H4/12.

71. Bachlin, "Deckung des Offiziersbedarf," pp. 22-23.

72. W. Keilig, *Truppe und Verbände der deutsche Wehrmacht*, 7 vols. (Wiesbaden, 1950-), 3:204/1.

73. Ibid., 3:204/4.

74. Palmer, "Procurement and Training," pp. 92-93.

75. Figures from Greenfield, *The Organization of Ground Combat Troops* (Washington, D.C., 1947), pp. 1-2, 210.

76. Replacement Board, "Replacement System World Wide," bk. 2 part 19.

77. Palmer, *Procurement and Training*, p. 105.

78. Adjutant General's Directive, 27 March 1942, No. AG 320 (3-20-1942), NA file 407/4103/12/3/B; also Department of the Army, ed., *The Personnel Replacement System of the U.S. Army*, p. 446.

79. Palmer, *Procurement and Training*, p. 105.

80. War Department, ed., *World Wide Strength Index*, p. 11.

81. That the high percentage of officers in the U.S. Army was not solely the result of greater mechanization is shown by a present Bundeswehr division containing only 3.6 percent of its personnel in officers.

82. Keilig, "Truppe und Verbände," 3:204/1.

83. For example, Sixth Corps (22 June 1941-2 October 1942) and Ninth Army (30 July-10 August 1942); BAMA file 29234/9. Also Army Group B during operations in France, 1 July 1944-31 December 1944, BAMA file HG 737.

84. Twentieth Mountain Corps (1 September 1939-31 January 1945), BAMA HG/737; Sixth Corps, 22 June 1941-2 October 1942, BAMA 29234/9; also Army Group South, 22 June 1941-31 October 1944, according to ObKdo HG Süd/IIa/Nr. 3052/44g, 16 November 1944, BAMA RH19/v/55.

85. Department of the Army, *The Army Almanac* (Washington, D.C., 1950) pp. 667-68. Other figures, different because they include nonbattle losses, can be found in Department of the Army, Statistical and Accounting Branch of the Adjutant General, *Army Battle Casualties and Nonbattle Deaths in World War II* (n.p., n.d.), p. 5.

86. Replacement Board, "Replacement System World Wide," bk. 3 part 42.

CONCLUSIONS 12

This concluding chapter has a twofold purpose. First, it is necessary to recapitulate the secret of the German Army's high fighting power, and to explain the very different setup that led to the U. S. Army's weakness in this respect. Second and more important, it is necessary to put the entire problem of fighting power into a much wider perspective. This we shall do by posing, and attempting to answer, three questions, namely: What are the distinct characteristics of military as opposed to civilian organization that make for fighting power? How, and to what extent, can fighting power be maintained under the impact of organizational change brought about by modern technology? What is the role of fighting power among other factors that govern modern war?

REFLECTIONS ON THE GERMAN ARMY

The German Army was a superb fighting organization. In point of morale, elan, unit cohesion, and resilience, it probably had no equal among twentieth-century armies.[1]

To some extent, indoctrination with National Socialist ideas, the exalted social status of the military, and (even) some odd quirks of national character may have contributed to this result; none of these would have availed, however, were it not for the army's internal organization. It was this organization, the product both of centuries-long development and of lessons consciously drawn from defeat, which succeeded in creating and maintaining fighting power.

The average German soldier in World War II was not psychotically inclined. He did not fight to gain social prestige, at any rate not after the winter of 1941. He did not as a rule fight out of a belief in Nazi ideology—indeed, the opposite may have been nearer the truth in many cases.[2] Instead, he fought for the reasons that men have always fought: because he felt himself a member of a well-integrated, well-led team whose structure, administration, and functioning were perceived to be, on the whole and in spite of the inevitable existence of Drückenberger (shirkers) and "Golden Pheasants" (party hacks in their gorgeous uniforms), equitable and just.

Constructed on the basis of Clausewitzan principles (war as a clash between independent wills) and traditionally hemmed in by severe economic and material constraints (both absolute and in comparison with the opponents it would have to face in a two-front war), the German Army responded by developing a single-minded concentration on the operational aspects of war to the deteriment, not to say neglect, of everything else. A fighting force first and foremost, the army's doctrine, training, and organization were all geared to fighting in the narrower sense. In striking a balance between function related and output related tasks, it spent comparatively few resources—sometimes, perhaps, too few—on logistics, administration, or management. It systematically and consistently sent its best men forward to the front, consciously and deliberately weakening the rear. In matters of pay, promotion, decorations, and so on, its organization was designed to produce and reward fighting men. It went for quality, and quality was what it got. In this, without a doubt, lay the secret of its fighting power.

Given its single-minded concentration on operations, the German Army did not have to develop scientific management to the same extent that the American one did and was, by modern and even contemporary standards, in many ways a crude organization. Much to the consternation of American officers who interrogated its personnel after the war, it employed neither mechanized methods of administration nor point systems.[3] It had no use for opinion polls, social workers, or psychoanalysis. It was content to collect only modest amounts of statistical information, and it did not as a rule employ mathematical models.

Much of this backwardness was due to negative factors, such as conservatism (in refusing to use business machines), lack of interest (in refusing to use polls), and Nazi ideology (in rejecting Freud). In part, however, it was the product of positive ones: the decision to do without certain kinds of detailed information, for example, prevented a threat to the position of subordinate commanders from developing and at the same time reflected a desire to reduce the burden of paperwork resting on the troops. In its attempts to simplify administration and cut red tape, the army was greatly helped by the fact that, from 1942 on, it was, in any case, short of almost everything; thus necessity could be turned into a virtue.

In many instances, therefore, information which an American headquarters would regard as indispensable was unavailable to a German one; and, conversely, when information was available, the absence of mechanized methods of data processing prevented its efficient utilization. To a far greater extent than their American counterparts, therefore, German commanders at all levels were compelled to select essentials and concentrate on them, while leaving the details to subordinates to work out. The system of mission-type tactics, the meticulous way in which officers were selected, and the distinction drawn between all efficiency reports and those of staff officers are but three examples of this remorseless concentration on essentials.

The differences between the two armies in this respect are reflected by their thought-processes and even by their language. A German officer, confronted by some task, would ask: worauf kommt es eigentlich an? (what is the core of the problem?) An American one, trained in the "engineering approach" to war, would inquire: what are the problem's component parts?[4]

Illuminating as such differences are, they do not by any means penetrate into the heart of the matter. In the final account, the German Army's system of organization reflected a deliberate choice, a conscious determination to maintain at all costs that which was believed to be decisive to the conduct of war: mutual trust, a willingness to assume responsibility, and the right and duty of subordinate commanders at all levels to make independent decisions and carry them out.

To generate independence, freedom had to be granted. To train men toward responsibility, authority had to be delegated. To create trust, reliability and long standing acquaintanceships had to be assured. A direct outcome of these considerations were, in the first place, the German regulations which, as compared to the American ones, did not go into great detail and did not attempt to prescribe solutions in advance. A decentralized system of administration left much to the discretion, not to say intuition, of individual commanders and men, but at the same time put complete and undivided responsibility squarely upon their shoulders. To help create the familiarity that is an indispensable prerequisite of both reliability and trust, the replacement system took considerable administrative and technical complications in stride.

The German Army, in other words, was built around the needs, social and psychological, of the individual fighting man. The crucial, indeed decisive, importance of the latter was fully recognized; and the army's doctrine, command technique, organization, and administration were shaped accordingly.

All this, however, did not mean that German troops—especially in comparison with American ones—were pampered. Rather, the opposite was true: the German Army at all times regarded itself as a fighting organization above all, and the treatment meted out to its personnel was designed solely in order to raise their combat effectiveness to the highest possible peak. In a German officer's instructions, the need to look after his men invariably figured well behind the imperative of maintaining fighting power, and as a function thereof.

Yet the coin also has a reverse side. Precisely because its power rested almost solely on the excellence of its organization per se, the German Army was capable both of fighting with the utmost stubbornness and of cold-bloodedly butchering untold numbers of innocent people. So strong was the grip in which the organization held its personnel that the latter simply did not care where they fought, against whom, and why. They were soldiers and did their duty, regardless of whether that duty involved carrying out an offensive in the south, a defensive in the north, or atrocities in the center.

Writing in his diary on the eve of Operation Barbarossa, the invasion of Russia that was the largest military undertaking of all time, Friedrich Sachsse said:

> Rumors follow each other. The vast German deployment is meant to make the Russians grant us free passage to Iraq. . . . Caucasus, Tiflis? A lieutenant says that his division is going to India. Some say we are going to fight the Russians. We shall see. In any case: we want to go somewhere, quickly.[5]

As Adolf Hitler, that great connoisseur of the German people, put it at about the same time in a different context, "the German soldier can do anything!"[6]

REFLECTIONS ON THE U.S. ARMY

Between 1940 and 1945 the U.S. Army grew from 243,000 officers and men into a force numbering over 8 million. With eighty-nine divisions, made up of men who had shortly before been civilians in one of the world's less militarized nations, it crossed the oceans and played a decisive role in the defeat of two of the most highly militarized powers the world has ever known. It is doubtful whether any other nation would have been capable of such feats: not for nothing, indeed, has General Marshall been called "the organizer of victory."

Many of the U.S. Army's shortcomings were the direct result of overrapid expansion. Other objective factors also played their part: long lines of communications, for example, prevented American officers from being trained as German ones were, that is, by service at the front, and were also partly responsible for the enormous divisional slices. There was, too, a desperate shortage of cadres. This helps explain why the system had to be so centralized, and why, in consequence, mechancial methods of administration had to be employed to the extent that they were.

Inexperience, too, played a role in shaping the American Army; yet inexperience as an explanation has its limitations. No amount of inexperience can excuse a cruel replacement system under which individual replacements were allowed to travel, without comrades or commanders, from one depot to the next and then to enter battle without even their names being known to the men around them.[7] No amount of inexperience can excuse a system under which it was those officers whose lives were least endangered that got the fastest promotions. No inexperience can excuse (given the first-class experience that was available from World War I) the way in which the whole question of psychiatric casualties was handled. Not inexperience but bureaucratic inefficiency pure and simple can explain the slowness of the decoration system. Not inexperience but a laxness intolerable in war—however admirable it may be in times of peace—can explain a justice system that treated military offenses committed by servicemen as if they were matters of no consequence.

A point to be noted about each of the above factors is the fact that they did not involve "mechanical" performance, in which respect the U.S. Army was for the most part as good as, and often vastly superior to, the German one. We saw, for example, that American divisions did not contain significantly more fat than did their German equivalents; that the U.S. Army developed logistic capabilities that the Germans could only dream about hardly requires mentioning. It was not here, but in the dearth of attention paid to the most elementary psychological needs of the soldier (combined, paradoxically, with a far-reaching readiness to accept "psychology" as an excuse) that the weakness lay. A case in point was the system under which technical NCOs, but not leadership-type ones, received special training. An even more glaring one was the treatment of the wounded; while the American medical services were considerably better at saving lives than were the German ones, the morale effect of this fact was counteracted by the way these men were handled after recovery.

Coming now to the true core of things, it would appear that the U.S. Army, backed by a gigantic productive engine and possibly looking across its shoulder at the organization of an automobile factory, chose to regard war not so much as a struggle between opposing troops but rather as one whose outcome would be decided largely by machines.[8] Rather than concentrating on fighting power, therefore, it aimed at confronting the enemy with the greatest possible firepower. Not attention to the needs of the soldier, but scientific management and the optimum distribution and deployment of resources became the name of the game. Not a single-minded concentration on *operativ* (the very word, incidentally, has no exact English equivalent) aspects of war but a balanced organization aimed at coordination and control was the result. This approach tended to turn men into adjuncts of their machines and largely explains the gulf between the army's "mechanical" efficiency and the scant attention it paid to social and psychological problems.

To deploy all resources as well as possible, to put every man and screw in their proper place, a highly centralized organization and vast amounts of detailed information were needed. Information being superabundant, mechanical means to process it were needed. Business machines being available, any- and everything had to be shaped in such a way as to enable them to process this information as efficiently as possible. Conversely, anything that could not be processed by mechanical means did not exist; and this, unfortunately, included precisely those seelische (psychical—the expression, once again, is difficult to translate) attitudes that constitute the core of fighting power.

These considerations, which ultimately derive from the peculiar American balance between men and machines, may explain why wounded and replacements were handled as they were; why units were put together without regard to geographic origins; and why men were allowed to enter combat without knowing either their commanders or their comrades. They also explain much about the way in which the divisions operated and the absence of a unit rotation system. From a purely managerial point of view aiming at the optimal coordination of available resources, a system which treats men as if they were interchangable cogs undoubtedly IS the most efficient. Again, the haste with which the army was organized probably played a role in this; equally important, however, was the determination of headquarters at all levels to put administrative efficiency above all else.

The addiction to information also had further unfortunate results. Since knowledge—as extensive and complete as possible—was regarded as the key to victory, the best and the brightest were, not unnaturally, put to the task of producing, procuring, and processing it. The number of—frequently commissioned—pen pushers in the rear was enormous, whereas the fighting arms were starved of high-quality manpower. The fact that Class I and II men were proportionally least numerous in the arms that suffered the most casualties, and the definitely low number of ground officers killed, leaves little doubt that the American democracy fought World War II primarily at the expense of the "tired, the poor, the huddled masses."

If it is indeed true, as is so often said, that the officer corps counts for everything in war, then the American officer corps of World War II was less than mediocre. Owing partly no doubt to pressure of time, the methods used to select and train officers were none too successful. Far too many officers had soft jobs in the rear, far too few commanded at the front. Those who did command at the front were, as the official history frankly admits and the casualty figures confirm, often guilty of bad leadership.[9] Between them and their German opposite numbers there simply is no comparison possible.

Yet when all is said and done, the fact remains that the American GI did win World War II. He did so, moreover, without assaulting, raping, and otherwise molesting too many people. Wherever he came—even within Germany itself—he was received with relief, or at any rate without fear. To him, no greater tribute than this is conceivable.

REFLECTIONS ON THE NATURE OF MILITARY ORGANIZATION

A question that remains to be answered and that has indeed haunted this study from the very beginning, is the following: if American military organization was so bad at producing fighting power, why was American economic and industrial organization so good at producing the material goods of war? Why was, for example, Volkswagen modelled on Ford, and not vice versa? Where lies the essential difference between business and war that enabled the U.S. to assemble the most efficient, most productive economic machine ever, but at the same time prevented its army from developing equally impressive fighting power?

In recent years, and especially since sociologists have started taking an interest in military organizations, it has become fashionable to talk of the similarities between armies and business corporations. Both are seen essentially as exercises in management, structures whose function is to coordinate human and material resources in such a way as to produce the greatest possible output at the lowest possible price—death by napalm, say, or instant coffee.

The more intensely technical armies become, the more sophisticated their bureaucratic structure, and the greater the temptation to draw parallels of this kind. Modern armies, it is correctly pointed out, employ only a small and diminishing fraction of their manpower on combat-related tasks. More and more of their personnel are managers, technicians, and specialists of every kind, whose jobs differ little, if at all, from those of their counterparts in civilian life with whom, indeed, they often have more in common than with the traditional image of the fighting man.[10] Even combat itself, it has been claimed, is no longer the raw and primitive business it once was; instead, it has become a highly complex, technological affair demanding from the tank driver, for example, skills that are not, according to one well-known authority, very different from those required in a crane operator.[11]

There is, admittedly, an element of truth in this. So long as he is engaged in mere maneuvers, the skills demanded of a tank driver are, in fact, quite similar to those of a crane operator. Both need spatial orientation, a certain manual dexterity, a good understanding of their machines, and the willingness to cooperate with others on a team.

Maneuvers, however, are in the final account mere games. In time of war—der Ernstfall, as the Germans say[12]—things are different. Vital as the skills of a crane operator are to the smooth functioning of an army, they cannot substitute for what, in this study, has been termed fighting power: namely the mixture, in one combination or another, of discipline and cohesion, morale and initiative, courage and toughness, the willingness to fight and the readiness, if necessary, to die. Without these, a crane operator is destined to remain just that—a technician fit for service (so long as things go well) in some safe spot far removed from the fighting.

It is the predominance of the above qualities—elusive, but absolutely vital—which distinguishes peace from war, business from military organization. This not only causes most studies concerning the similarities between armies and business corporations to miss their target; on a deeper level, it means no less than that an army—and it is here that its unique character lies—neither can nor should be constructed on the basis of utilitarian considerations alone. Reason acting in the service of interest may, to be sure, serve as the foundation of a nation's decision to go to war, and even of an army's readiness to fight; it is a matter of definition, however, that no kind of utilitarian reasoning in the world can render the individual willing to lay down HIS life. It is at this point, the very essence of fighting power, that a completely different set of nonrational, socio-psychological factors enters the picture.

Business life, in other words, is based on self-interest and the reason serving it; armies, on the other hand, cannot be based on either. Much as armies should encourage reason and make use of it, the latter cannot in the final account serve as the cornerstone on which they are built. Reason is essential, to be sure, but the vital Something Else is more essential still.

The problem of balancing between rationality and irrationality, efficiency and psychology, is complicated further by the fact that armies do not spend all of their time in either peace or war. Unlike business corporations, which do their thing yesterday, today, always, armies are faced with the additional problem of switching—often at great speed and without warning—from one type of activity to another. When such a change takes place, systems of command, channels of communications, relations with comrades, attitudes toward various kinds of resources, and indeed to human life itself all assume very different forms. The entire structure is shaken to its foundations, altered, metamorphosed, flooded by enormous quantities of adrenalin.

How, given the inexorable advance of technology, is the balance between rationality and irrationality struck? Can fighting power be built up in peace, utilitarian reasoning be preserved in war? To what extent, if at all, can the demands of modern technology and organization be reconciled with the need for fighting power?

REFLECTIONS ON THE IMPACT OF TECHNOLOGY

Technology, it has been known since at least Adam Smith, brings specialization in its wake, and specialization inevitably implies a decreasing degree of flexibility and all-around capability. The more specialized the components—human or material—of a given machine (military or other, it does not matter), the more important it becomes to make sure that each one is employed in its proper place and supported in concert by all others. Consequently, top-level planning, control, and coordination, detailed and continuous, gain in importance; that these functions can only be carried out with the aid of mechanized (and therefore digital) data processing systems is, given the sheer complexity of modern armies, beyond dispute. Thus, to mention but a single example, the mere fact that a present-day Bundeswehr division contains 900 different MOS, as against only 40 in a World War II infantry division, is itself sufficient to turn the Wehrmacht's entire loose and decentralized personnel management system into a historical curiosity.[13]

That the advance of technology has rendered out of date much of the German Army's organization as here described is thus readily granted, but this does not mean that its experience has lost all relevance, much less that we should now sacrifice everything to efficiency to the exclusion of fighting power. This applies in the first place to those aspects of manpower management that are eternal in the sense of being largely independent of technology. The principle that officers should be the leaders and educators of their men in every field; a system of military terminology and customs that will emphasize the basic unity among officers and men as well as the differences between them; a pay, decorations, and promotions system that will ensure proper rewards to those men whose lives are in the greatest danger; a justice system that will be as swift and effective in protecting the individual (something made all the more necessary by the authoritarian nature of all military organizations) as it is in enforcing discipline; and an outlook that will condemn military offenses, directed as they are not merely against private individuals but against the nation as a whole, at least as severely as it does civilian ones—without all of these, no army can hope to develop, much less maintain, fighting power.

While an organization as specialized for operations as was the German Army is inconceivable under modern conditions, the opposite extreme, that is, that of overemphasizing the role of technical and supporting services, should also be avoided. An army's first and overriding function, after all, is to fight; it is not primarily to administer personnel, gather intelligence, or even bring up supplies and repair vehicles.[14] To the extent that the German Army's selection, training, and promotion systems took this fact into account, something might still be learnt from it today.

Passing to fundamental principles of organization, there would appear to exist no prima facie reason why the armed forces of a large nation should not employ a regional structure in order to secure a modicum of social cohesion inside the units (as is in fact the practice of the Bundeswehr), nor why a regimental system on the British model should not be retained in spite of the administrative complications involved. There appears to be no reason, furthermore, why large units should not be tied to specific training centers, receive their recruits and replacements by means of closed marching battalions, and absorb them by way of field replacement battalions; both institutions do, in fact, exist in the Bundeswehr.

Regarding the details of personnel management, the German Army's system of assigning responsibility for the appointment and discharge of NCOs to company and battalion commanders would appear to be still relevant and has, indeed, been retained by several armies. Nor, in principle, is there any a priori reason why it should not be possible to go even farther and give regimental commanders a measure of control over the selection, training, and commissioning (possibly by means of a probationary period) of their own officers. Both measures would undoubtedly involve a degree of administrative inefficiency and even waste; whether these would not be outweighed by the increased cohesion of units, however, should be carefully considered in each case. Such a system, with its delegation of important responsibilities, might also do something to correct the low social status under which the officer corps of most highly developed countries seems to labor.

In many cases, the organization of modern armies along such lines would be facilitated rather than retarded by the availability of modern data-processing systems, which could easily be programmed to match, for example, a man's regional origins against his professional qualifications on one hand and available vacancies on the other. Computers and mathematical models could also be used, to adduce another example, to regulate "churning" in such a way as to make possible the return of junior officers to their own units after training. The availability and capacity of modern means of communication and transport might be used to maintain ties between front and rear, ZI, and overseas theaters, to an extent that was impossible in World War II.

The advance of technology, in brief, has not rendered the German Army's experience in achieving high fighting power meaningless. This experience has retained enough of its relevance to make learning possible. However, learning should not involve any return to some more primitive methods of organization and administration. Rather, true learning would consist of attempting to design a system that, in addition to meeting the necessary technical and professional requirements, would take into account the social and psychological needs of man.

In this context, a warning is in place. The German Army had extremely high fighting power, it is true, but only at the cost of producing troops to whom an order, regardless of its nature, was an order and who could therefore be relied upon not only to fight hard but to commit any kind of atrocity as well. To produce fighting power without paying as high a price; that is the true challenge facing the armies of the West.

REFLECTIONS ON FIGHTING POWER

The end of our journey is approaching, and it is already possible to hear the critics ask: does not this study, by concentrating on fighting power to the virtual exclusion of all other factors that govern modern war, misrepresent the latter's nature? Does it not do an injustice, not merely to the U. S. Army but to the entire social-economic-industrial-military complex with which the U. S. waged, and won, World War II? The German Army, after all, may have developed awesome fighting power, but only at the expense of neglecting numerous other factors that were just as important. Behind it, moreover, there stood a political and industrial system which, for sheer efficiency, could not begin to compete with American might.

To put the same point more bluntly still: trusting to fighting power, Germany's leaders in 1939-45 may be said to have given proof of their criminal misjudgment of the forces that shape today's world and, as their just reward, ended up by sacrificing the lives of perhaps four million of their countrymen and reducing the country to a shambles such as has been rarely equalled in history. America's leaders, by contrast, relying on high technology and an enormously productive system of economic organization, demanded the lives of but 300,000 of their compatriots—and, at this comparatively trifling cost, not only won the war but also propelled their country into the position of the world's greatest, indeed almost sole, superpower. Does not this prove that modern war, and indeed the modern world as a whole, is governed by forces other than fighting power?

My reply to this objection is this: it uses results, in this case final victory, as the sole measure of performance, thereby falling into the very trap against which warning was served on the first page of the present study. By ignoring a host of fundamental factors that led to Germany's defeat (the difference in relative size between the opponents, to mention the most obvious one only) and by neglecting to look for intrinsic qualities for measuring excellence, such an approach distorts reality just as much as does one that regards fighting power as the sole constituent of victory.

To recall the formula used on the first page of this study: within the limits of its size, the military worth of an army equals the quantity and quality of its equipment multiplied by its fighting power. This formula does justice to both factors, the moral and the material, implying as it does that each can make up for the other only to a limited extent and that each without the other is utterly worthless. This is as true today as it ever was in the past. Fashionable talk about electronic battlefields and push-button wars to the contrary, there is nothing in the history of armed conflict as waged since 1945 to indicate that fighting power has become at all less decisive; against a nation relying solely on technology and scientific management, it could well be very decisive, indeed.

NOTES

1. A parallel that does come to mind is the Israeli Army of 1967—but that war lasted six days rather than six years.

2. During the thirties many people "emigrated" into the Army precisely because it was regarded as non- or anti-Nazi.

3. It was out of these interrogations that the studies by German exofficers, on which much reliance was placed for the present work, were born.

4. It is interesting and by no means insignificant that many key terms used in German military writing have no English equivalents and are indeed almost untranslatable. Among them are "Truppenführung," "Verantwortungsfreudigkeit," and, of course, "Kampfkraft" itself.

5. F. Sachsse, *Roter Mohn* (Frankfurt am Main, 1972), pp. 94-95.

6. "Dem deutsche Soldat is nichts unmöglich!" Speech of 31 May 1941 in honor of the fall of Crete.

7. In the Korean War the "buddy system," designed to allow four men to train, travel, and fight together, was adopted to remedy this fault.

8. See E. N. Luttwak and S. L. Canby, "Mindset: National Styles in Warfare and the Operational Level of Planning, Conduct and Analysis," Canby and Luttwak, Washington, D. C., 1980, especially p. 4.

9. Greenfield, *The Organization of Ground Combat Troops* (Washington, D.C., 1947), p. 316.

10. See E. A. Fleischman, "Differences between Military and Industrial Organizations," in *Patterns of Administrative Performance,* ed. R. M. Stodgill and C. L. Shartle (Columbus, Ohio, 1956), pp. 31-38.

11. J. van Doorn, *The Soldier and Social Change* (London, 1975), pp. 19-20.

12. Another untranslatable term: "the real thing" would be closest.

13. Whether such extreme specialization is in fact necessary may perhaps be doubted but is beyond the author's competence to judge: see the *Bericht des Kommission des Bundesminister der Verteitigung zur Stärkung der Fürungsfähig-*

keit und Entscheidungsverantwortung in der Bundeswehr (Bonn, 1979). Specialization, of course, is but one link in a long chain, many of whose parts would seem to militate against the attainment of high fighting power by the methods described in the present study. In typically "modern" organizations, authority tends to be diffused. Horizontal channels of communication often supplement or even replace vertical ones, thus undermining the position of commanders or superiors. Justice, especially the distribution of rewards for performance, becomes more difficult to carry out. The many different types of training courses that different individuals go through may well lead to a drop in homogeneity and cohesion. The list of difficulties could be carried on infinitely.

14. This remains as true in today's age of deterrence as it was in every previous one. Today's armies' function can be summed up in Helmut Schmidt's words: "kämpfen zu können, um nich zu mussen" (to be able to fight, so as not to be compelled to).

Appendix A

NOTES ON METHOD

The purpose of the present study has been to find out the secret of the German Army's exceptional fighting power. To do this, the comparative method was selected, because it alone allows the facts to speak out for themselves.

In order to lay any claim to objectivity, the comparison had to be "thick," that is, embrace as many different points as it was technically feasible to do. Conversely, it meant leaving out—with few unimportant exceptions—any but passing references to other forces, that is, the British, or Russian, or Japanese, which for one reason or another could not be studied in equal depth. A detailed reference to the British regimental system, for example, would have been interesting by way of offering additional proof of the importance of geographical homogeneity and unit cohesion; within the framework of the present study, however, an isolated reference of this kind would have amounted to mere demagoguery.

A study comparing two forces only does, of course, run certain methodological dangers. Since no historical phenomena, let alone two armies, are ever alike, one may always be accused of not comparing like with like. Without a doubt, the U. S. Army was different from the German one; it was far less experienced, placed much greater reliance on material resources, and was not nearly as important within the American armed forces as a whole as was the German land army within the Wehrmacht.

The differences between the two forces should not, on the other hand, be exaggerated. Both were made up, for the most part, of men of similar Caucasian stock. Both were in some way part of the Western world—if only in the sense that neither contained a significant number of Buddhist or Shinto troops. Both were, for their time, modern, technological organizations operating a roughly similar array of weapons and equipment. Finally, both armies embodied their nations' will to win victory on land, and to that extent they possessed a similar mission.

Seen from another point of view, moreover, a comparison between dissimilar forces is the only one possible; for what is to be gained by comparing two identical spheres?

Putting these by no means inconsiderable difficulties to one side, it was necessary to find a way of making the comparison itself objective. The sole way in which this could be done was by placing a very heavy reliance on statistics, to the exclusion, indeed almost neglect, of all other kinds of evidence. This made it impossible for me to show, for example, that the German Army contained more tough peasants (supposed to be excellent infantry material) or that U. S. troops were better with machines, though both propositions, often found in history books, may very well have been true. It also prevented me from making use of the fact that every single historian to whom I talked agreed that the German Army fought harder than any other in World War II—for no systematic poll on the question has ever been taken.[1] Historians, unfortunately for them, cannot manufacture their own material to order; nor is there any way in which questionnaires, or impressionistic accounts, can conjure up an age long past.

Consequently, what material the present study contains besides statisitcal tables has been used, as a rule, not to make points, but merely to illustrate them. The major exceptions, of course, are the discussions of command principles on one hand and of the officers' image and position on the other. Since statistical data on these vital points were clearly not to be had, long quotations from the official regulations have been included to enable the reader to draw his own conclusions.

To study history, especially military history, on the basis of written records, is always a hazardous undertaking. Much that mattered was never recorded. Much that was recorded did not matter. To check on the trustworthiness of official records, one could occasionally use personal reminiscences and even fiction—but these, by their very nature, are subjective and for that reason probably unrepresentative. There is, in short, no fail-proof way to discover whether and to what extent official records—on the distribution of leave, for example, or on methods of training—reflected actual practice in the field.

Yet for a comparative study such as the present one, the untrustworthiness of written records is of comparatively little importance. Such records may not give a true picture of what an army was, but they do at any rate demonstrate what it wanted to be. Probably few soldiers read, much less digested, the bellicose reflections on the nature of war contained in the *Truppenführung* of 1936 (or the more managerial ones in the regulations of 1941); yet, in both cases, the views put forward constituted an ideal to be striven for which, directly and indirectly, affected practice in a thousand ways.

One final point. The present study is focused on the German Army. For this reason, it mostly follows German practices in regard to terminology, classification, organization, and so on. This sometimes gave rise to difficulties. It was, for example, by no means easy to decide just which parts of an American division constituted the equivalent of a German divisional headquarters (Kommand). As far as possible, I tried to compare like with like.

NOTE

1. For the same reason, I generally avoided using an enormous body of American material for which there exists no German equivalent at all—namely the very numerous opinion surveys carried out among U.S. troops during the war and published in *The American Soldier*. Since the Germans for many reasons lagged behind in sampling and polling techniques and were in any case little interested in them, there just is no way for a historian to discover whether, for example, German

troops were more or less satisfied with their army lives than American ones. Great as is the temptation to use this material as an indication of the results of organization, faulty or otherwise, the temptation in most cases had to be resisted.

Appendix B

ENGAGEMENTS FROM TABLE 1.1

NO.	ENGAGEMENT
1	Port of Salerno, 9-11 September 1943
2	Amphitheater, 9-11 September 1943
3	Sele-Calore Corridor, 11 September 1943
4	Tobacco Factory, 13-14 September 1943
5	Vietri I, 12-14 September 1943
6	Battipaglia I, 12-15 September 1943
7	Vietri II, 12-14 September 1943
8	Battipaglia II, 17-18 September 1943
9	Eboli, 17-18 September 1943
10	Grazzanise, 12-14 October 1943
11	Capua, 13 October 1943
12	Triflisco, 13-14 October 1943
13	Monte Acero, 13-14 October 1943
14	Caiazzo, 13-14 October 1943
15	Castel Volturno, 13-15 October 1943
16	Dragoni, 15-17 October 1943
17	Canal I, 15-20 October 1943
18	Canal II, 17-18 October 1943
19	Francolise, 20-22 October 1943
20	Monte Grande, 16-17 October 1943
21	Santa Maria Oliveto, 4-5 November 1943
22	Monte Lungo, 6-7 November 1943
23	Pozzilli, 6-7 November 1943
24	Monte Camino I, 5-7 November 1943
25	Monte Camino II, 8-12 November 1943
26	Monte Rotondo, 8-10 November 1943
27	Monte Camino III, 2-6 December 1943
28	Calabritto, 1-2 December 1943
29	Monte Maggiore, 2-3 December 1943
30	Aprilia I, 25 December-6 January 1944

31 The Factory, 27 January 1944
32 Campoleone, 29-31 January 1944
33 Campoleone counterattack, 3-5 February 1944
34 Carroceto, 7-8 February 1944
35 Moletta River defense, 7-9 February 1944
36 Aprilia II, 9 February 1944
37 Factory counterattack, 11-12 February 1944
38 Bowling Alley, 16-19 February 1944
39 Moletta River II, 16-19 February 1944
40 Fioccia, 21-23 February 1944
41 Santa Maria Infante, 12-13 May 1944
42 San Martino, 12-13 May 1944
43 Spigno, 14-15 May 1944
44 Castellonorato, 14-15 May 1944
45 Monte Grande, 17-19 May 1944
46 Formia, 16-18 May 1944
47 Itri-Fondi, 20-22 May 1944
48 Terracina, 22-24 May 1944
49 Moletta Offensive, 23-24 May 1944
50 Anzio-Albano Road, 23-24 May 1944
51 Anzio Breakout, 23-25 May 1944
52 Cisterna, 23-25 May 1944
53 Sezze, 25-27 May 1944
54 Velletri, 26 May 1944
55 Villa Crocetta, 27-28 May 1944
56 Campoleone Station, 26-28 May 1944
57 Ardea, 28-30 May 1944
58 Lanuvio, 29 May-1 June 1944
59 Campoleone, 29-31 June 1944
60 Tarto-Tiber, 3-4 June 1944
61 Seine River, 23-25 August 1944
62 Moselle-Metz, 6-11 September 1944
63 Metz, 1 September 1944
64 Chartres, 16 August 1944
65 Melun, 23-25 August 1944
66 Chateau Salins, 10-11 November 1944
67 Morhange-Cohthill, 13-15 November 1944
68 Bourgaltroff, 14-15 November 1944
69 Baerendorf I, 24-25 November 1944
70 Baerendorf II, 26 November 1944
71 Burbach-Dursel, 27-30 November 1944
72 Sarre Union, 1-2 December 1944
73 Singling-Bining, 6-7 December 1944
74 Seille River 8-12 November 1944
75 Morhange-Faulquemont, 13-16 November 1944
76 Francaltroff-St. Avold, 20-27 November 1944
77 Durstil-Faversviller, 28-29 November 1944
78 Sarre River, 5-7 December 1944

Appendix C

GLOSSARY OF GERMAN TERMS[1]

Abitur	matriculation
Armeegruppe	Army Group
Auffrischung	refreshment (of troops)
Auftragstaktik	mission-oriented command system
Aushebung	enrollment
Beamter	official, clerk
Befehl	order
Beurteilung	Officer Evaluation Report (literally: assessment, estimate)
Bildungsoffizier	education officer (World War I)
Drückberger	shirker
Einjährige	one year volunteer (before 1919)
Einzelkampfer	single combat warrior
Erholungsheim	recovery home (military)
Ernstfall	the real thing (war, as opposed to training)
Ersatzheer	Replacement Army
erster Generalstabsoffizier (Ia)	first general staff officer (op.)
fechtende Truppen	fighting troops
Feldausbildungsdivision	field training division
Feldersatzbattalion	field replacement battalion
Feldheer	Field Army
Feldwebel	sergeant major

[1] The list is neither comprehensive nor systematic. It consists simply of the German terms appearing in the text.

Garnisonverwendungsfähig (Gv)	fit for garrison type duty
Gefreiter	corporal
geistige Betreuung	troop indoctrination (literally: spiritual reinforcement)
Generalstab	General Staff
Hauptfeldwebel	first sergeant major
Heer	land army
Heeres Dienstvorschrift (HDv)	Army Regulations
Heeres Personal Amt (HPA)	Army Personnel Office
Heimat	Zone of the Interior
Kampfgemeinschaft	fighting community
Kampfkraft	fighting power
Kriegsakademie	War Academy
Kriegsverwendungsfähig (Kv)	fit for combat
Laufbahn	career
Marschbattalion	marching battalion
Musterung	preliminary callup (of recruits)
Nachprüfung	final officer candidate's exam (for men without high school diploma)
Nazionalsozialistische Führungsoffizier (NSFO)	National Socialist Leadership Officer
Oberfeldwebel	sergeant first class
Oberkommando der Wehrmacht (OKW)	Armed Forces High Command
Oberkommando des Heer (OKH)	Army High Command
Offizierstellvertreter	sergeant-lieutenant
Panzergruppe	Armoured Group
Reichs Arbeits Dienst (RAD)	Reich Labor Service
Reifeprüfung	high school diploma
Stab	staff
Stabsfeldwebel	master sergeant
Trosse	organic support troops
Truppenamt	General Staff (Weimer period)
Truppenführung	command, leadership, of troops
Truppengeneralstab	General Staff with the Troops

Verantwortungsfreudigkeit	readiness to take responsibility (literally: joy in responsibility)
Versorgungstruppen	supply troops
Volksdeutsche	ethnic Germans
Vorprüfung	preliminary officer candidate exam (for men without high school diploma)
Wehrkreis	Defense District
Wehrkreisprüfung	general staff candidate exam
Wehrunfähig (Wu)	unfit for duty (literally: unfit for defense)
Weisung	directive
Zersetzung der Wehrkraft	undermining fighting power (military offense)
Zulage	allowance (financial)

BIBLIOGRAPHY

GENERAL

Unpublished

Luttwak, E. N. and Canby, S. L. "Mindset: National Styles in Warfare and the Operational Level of Planning, Conduct and Analysis." Canby and Luttwak. Washington, D. C., 1980.

Published

Andreski, S. *Military Organization and Society*. Berkeley, California, 1968.

Barnett, C. "The Education of Military Elites." *Journal of Contemporary History* 2 (1967):15-35.

Bericht des Kommission des Bundesminister der Verteitigung zur Stärkung der Führungsfähigkeit und Entscheidungsverantwortung in der Bundeswehr. Bonn, 1979.

Bidwell, S. *Modern Warfare*. London, 1973.

Creveld, M. van. *Supplying War; Logistics from Wallenstein to Patton*. Cambridge, England, 1977.

Doorn, J. van, ed. *Military Profession and Military Regimes*. The Hague, 1969.

———. *The Soldier and Social Change*. London, 1975.

Du Picq, A. *Combat Studies*. Harrisburg, Pa. 1947.

Dupuy, T. N. *Numbers, Predictions and War*. New York, 1979.

Erikson, E. H. *Childhood and Society*. London, 1965.

Etzioni, A. *A Comparative Analysis of Complex Organizations*. New York, 1961.

Fleishman, E. A. "Differences between Military and Industrial Organizations." In *Patterns of Administrative Performance*, edited by R. M. Stogdill and C. L. Shartle. Columbus, Ohio, 1956.

Granahan, D. V. "A Comparison of Social Attitudes among American and German Youth." *Journal of Abnormal and Social Psychology* 41 (1946):244-57.

Harkabi, Y. "Basic Factors in the Arab Collapse during the Six Day War." *Orbis* 2 (1967):677-91.

Harrell, T. W., and Churchill, R. D. "The Classification of Military Personnel." *Psychological Bulletin* 38 (1941):331-53.
Janowitz, M., and Little, R. W. *Militär und Gesellschaft.* Boppard am Rhein, 1968.
Lang, K. *Military Institutions and the Sociology of War.* London, 1972.
McClelland, D. C. "The United States and Germany; a Comparative Study of National Character." In *The Roots of Consciousness.* New York, 1965.
______. Sturr, J. F.; Knopp, R. N,; and Wendt, H. W. "Obligations to Self and Society in the US and Germany." *Journal of Abnormal and Social Psychology* 56 (1958):245-55.
Nöbel, W. "Das Verhalten von Soldaten im Gefecht." *Wehrwissenschaftliche Rundschau* 28 (1979):113-21.
Parsons, T. *Essays in Sociological Theory.* Glencoe, Ill., 1954.
Richardson, F. M. *Fighting Spirit.* London, 1978.
Schall, W. "Fürungsgrundsätze in Armee und Industrie." *Wehrkunde* 14 (1964): 10-18, 75-81.
Seashore, S. E. *Group Cohesiveness in the Industrial Work Group.* Ann Arbor, Mich., 1954.
Watson, P. *War on the Mind.* London, 1978.
Wright, Q. *A Study of War.* Chicago, 1965.

GERMAN ARMY

Archival Material

Files at the Bundesarchiv/Militärarchiv (BAMA), Freiburg i. B.:

29234/2	H20/477	Rh7 v 297
29234/9	H20/480	Rh7 v 299
29234/11	H20/481	RH19/III/494
32878/26	H20/482	RH19/v/55
52535/18	H20/485	RHD6/18b/31
H4/12	H20/500	W-05-165
H20/90	H20/502	W-05-166
H20/122	H20/574	

Other Unpublished Material

Bachlin, G. "Deckung des Offiziersbedarf im deutschen Heer Während des 2. Weltkrieg." U. S. Army Historical Division (USAHD) Study D 110. n.p., n.d.
Blumentritt, G. "Das alte deutsche Heer von 1914 und das neue deutsche Heer von 1939." USAHD Study B 296. Allendorf, 1947.
______. "Warum hat der deutsche Soldat in aussichtlosser Lage bis zum Schluss des Krieges 1939-1945 gekämpft?" USAHD Study B 338. Allendorf, 1947.
Denkert, "Einsatz der 3. Panzer Grenadier Division in der Ardennen-Offensive." USAHD Study B 086. n.p., 1946.

Hofmann, R. "Beurteilungen und Beurteilungnotizien im deutschen Heer." USAHD Study P 134. Koenigstein Ts., 1952.

Karldrack, G. "Offizier und Politische Bildung." Ph. D. diss., Munich University, 1970.

Messerschmidt, M. et al. "Verhältniss von algemeinbildenden und fachlichen Inhalten in der Ausbildung zum Offizier." Militärgeschichtliches Forschungsamt. Freiburg, 1971.

Mueller-Hillebrand, B. "Division Slice." USAHD Study P 072. Koenigstein Ts., 1951.

______. "Personnel and Administration." USAHD Study P 005. Koenigstein Ts., 1948.

______. "Statistisches System." USAHD Study PC 011. Koenigstein Ts., 1949.

Nothaas, J. "Social Ascent and Descent among Former Officers in the German Army and Navy after the World War." New York, 1937.

Quinett, R. L. "Hitler's Political Officers; the National Socialist Leadership Officers." Ph.D. diss., Oklahoma University, 1979.

Reinhardt, H. "Grosse und Zusammenstellung der Kommandobehörden des deutschen Feldheers im II. Weltkrieg." USAHD Study P 139. n.p., n.d.

Robertson, W. A. "Officer Selection in the Reichswehr 1918-1926." Ph. D. diss., University of Oklahoma, 1978.

Simoneit, M. "Die Anwendung psychologischer Prüfungen in der deutschen Wehrmacht." USAHD Study P 007. Koenigstein Ts., 1948.

Spires, D. N. "The Career of the Reichswehr Officer." Ph.D. diss., University of Washington, 1979.

Published

Absalon, R. *Wehrgesetz und Wehrdienst 1935-45*. Boppard am Rhein, 1960.

Altrock, C. von. *Vom Sterben des deutschen Offizierkorps*. Berlin, 1922.

Ansbacher, H. L. "Attitudes of German Prisoners of War: a Study of the Dynamics of National Socialistic Fellowship." *Psychological Monographs*, no. 62. Washington, D. C., 1948.

______. "German Military Psychology." *Psychological Bulletin* 38 (1941):370-92.

Bald, D.; Lippert, E.; and Zabel, R. *Zur Sozialen Herkunft des Offiziers*. Bonn, 1977.

Bigler, R. F. *Der einsame Soldat*. Frauenfeld, 1963.

Blecher. "Gedanken zur Erneuerung des Eisernen Kreuzes vor 25 Jahren." *Soldatentum* 6 (1939):242-46.

Brickner, R. M. "The German Cultural Paranoid Trend." *American Journal of Orthopsychiatry* 12 (1942):611-32.

Buchbender, O. *Das tonende Erz, Deutsche Propaganda gegen die Rote Armee im Zweite Weltkrieg*. Stuttgart, 1978.

______, and Schuch, H. *Heil Beil. Flugblattpropaganda im Zweiten Weltkrieg*. Stuttgart, 1974.

Bullock, A. *Hitler, a Study in Tyranny*. London, 1962 ed.

Cooper, M. *The German Army 1933-1945*. London, 1978.

Creveld, M. van. "Warlord Hitler; Some Points Reconsidered." *European Studies Review* 4 (1974):57-79.

Demeter, K. *Das deutsche Offizierkorps*. Berlin, 1965.

Dicks, R. V. *Licensed Mass Murder; a Socio-Psychological Study of Some SS Killers*. London, 1972.

Doepner, F. "Zur Auswahl der Offizieranwärter im 100,000 Mann Heer." *Wehrkunde* 22 (1973):200-203, 259-63.

Dupuy, T. N. *A Genius for War*. London, 1977.

Ein Stabsoffizier. *Das alte Heer*. Charlottenburg, 1920.

Erfurth, W. *Die Geschichte des deutschen Generalstab von 1918 bis 1945*. Göttingen, 1957.

Frahm, H. *Wehrbeschwerdeordnung*. Berlin, 1957.

Generalstab, ed. Heeres Dienstvorschrift 26. *Richtlinien für die psychologischen Prüfstellen*. Berlin, 1935.

______. Heeres Dienstvorschrift 29/a. *Bestimmungen über die Beförderungen und Ernennungen der Unteroffizieren und Mannschaften bei besonderen Einsatz*. Berlin, 1939.

______. Heeres Dienstvorschrift 81/15. *Wehrmachtersatzbestimmungen bei besonderen Einsatz*. Berlin, 1942.

______. Heeres Dienstvorschrift g. 151. *Mobilmachungsplan für das Heer: E. Erhaltung des Heeres im Kriegszustand*. Berlin, 1939.

______. Heeres Dienstvorschrift 209/2, Nr. 126. "Richtlinien für die Beurteilung von Soldaten mit seelisch-nervösen Abartigkeiten (Psychopathen) und seelisch-nervösen Reaktionen sowie für die Uberweisung in Sonderabteilungen." Berlin, 1 August 1942.

______. Heeres Dienstvorschrift 252/1. *Vorschrift über militärärtzliche Untersuchungen der Wehrmacht* part I. Berlin, 1937.

______. Heeres Dienstvorschrift 299/lb. *Ausbildungsvorschrift für die Panzertruppen*. Berlin, 1943.

______. Heeres Dienstvorschrift 300. *Truppenführung*. 2 vols. Berlin, 1936.

Goerlitz, W. *History of the German General Staff, 1657-1945*. New York, 1953.

Haffner, S. *Anmerkungen zu Hitler*. Munich, 1978.

Halder, F. *Kriegstagebuch*, vol. 2. Stuttgart, 1962.

Heeres-Sanitätsinspekteur, ed. *Die Wiedereinsatzfähigkeit nach Verwundungen, Erfrierungen, Erkrankungen*. Berlin, 1944.

Hellpach, W. *Der Deutsche Charakter*. Bonn, 1954.

Hennicke, O. "Auszüge aus der Wehrmachtkriminalstatistik." *Zeitschrift für Militärgeschichte* 5 (1966):438-56.

______. *Soldatendienst im neuen Reich*. Berlin, n.d.

Hesse, K. *Der Geist von Potsdam*. Mainz, 1967.

Hobohm, M. *Soziale Heeresmisstände als Teilursache des deutschen Zusammenbruchs von 1918*. Berlin, 1929.

Horn, D. *Mutiny on the High Sea, the Imperial German Naval Mutinies of World War I*. London, 1969.

Keilig, W. *Truppe und Verbände der deutsche Wehrmacht*. 7 vols. Wiesbaden, 1950-.

Kecskemeti, P., and Leites, N. "Some Psychological Hypotheses on Nazi Germany." *Journal of Social Psychology* 27 (1948):91-117.

Kitchen, M. *The German Officer Corps, 1890-1919*. Oxford, 1968.

Knight, M. E. *The German Executive 1890-1933*. Stanford, Calif., 1952.
Kortzfleisch, Captain von. "Der Offizierberuf im Reichsheer." *Deutschen Adelsblatt* 39, no. 22.
Lahne, W. *Unteroffiziere*. Munich, 1965.
Lerner, D. *Psychological Warfare against Nazi Germany; the Skywar Campaign, D Day to VE Day*. Cambridge, Mass., 1971.
Loewenberg, P. "Psychohistorical Perspectives on Modern German History." *Journal of Modern History* 47 (1975):229-79.
Lossow, W. von. "Mission-Type Tactics versus Order-Type Tactics." *Military Review* 52 (June 1977):87-91.
Macksey, K. *Guderian, Panzer General*. London, 1975.
Madej, W. V. "Effectiveness and Cohesion of the German Ground Forces in World War II." *Journal of Political and Military Sociology* 6 (1978):233-48.
Martin, A. H. "Examination of Applicants for Commissioned Rank." In *German Psychological Warfare*, edited by L. Farago. New York, 1941.
Masuhr, H. "Zur Unterstützung militärischer Menschenauslese durch soziologische Statistiken." *Soldatentum* 1 (1934):145-61.
Meier-Welcker, H. *Untersuchungen zur Geschichte des Offizier-Korps*. Stuttgart, 1962.
Messerschmidt, M. *Die Wehrmacht im NS Staat*. Hamburg, 1969.
Militärgeschichtliches Forschungsamt, ed. *Handbuch zur deutschen Militärgeschichte*. 7 vols. Frankfurt am Main, 1965-.
Model, H-G. *Der deutsche Generalstabsoffizier*. Frankfurt am Main, 1968.
Mueller-Hillebrand, B. *Das Heer*. 3 vols. Frankfurt am Main, 1968-.
Nass, G. "Persönlichkeit des Kampfwagenführers." *Beihefte zu angewendete Psychologie* 79 (1938).
Nuber, H. *Wahl des Offizierberuf*. Leipzig, 1935.
O'Neill, R. J. *The German Army and the Nazi Party*. London, 1966.
Preradovich, N. von. *Die Militärische und Soziale Herkunft des deutschen Heeres 1 Mai 1944*. Onasbrück, 1978.
Rodnick, D. *Postwar Germany*. New Haven, 1948.
Roth, N. "Zur Formulierung psychologischer Gutachten bei Wehrpsychologischen Eignungsuntersuchungen." *Soldatentum* 5 (1938):175-85.
Rumschöttel, H. "Bildung und Herkunft der bayerischen Offiziere 1866 bis 1914." *Militärgeschichtliche Mitteilungen* 2 (1970):81-131.
Sachsse, F. *Roter Mohn*. Frankfurt am Main, 1972.
Schaffner, B. *Father Land; a Study of Authoritarianism in the German Family*. New York, 1948.
Schmirigk. "Die psychologische Beurteilung Dienstpflichtiger bei Musterung und Aushebung." *Soldatentum* 6 (1939):24-27.
Schwinge, E. *Die Entwicklung der Manneszucht in der deutschen, britischen und französischen Wehrmacht seit 1914*. Berlin, 1941.
Seidler, F. W. "Alkoholismus und Vollrauschdelikte in der deutschen Wehrmacht und bei der Waffen SS während des Zweiten Weltkrieges." *Wehrwissenschaftliche Rundschau* 28 (1979):183-87.
______ . "Die Fahnenflucht der deutschen Wehrmacht während des Zweiten Weltkrieg." *Militärgeschichtliche Mitteilungen* 22 (1977):23-42.

———. *Prostitution, Homosexualität, Selbstverstümmelung, Probleme der deutschen Sanitätsführung 1939-1945.* Neckargemund, 1977.

Shils, E. A., and Janowitz, M. "Cohesion and Disintegration in the Wehrmacht in World War II." *Public Opinion Quarterly* 12 (1948):280-315.

Simoneit, M. *Leitgedanken über die psychologische Untersuchung des Offizier-Nachwuchs in der Wehrmacht.* Berlin, 1939.

———. *Wehrpsychologie.* Berlin, 1943.

Statistisches Reichsamt, ed. *Statistisches Jahrbuch für das deutsche Reich,* vol. 57. Berlin, 1938.

Steinert, M. G. *Hitlers Krieg und die Deutschen.* Düsseldorf, 1970.

Volkmann. *Soziale Heeresmisstände als Mitursache des deutschen Zusammenbruchs.* Berlin, 1929.

Wedel, H. von. *Die Propagandatruppen der deutschen Wehrmacht.* Neckargemund, 1962.

Weltz, R. *Wie Steht es um die Bundeswehr?* Hamburg, 1964.

Weniger, E. *Wehrmachtserziehung und Kriegserfahrung.* Berlin, 1938.

Wezell, ed. *Die deutsche Wehrmacht.* Berlin, 1939.

Zimmer, ed. *Wehrmedizin, Kriegserfahrungen 1939-1943.* Vienna, 1944.

Zwimmer, E. "Psychologische Lehren des Weltkrieges." *Soldatentum* 2 (1935): 181-85.

U.S. ARMY

Archival Material

Files at the National Archives, Washington, D.C.

204-58(87)	332/52/268	RG/332/52/265
204-58-90(22-819)	322/Admin. File ETO 7/38	
204/58/106-253	322/Admin. File ETO 38/183	

Other Unpublished Material

Command and General Staff College, Fort Leavenworth. "History of the Army Personnel Replacement System." 1948.

Haggis, A. "An Appraisal of the Administration, Scope, Concept and Function of the US Army Troop Information Program." Ph.D. diss., Wayne State University, 1961.

Halder, F. "Gutachten zu Field Service Regulations." USAHD Study P 133. Bonn, 1953.

Historical Division, U.S. Forces, ETO. "Basic Needs of the ETO Soldier." n.p., 1946.

Office of the Chief Military Historian. "Study of Information and Education Activities, World War II." Washington, D. C., 1946.

Replacement Board, Department of the Army. "Replacement System World Wide, World War II." Washington, D. C., 1947.

Published

Anderson, R. S. *Neuropsychiatry in World War II.* 2 vols. Washington, D. C., 1966.

______. *Physical Standards in World War II.* Washington, D. C., 1967.

Bendix, R. *Higher Civil Servants in American Society.* Boulder, Colo., 1949.

Blumenson, M. *Breakout and Pursuit.* Washington, D. C., 1961.

______, ed. *The Patton Papers 1940-1945.* 2 vols. Boston, 1974.

Coates, C. H., and Pellegrin, R. J. *Military Sociology; a Study of American Military Institutions and Military Life.* Washington, D. C., 1965.

Cole, H. M. *The Lorraine Campaign.* Washington, D. C., 1950.

Cooke, E. D. *All but Me and Thee, Psychiatry at the Foxhole Level.* Washington, D. C., 1946.

Department of the Army, ed. *The Army Almanac.* Washington, D. C., 1950.

______. *The Personnel Replacement System of the US Army.* Pamphlet No. 20-211. Washington, D. C., 1954.

______. Statistical Accounting Branch of the Adjutant General. *Army Battle Casualties and Nonbattle Deaths in World War II.* n.p., n.d.

Duncan, A. J. "Some Comments on the Army General Classification Test." *Journal of Applied Psychology* 31 (1947):143-49.

Eaton, J. W. "Experiments in Testing for Leadership." *American Journal of Sociology* 52 (1947):523-35.

Elkin, H. "Agressive and Erotic Tendencies in Army Life." *American Journal of Sociology* 51 (1946):408-13.

Ellis, G., and Moore, R. *School for Soldiers, West Point and the Profession of Arms.* New York, 1974.

FBI, ed. *Uniform Crime Reports for the US and its Possessions.* Washington, D. C., 1939.

Field Manual 100-5. *Field Service Regulations.* Washington, D. C., 1941.

Forty, G. *US Army Handbook 1939-1945.* New York, 1979.

Gabriel, R. A., and Savage, P. L. *Crisis in Command; Mismanagement in the Army.* New York, 1978.

Ginzberg, E. *The Ineffective Soldier,* 3 vols. New York, 1949-.

Greenfield, K. *The Organization of Ground Combat Troops.* Washington, D. C., 1947.

Henderson, S. T., "Psychology and the War." *Psychological Bulletin* 40 (1942): 306-13.

Hittle, J. D. *The General Staff, Its History and Development.* Harrisburg, Pa.,1961 ed.

Huie, W. D. *The Execution of Private Slovik.* New York, 1954.

Huntington, S. P. *The Soldier and the State.* Cambridge, Mass., 1957.

Janowitz, M. *The Professional Soldier, a Social and Political Portrait.* New York, 1960.

Little, R., ed. *Handbook of Military Institutions.* London, 1971.

Mantell, D. N. *True Americanism: Green Berets and War Resisters, a Study of Commitment.* New York, 1974.

Marshall, S. L. A. *Soldaten im Feuer.* Frauenfeld, 1951.

Menninger, W. C. *Psychiatry in a Troubled World.* New York, 1948.

Moskos, C. C. "Eigeninteresse, Primärgruppen und Ideologie." In *Beiträge zur Militärsoziologie,* edited by R. König. Cologne, 1968.

Palmer, R. D. *The Procurement and Training of Ground Combat Troops.* Washington, D. C., 1948.

Pappas, G. S. *Prudens Futuri; the US Army War College 1901-1967.* Carlisle, Pa., n.d.

Parish, N. F. "New Responsibilities of Air Force Officers." *Air University Review.* 3 (March-April 1972).

Pennington, L. A. *The Psychology of Military Leadership.* New York, 1943.

Pershing Report. *Infantry Journal* 15 (1919):691-706.

Personnel Research Section, the Adjutant General's Office. "Personnel Research in the Army: vi. the Selection of Tank Drivers." *Psychological Bulletin* 41 (1943): 499-508.

Report of the Secretary of War's Board on Officer-Enlisted Men Relationships. Washington, D. C., 1946.

Rose, A. M. "The Social Psychology of Desertion from Combat." *American Sociological Review* 16 (1951):614-29.

Savage, P. L., and Gabriel, R. A. "Cohesion and Disintegration in the American Army." *Armed Forces and Society* 2 (1976):340-76.

Seidenfeld, M. A. "The Adjutant General's School and the Training of Psycholigical Personnel for the Army." *Psychological Bulletin* 40 (1942):381-84.

Sissoh, E. D. "The New Army Rating." *Personnel Psychology* 1 (1948):365-81.

Steele, R. W. "'The Greatest Gangster Movie Ever Filmed': *Prelude to War.*" *Prologue* 11 (1979):211-35.

Stouffer, S A. et al. *The American Soldier.* 4 vols. Princeton, 1949.

U.S. Army, Medical Department. *Medical Statistics in World War II.* Washington, D. C., 1975.

______. *Personnel in World War II.* Washington, D. C., 1963.

War Department, ed. *Absence Without Leave.* Washington, D. C., 1944.

______. *Decorations and Awards.* Washington, D. C., 1947.

______. *Technical Manual TM 14-509, Army Pay Tables.* Washington, D. C., 1945.

______. *World Wide Strength Index.* n.p., n.d.

Weigley, R. F. "A Historian Looks at the Army." *Military Review* 52 (February 1972):25-36.

______. *History of the United States Army.* New York, 1967.

______. "To the Crossing of the Rhine, American Strategic Thought to World War II." *Armed Forces and Society* 5 (1979):302-20.

Other Material

War Office, ed. *Statistics of the Military Effort of the British Empire during the Great War.* London, 1922.

INDEX

About the Author

MARTIN L. VAN CREVELD is a senior lecturer in the History Department of the Hebrew University in Jerusalem. He is the author of *Hitler's Strategy* and *Supplying War*, a well as a great many articles which have appeared in *Journal of Contemporary History*, *European Studies Review*, *The Washington Quarterly*, *The Jerusalem Quarterly*, and *The Journal of the Royal United Services Institute*, among others.